# Beyond the Home Ranch

# Beyond the Home Ranch

Diana Phillips

HARBOUR PUBLISHING

**Harbour Publishing Co. Ltd.**
P.O. Box 219, Madeira Park, BC, V0N 2H0
www.harbourpublishing.com

All photographs from the author's collection unless otherwise noted
Front dust jacket: *Diana Phillips at Tsetzi Lake*, Vance Hanna photo. Back: *Sleepy
Hollow*. Back flap: *Diana Phillips*, Leslie Michaud photo. Pages 2–3: *Driving cattle
down Kluskus Road*, Wanda Simpson photo.
Edited by Pam Robertson
Cartography by Bernie Neary and Terra Firma Digital Arts
Digital mapping from the National Topographic Database, Natural Resources Canada.
Indexed by Ellen Hawman
Dust jacket design by Teresa Karbashewski
Text design by Mary White
Printed and bound in Canada

Harbour Publishing acknowledges financial support from the Government of
Canada through the Canada Book Fund and the Canada Council for the Arts,
and from the Province of British Columbia through the BC Arts Council and the
Book Publishing Tax Credit.

 Canada Council    Conseil des Arts      BRITISH COLUMBIA
for the Arts    du Canada     ARTS COUNCIL
An agency of the Province of British Columbia

**Library and Archives Canada Cataloguing in Publication**

Phillips, Diana, 1945–
    Beyond the Home Ranch / Diana Phillips.

Sequel to: Beyond the Chilcotin.
ISBN 978-1-55017-541-7

    1. Phillips, Diana, 1945–. 2. Women ranchers—British Columbia—
Chilcotin River Region—Biography. 3. Ranch life–British Columbia—Chilcotin
River Region. 4. Phillips, Pan, 1910-1983. 5. Chilcotin River Region (B.C.)—
Biography.
I. Title.

FC3845.C445Z49 2011        971.1'7504092        C2011-904602-4

*This is in the memory of Judy Christensen,*
*My friend for more than five decades.*
*You cheered me with your beautiful smile,*
*You made me laugh with your sense of humour.*
*When I am alone and I think of you*
*I imagine in the distance I hear your laughter*


*To my family,*
*I love you all*

*Cattle swim across the Blackwater River.*

# Contents

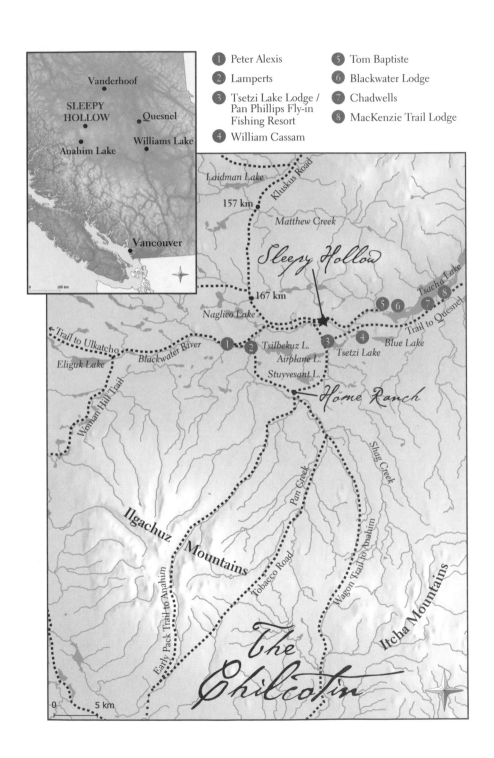

1 Peter Alexis    5 Tom Baptiste

2 Lamperts    6 Blackwater Lodge

3 Tsetzi Lake Lodge /
Pan Phillips Fly-in
Fishing Resort    7 Chadwells

                  8 MacKenzie Trail Lodge

4 William Cassam

Vanderhoof

SLEEPY
HOLLOW    Quesnel

Anahim Lake    Williams Lake

Vancouver

Laidman Lake

Kluskus Road

157 km

Matthew Creek

*Sleepy Hollow*

Tsacha Lake

167 km

Naglico Lake

Trail to Quesnel

Trail to Ulkatcho

Blackwater River

Eliguk Lake

Tsilbekuz L.

Airplane L.

Tsetzi Lake

Blue Lake

Stuyvesant L.

Woman Hill Trail

*Home Ranch*

Shag Creek

Ilgachuz
Mountains

Pan Creek

Itcha Mountains

Tobacco Road

Wagon Trail to Anahim

Early Pack Trail to Anahim

*The
Chilcotin*

0    5 km

# The Early Years

I had a childhood that was different from that of most other kids. I was raised in the remote Blackwater country, and until I was older I thought we lived like everyone else. As far as I was concerned my childhood was a very happy one, with all the animals to play with and horses to ride. My siblings may have had another opinion. There were always so many things to do: unlimited bush to cut trails through (we always had access to axes) and build forts in. Sloughs and creeks to sail homemade boats on, or our own rafts. We would be gone all day and no one worried or looked for us till evening, and by then hunger brought us home. And we always had a mongrel dog or two that was devoted to us kids and never left us, so I thought I had the best of all worlds.

My dad, Pan Phillips, settled in the Blackwater country in 1935, with Rich Hobson as his business partner, after leaving Wyoming in the fall of 1934. He dreamed of starting a cattle ranch, and his dreams had led him to British Columbia and the uncharted country north of Anahim Lake and the Ilgachuz Mountains. There, Dad and Rich found the large grasslands where they started the Home Ranch and formed the Frontier Cattle Company. Over the next four years, they developed the land and purchased and built up cattle herds, along with buying and raising a lot of horses.

*Maude and Andy cross Pan Creek with Maude's colt Nicki (Don and Charlie White in the wagon).*

People living in that country were few and far between; those considered to be neighbours might have lived seven to twenty miles away. George Dagg and Joe Stover had trapped and hunted in the Itcha Mountains around the turn of the century, and Jack Day had trapped in the Blackwater area in the early 1930s, coming from Nazko, but they were gone by the time my dad arrived. By then, there were no white people living in the area north of the Ilgachuz Mountains, on the headwaters of the Blackwater River. The only people scattered through the area were the people known as the Carrier Indians. They were from the Ulkatcho Band to the west and the Kluskus Band to the east. Most of them lived along the Blackwater River, in small, overcrowded log cabins. In winter they trapped and hunted, and in the summer they lived in tents, camping where there was good fishing and hunting. Later on, most began raising small herds of cattle.

Any supplies that were needed to build up the ranch were brought in by pack horses, all the way from the small coastal town of Bella Coola on the North Bentinck Arm. There was a Hudson's

Bay trading post there, and a steamship arrived weekly to deliver supplies to the small village. It was there that all the haying equipment, windows, stoves, clothing and groceries were purchased and then packed the 130 or so miles to the Home Ranch. Leaving Bella Coola the trail travelled up the valley for forty miles, with a very steep climb out of the valley's end on the Zig Zag Trail (Sugar Camp Trail), then down into the Precipice Valley. Another climb would take the pack string up to the Chilcotin Plateau, where the little settlement of Anahim Lake was situated.

After leaving Anahim Lake, the pack trail slashed through the timber and swampland, skirting muskeg bogs, over a pass in the Ilgachuz Mountains, and then took a steep drop into Carnlick Valley. From there the trail followed Carnlick Creek for another ten or twelve miles, till the creek met up with what came to be called Pan Creek, after my dad. Where these two creeks joined was the start of the wild meadows that ran to the east. And in the summer of 1935, that's where my dad and Rich built their first cabin. The following year they built a large house (well, considered large back then) and a barn. This is the property that would come to be known as the Home Ranch. A few years later they purchased the Batnuni Ranch, about eighty miles east; a lot of their cattle were wintered on the Batnuni place.

In 1939, with the outbreak of the war, many of the cowboys in the Chilcotin enlisted and went off to serve their country. The cattle market reached rock bottom that year, and Frontier Cattle Co. began having financial trouble. It was decided by 1944 that the company could no longer keep operating, so it was liquidated. My dad kept the Home Ranch, a small herd of cattle and the horses, while Rich took the Batnuni Ranch and some cattle. The rest of the cattle herds were sold to pay off much of their debt, and none of the leases on the wild meadows scattered from the Home Ranch to Batnuni that were held by the Frontier Cattle Co. were renewed.

My mom was raised on a small farm near Cultus Lake, in a small community just north of the US border in southwestern BC. After leaving the farm in her late teens she went to Vancouver, working for a time in the fish canneries. Later, when the war broke out, she made her way up the coast to the coastal village of Ocean Falls to work in the pulp and paper mills. There she met a friend of my dad's, who talked her into venturing inland to the remote Home Ranch to work as a cook. She loved the lonely, beautiful country— and my dad—and outlasted my dad's other two wives (one he had left behind in Wyoming when he came north, and the other, from Bella Coola, had only lasted a few years at the ranch).

I was born in 1945. It was a great year! World War II ended and Hitler took his own life. The microwave oven was patented. Ballpoint pens, Tupperware and frozen orange juice hit the market. People who could afford it had TVs in their homes. Famous people like Goldie Hawn, Bette Midler and Anne Murray were born that year, and Bing Crosby was singing "White Christmas."

My brother Ken was sixteen months old when I was born. And when I was eleven years old my brother Robert was born. (I also had two half-brothers in the States from Dad's first marriage and a half-sister, Gayle, from his second marriage.) We were raised with no plumbing and no electricity, in a log house with wood heat. Our lights were kerosene lamps and in later years gas lanterns. We bathed in a round tin tub in front of the kitchen range in water we heated on the wood stove, after first packing it in pails the hundred yards or so from Pan Creek. The only schooling we got was what Mom taught us around the kitchen table from the government's home correspondence courses.

Other families lived a similar lifestyle, but not in the remote area that we did. When we were young, twice-a-year trips to civilization were all we had. In July of every year we would go to Anahim Lake for the rodeo. In October of every year we took our cows to market in Quesnel. Other than that, Mom and us kids stayed home. Dad went out more often to Anahim Lake, as he had to freight supplies into the ranch. Our animals were our only playmates, unless some of the local Indian children happened to stop by. At first we could not speak the same language, but in time they learnt to speak English and we learned to understand the Carrier language.

Any visitors to our ranch rode the fifty miles from Anahim Lake to the south, following the old pack trail through the Ilgachuz Mountains, or took the wagon trail cut in 1941 over the pass between the Ilgachuz and the Itcha Mountains, or rode ninety miles from Nazko to the east. This is seldom done today, but from the 1930s through to the 1970s it was common practice. In the summer, teams and wagons were the main way of transporting families and freight. In the winter, it was teams and sleighs.

I loved to travel with the team and sleigh. The runners of the sleigh slid smoothly over the snow, especially on warm days, and unless the sleigh was heavily loaded the team trotted right along, with leather harness slapping their bodies and the trace chains jingling. The team would often lope down steep hills and as the trees sped by, hunks of snow would fly from the horses' hooves, often landing in the sleigh with us. Going back up those hills was much slower, of course. On warm days the squirrels would be out and about and would sit on the tree branches chattering at us as we passed by.

Travelling with team and wagon was not as nice. The trails were strewn with roots from pine trees and lots of rocks. In softer ground there were still rocks but also hummocks and mudholes. There were no springs on those rubber-tired wagons, and as the tires hit roots and rocks you would be bounced all over. The person driving had the advantage, hanging onto the leather driving reins, but passengers were thrown about. Usually we had the flies to deal with as well, and the teams were constantly trying to rub on passing bushes and trees or each other trying to rid themselves of the biting insects. We learnt to appreciate the few smooth stretches of trail that we came across.

Every October we would drive our cattle to market. In the fifties we drove them all the way to Quesnel, which took us twenty-one days, but when the road between Nazko and Quesnel was gravelled we started trucking from Nazko, as the cattle would become too sore-footed. Our last drive was in the fall of 1969, and was filmed by CBC—it aired in 1970 on *This Land of Ours*.

My brother Ken left home at sixteen and went to work in Bella Coola. Rob was boarded out to school from a tender age. And as I got older, I found the winters and the remoteness far too lonely, so I would find work away from the ranch for the cold winter months and return to the ranch the beginning of March to help with the calving and the haying through the summer. When the cattle were driven to the market in the fall I would leave again till the next year. I never spent a summer anywhere else; by early spring, it did not matter where I was, the homesickness would always draw me back to the home of my childhood.

These early years are all described in my first book, *Beyond the Chilcotin*, which I wrote about my experiences while growing up on the Home Ranch, and covers up to my parents' decision to sell the Home Ranch in 1969. This book continues on to cover the next thirty-four years I spent in the Blackwater country, living a similar lifestyle. I married, started a ranch of my own and raised my three sons. I also saw the passing of my parents, the slow changing of the land and the dying out of a unique lifestyle.

# CHAPTER 1

# Early Days at Tsetzi Lake

Growing up with a love of ranch life, and it being so important to me, I was not keen on the Home Ranch being sold. It was the only home I had ever known, but my parents felt it was time to move on. My mother was not well and had not been for some time. She had bad arthritis, as well as other medical problems. My dad was just discouraged, as we had recently had a number of years of bear troubles, with a huge loss in cattle each summer, due to the grizzlies on their killing sprees.

Bob Anthony from Utah looked at the ranch in the spring of 1969 and an agreement was drawn up. He would take over the ranch a year later, giving my parents a year to reorganize their lives. In the end I think it was the hardest for my mom to leave her home. There were a lot of tears as she slowly packed up her most precious belongings, of which there were very few. She was the one making the biggest change, moving from the ranch to town. If she did not move to town she would have had to move to a small one-room log cabin on Tsetzi Lake, which my dad had decided was to be his next home. Even the rather rough lifestyle at the ranch was a lot better than starting from scratch, like Dad would be at Tsetzi Lake. At that time I could not truly understand the pain Mom was going through, and I wouldn't until years later.

*My dad at the front door of the "Pan Phillips Fly-in Fishing Resort" lodge, 1970s.*

My dad, at fifty-eight, was off on a new venture, after forty-two years as a horseman and cattleman. He was now getting set up to cater to fly-in fishermen and big-game hunters. Rick Boland, who had lived with us off and on since he was fourteen and was considered one of the family, was partnering up with Dad in the fishing camp and guiding business. Since I no longer had a home on the ranch I was going with Dad. My brother Rob would spend time with Mom in Quesnel while in school, as well as some time out with us at Tsetzi Lake.

Bob Anthony, with his wife, Dorthea, and four children—Terry, Tim, Ted and Tammie—moved onto the ranch in the late spring of 1970, along with a variety of dogs, horses, a pet monkey and a myna bird. While they were moving in, we were moving out. Our move to Tsetzi Lake, four miles north of the Home Ranch, didn't involve a great deal. Mom had taken very little when she left the ranch, not that there was anything much of value to take. She traded her treadle sewing machine and gas washing machine to Dorthea for Dorthea's electric sewing machine and automatic washing machine. Dad took the kitchen table and chairs, his desk, a rocking chair, another hand-carved chair and the contents of the tack shed. He also took several wagonloads of lumber, leaving the sawmill behind. The cabin we were moving into, one that Rick and I had built five years before on the banks of Tsetzi Creek, close to Tsetzi Lake, was very small. We didn't have room for much of anything.

Dad kept about fifteen head of his good hunting horses, leaving the rest to go with the ranch. Rick had his horses and I had mine so the horse bunch was still fairly large. That spring those horses were moved from the Home Ranch range to Sleepy Hollow. Sleepy Hollow was the old Jack "Happy" Thompson place, seven miles north of the Home Ranch on the Blackwater River. Before Happy settled there in the late forties it was one of the hay meadows controlled by the Frontier Cattle Co. Ed Adams, the retired dairy farmer from New York state who had come to visit us at the Home Ranch in September 1960 and never left, had purchased the two quarters of land in the early 1960s. Ed was like a member of our family, and had been working on the Home Ranch with us for a decade. The horses would now run on the north side of the river west to Naglico Lake. In later years their area expanded, as horses are inclined to drift around, and they spent a lot of time in the Tommy Valley and Wolf Lake areas north and west of Naglico Lake. I still had my cattle, too, which had been turned onto the Home Ranch range for the summer. I was to move them by mid-October. I was not ready to sell my cattle yet. All the other cattle belonging to my parents went with the ranch.

Mom, after living twenty-six years in the bush, was by then back living in civilization. She had rented the Gunson home, on Elliott Street in Quesnel, and for the first time in her life had some nice things. She had never had indoor plumbing or electricity at the ranch, or even when she was growing up, so they were a real treat to her. She furnished the house with plain, serviceable items, nothing elaborate: her first TV, a comfortable recliner and a decent bed. The place had a wood cookstove as well as an electric one, which made the transfer from old to modern easier. She still hung her clothes outdoors on the line to dry even though she had purchased a dryer. The house was kept very neat and clean, as the ranch house had been, but was much easier to keep. Having the place to herself most of the time, she did not have to put up with muddy boots or dirt being tracked in.

At the ranch Mom was constantly cleaning and cooking. Now she had time to pursue interests of her own. She even started taking driving lessons! Never ever having driven before. This was pretty scary, as Mom was forty-nine years old. She bought a used car, which she was extremely proud of. I think it represented a form of freedom to her that she had not had at the ranch. She took up bowling in a league and made a lot of friends around town; she also took up the hobby of hooking rugs and made some very pretty ones. In her new yard, she could now grow more flowers—and especially roses, one of her favourites. She also planted a small vegetable garden. But she missed farm eggs and had to drive out to Dragon Lake to a friend's place to buy fresh eggs, not liking the store-bought ones.

Ed Adams stayed on at the ranch. He was treated with respect and pretty well left to do his own thing. He had the privacy of his own cabin, which he had lived in since arriving at the ranch back in 1960. He continued to follow his same routine of rising early and making his cup of tea, then doing chores. He retired early as well, to read in his cabin after the evening meal.

Dad moved to Tsetzi Lake in June of 1970, and Rick immediately began cutting and peeling logs for the construction of the lodge. Things were coming together for the beginning of the "Pan Phillips Fly-in Fishing Resort." The Vaughans and the Blackwells, who had moved from Oregon the year before and settled some twenty miles west of us on Moose Lake, had a bulldozer. Dad had made arrangements for one of them to build an airstrip at Tsetzi Lake. That work started a month or so after the move.

As for myself, I stayed on at the ranch for about six weeks to work for the new owners. Rick's girlfriend Delores and her baby son, who was about a year old at the time, were at Tsetzi Lake, so the guys had someone to cook for them there. But Delores lasted at the lake about as long as I lasted at the ranch. She was a town gal and not used to bush living. My dad could be very overbearing and his frugal ways didn't allow for many mistakes. Packing water, chopping wood and bathing in a tin tub or in the creek took some getting used to. Then with her baby not diaper trained, using the scrub board to wash diapers was a chore on its own. The mosquitoes were bad too, and allowed very little relief day or night. The baby could not be kept under the mosquito netting every hour of the day, and looked like he had measles from the bites. On a few occasions Delores left the baby with Rick and went fishing for the evening meal, but Rick was not used to babies. The baby would cry for his mother and Rick could not console him, and the sobs would soon turn into screams. Once when he was outside with the baby he started the chainsaw and ran it full throttle. He much preferred the screaming of the saw to the screams of the baby. Needless to say Delores soon packed up and returned to Smithers, and I couldn't say that I blamed her.

When the Anthonys moved in, there was a big change in the

running of the Home Ranch. Catering to paying guests and raising horses were given priority over the cattle operation. This was the era when the city folks paid good money to be flown into remote areas to fish and ride horses. In the evening they would sit around the fireplace with cocktails in hand, inhaling the aromas of the evening meal filtering in from the kitchen, and discuss the events that had taken place during the day. Later they would retire to their private log cabins for a restful night of sleep. It was called experiencing the wilderness dream.

The new house that we had built on the ranch but never occupied was turned into a lodge, with a big kitchen and dining area with a fireplace. A full-time cook was hired. Bob had a six-passenger Piper Cherokee aircraft so he flew in and out of Quesnel and Williams Lake, constantly hauling people back and forth.

Dorthea remodelled the old ranch house by stripping the walls of cardboard and wallpaper, which my mother had put up to keep the mud chinking from falling, and recovering them in rough lumber nailed up horizontally with narrow strips of rough lumber nailed over the cracks. The curtains were removed from the windows, and Mom's beloved kitchen cabinets were moved over into what was then referred to as "the lodge," as was the cookstove. The heater was taken out of the living room and a rock fireplace was installed in there as well. Dorthea also had the guys remove all the dirt from the roof of the ranch house and was so pleased when the rafters rose up several inches. But the dirt was also the roof's insulation, so the house was always cold after that, or too hot in summer. A barrel heater had to be put back into the living room when fall came to keep things from freezing, and had to be kept going most of the time as soon as the days cooled off at summer's end.

The ice house and the chicken coop were turned into bunkhouses and two new guest cabins were built across the slough west of the house; wooden walkways with handrails were built across the marshy ground to reach them. A cabin for laundry and showers was built on the site of the ranch's old root cellar. The only buildings left untouched were Ed's bunkhouse (the cabin built in 1935), the meat house (which no one used) and the small bunkhouse just out front of the main ranch house, which accidentally burnt down the first winter Anthonys were living there.

I am not sure who wanted goats, but the family got two kid goats right away. Well of course they were the sweetest little things. It was my first experience with goats, and I discovered they are very good for getting into everything and eating everything. One evening I went out with the twin-mantle gas lamp to fill it. I set the lamp down on the porch step and went to get the gas jug, and the goats promptly ate the mantles off the lamp. They would run through the house whenever the doors were left open, jumping onto the furniture and racing into the bedrooms and over the beds, leaving their droppings scattered everywhere. But they weren't the only animals causing havoc. The monkey was taken from his cage one day and escaped up into the rafters of the main house and could not be lured down. Bob and Dorthea's daughter Terry finally lost her patience and hit the monkey with a broom, knocking it unconscious, or maybe when it fell from the rafter to the floor it knocked itself out. She rocked him in her arms till he came to and nearly escaped a second time, before being stuck back in his cage.

I flew with Bob a bit in his Cherokee but some of the things he did scared me. I was not fond of flying anyway. We once left Anahim so heavily loaded I don't know how we got off the runway. I prayed all the way to the Home Ranch strip, as the plane seemed to barely move, its engine labouring just above the treetops. We had to keep gaining elevation even to get over the lowest pass between the mountains, and it was still touch and go. Once that hurdle was crossed we could lose elevation and things went more smoothly, but by then I was nearly paralysed from fear.

Another time, leaving Williams Lake, it was me, Bob, Dorthea, the four kids—two of whom were teenagers—my brother Ken and a friend of his who we were dropping off at the landing strip at the old Punzi airbase, making nine people in a six-seater aircraft. Bob was singing the song "Tennessee Bird Walk" at the top of his lungs when the gas tank the plane was running on ran dry. The motor quit, and there was sudden silence, except for Bob's booming voice. The aircraft started on its descent towards the timbered landscape some thousand feet below us. The prop slowed down to the point where you could see the full blade as it turned. Bob quit singing and stared at the gauges. One of the kids seated behind me promptly threw up all over my back. Suddenly Bob's thinking kicked in and he switched tanks and restarted the motor, which fired right up, and the roar of the engine could be heard in the cabin again—but only the engine. There was no more singing or conversation. We landed at Punzi and dropped off Ken and his friend then continued on to the Home Ranch. That was probably my last ride in the Cherokee with Bob at the controls.

Bob was also loud and crude, especially to women, when he'd had a drink or two. On one of these occasions I sat holding a heavy riding boot that I'd found beside the door. I was tired of his crude remarks, and when he got close enough I grabbed the boot with both hands and began hitting his face and head with it as hard as I could. He was a big man, and I think a Hereford bull would have backed down first. I hit him a good dozen times—and I was strong in my younger days—before he backed off. The next day his face was discoloured where most of the blows had landed. My life was more peaceful after that.

Bob and his hired hands drank a great deal and the local Indians hired to build fences were constantly drunk. When haying started later in the summer, one of the hired hands who was raking hay with a team of horses had a gallon jug of Calona Red wine tied around his neck with a piece of rope. I think this was about when I decided it was time I left. I took my cat Jimmie and my saddle horses and moved down to the lake with Rick and Dad, as Delores had left by then.

There had been a lot of plane traffic at the Home Ranch, and it was pretty quiet without it at Tsetzi Lake. We did get aircraft buzzing us, though, and we did get float plane traffic: it was only a few hundred yards to the building from Tsetzi Lake, whereas it was about two and a half miles from Styvie Lake to the Home Ranch. The airstrip was just being built, using John Blackwell's bulldozer. The strip would run north to south between Tsetzi Lake and Airplane (Cluchata) Lake. From where the building site was, going south there was a gradual rise, giving the strip a slope. Most of it was gravel, but the part closer to the building was dirt and whenever the wind blew there was plenty of dust to coat everything. When it rained the area turned to mud, which would be tracked into the cabin.

Even without the airstrip, we had a lot of company. I recall that summer as a busy one. The Anthony kids came and went and people rode in regularly. Some flew into the ranch strip, where we picked them up and brought them down to Tsetzi Lake. Our living space was fairly small but somehow we managed. We pitched tents for sleeping quarters and had a lot of fun. At the same time, living in close quarters wasn't easy. The cabin was crowded. We had no washing machine, so it was the scrub board and a tin tub on the porch of the cabin. This was how my Mom had had to do laundry for a number of years before she was able to afford to buy a gas washing

*Ilgachuz hunting camp—Dad and I are in the back with the four hunters and (left to right) Dave Helkenberg, Peter Alexis and Rick Boland are in front.*

machine, and it was not a pleasant chore. My knuckles became red and bruised. My hands wrinkled like prunes. Wringing out the clothes made my palms sore. It was bad enough to wring them out after washing them in warm water but then they had to be rinsed in cold water and wrung again, then hung out on the clothesline. Dad was not known to change his jeans often. They were usually able to stand by themselves when he'd finally change them, and they required a great deal more scrubbing to get clean. We had heated discussions about this. My cat Jimmie helped me once by peeing on Dad's jeans during the night as they lay on the floor. Least he changed them then! Dad did a lot of swearing about it, but I pointed out that the cat thought the soiled jeans were a litter box because they were so filthy.

The log work on the lodge was pretty well completed before the hunting season started that fall. The landing strip was also ready for planes. Quite a number of hunting parties were booked. I did have a guide licence but mainly I was to cook on the September hunts, and then I had to move my cows. Rick and Peter Alexis—a local Indian, friend and long-time neighbour—were the guides and Dad packed meat. We would take four hunters on a ten-day hunt for moose, caribou, mountain goat or grizzly bear, whatever they had bought tags for. We never hunted deer or black bear. Rick and Dad both took teams and wagons to the hunting camp up in the Ilgachuz Mountains on Carnlick Creek, following the original trail first cut to the Home Ranch, while Peter and I took the hunters on horseback. We hunted out of the Carnlick Canyon base, where a small cabin had been built a couple years before. (A year or so later a second cabin was built for the hunters' own use.)

It would take a full day to reach the hunting camp, arriving about dark. The horses were taken down to the creek and hobbled and put across on the south side. With all of us in the cabin there wasn't much room, so we ate in relays at the table. The six bunks were for the hunters, Dad and me. Rick and Peter got the floor. Peter snored worse than anyone can imagine, and no one else was much better. You had to be tired to sleep in there! Dad would have everyone up at the crack of dawn and send Rick and Peter after the horses, which during the night generally hobbled a couple miles downstream. On the early hunts, when feed was still good, a couple horses would be staked, but as feed got scarcer they would be hobbled too. This meant that Rick and Peter had to walk after the horses, packing enough halters to catch them all, then tail them up and return to camp riding bareback.

In the meantime I prepared breakfast and fed the hunters and made lunches while Dad filled grain boxes with oats and brought in wood or water, whatever was needed. When Rick and Peter returned, Dad saddled the horses while the guys ate and then everyone took a lunch and left for the day. On days that Dad was in camp he kept me busy, usually cutting and splitting wood. On days that he was out packing meat I was on my own. I would clean up the cabin and plan supper, and then I was free to read or go for a walk. Generally the guides and hunters never returned till after dark.

On the ride into the base camp with two American moose hunters on the first hunt, it was a cool day with a light rain falling. We were about halfway to camp and the guys were already feeling the effects of the saddle when a young bull moose crossed the trail ahead. We had been riding for some time in an old burn sparsely covered by small second growth and the few dry trees still standing. I stopped my horse and told them it was a good shot as the bull stopped broadside and watched us. They were not interested, pointing out it was the first day, and besides it was raining. I urged them strongly to shoot it, and I would gut it out, but to no avail. The young bull trotted off for the cover of heavy pine. As the ten-day hunt wore on with warm weather and long, hard riding, I couldn't resist poking some fun at them for not taking one on the first day. They had good luck, however, and did get two bull moose on the last day.

# CHAPTER 2

# On the Trail Again

After two hunts to the mountains, I had to get ready to move my cattle to Nazko, about ninety miles towards Quesnel. I had made arrangements earlier in the summer with Lloyd Bennett, who managed the Malfait Ranch, to winter my cattle for me. I still hoped that somehow I would be able to keep my cows, and this was the first step in trying to do that. Herb, a young fellow who was working for Lloyd at Nazko, was to help me with the cattle. Herb arrived at Tsetzi Lake on his saddle horse the day before I wanted to leave, with his bedroll and belongings tied behind the saddle. He had left Nazko two days earlier, pushing his horse hard to cover the distance and arrive on time. I had moved my cattle from the Home Ranch to Tsetzi Lake a few days before, so they had had a few days to get used to being away from the main bunch.

We left the following morning with the first light. It was a cool October morning, the frost sparkling on the ground, the grass crunchy under the hooves of the animals. When a cow bawled, its breath was like a cloud of fog. I had belled a couple of the older cows so we could keep track of their movements during the nights to come. It was a small bunch of about thirty-five head of cattle, so they were easy to manage. The few yearlings would stay with the cows and calves; there were not enough of them to split and cause

*Here's me with Apache, one of my many horses, in the early 1970s.*

problems. I took a pack horse to pack food, a fry pan, a coffee pot
and another pot, a small tent, tarps, picket ropes and hobbles, a
change of clothes, rain gear and gumboots. On my saddle horse
I packed a .22 rifle for grouse hunting. That would be our fresh
meat supply for the trip. One person had to do most of the bush
riding, as it was hard to get into the thick bush or timber leading a
pack horse.

We would follow the wagon road east, a route we had used to
drive cattle to market since the fall of 1952. On previous drives we'd
normally cover from the Home Ranch to what was called Paul's
Meadow, above Tsacha Lake, on the first day. On this drive we were

already four miles down the trail at Tsetzi Lake, so we pushed the cattle all the way to Antoine Baptiste's place on Kushya Creek, near the east end of Tsacha Lake, a good twenty-two miles. One of the reasons for this was that Bob Anthony's Home Ranch cattle drive was leaving the day after me, and I wanted to have a day in between us. But it was a long day for the calves.

We stopped for awhile at Francis Cassam's summer place near Tsacha Lake and let the cows graze on the little hay meadow there, but there was no water so they were soon on the move down the trail, till they found water at the first small creek. The next stop was at Paul's Meadow, where they fed for only a short time and bedded down to rest. When they got up to feed we pushed them off the brush flat and onto the trail. The next eight miles was a good area for mushrooms. In September and October cattle love to feed on the mushrooms that grow throughout the pine timber. This made the rest of the day hard, with the cattle scattering through the trees. Darkness caught us a good hour from Antoine Baptiste's place. When we did arrive we put the cattle behind a fence into a pasture and staked our tired horses down by the creek. We started a roaring fire and snacked on a cold supper, then threw our beds down near the dying fire a short time later. Nothing moved during the night.

We broke camp in the morning and gathered up the cattle. After counting them, I was happy to find that we had lost none in the dark the night before. We then got them started on the trail to Kluskus, the abandoned Indian village. The day was hot and muggy with a drizzle of rain. The cattle moved slowly, still weary from the long drive the day before. But by now they were far enough from home—they were not willing to stray from each other, and stayed together on the rutted wagon trail that wound its way east through the spruce and poplar. Five miles down the trail we came to the west end of Squirrel Lake (part of the Kluskus Lakes chain), where there was a grassy opening on the lakeshore with an abundance of feed. The cattle grazed for a time and drank from the rocky shoreline of the lake, causing the local loons to call across the water that there were unknown animals on the shore.

We let the cattle bed down for a rest while we ate our lunch sitting under a large spruce tree, which gave us shelter from the misty rain drifting down. A light breeze stirred the leaves and some drifted slowly to the ground.

From there the trail stayed back from the lake a bit, following the hillside for several miles to the east end of the lake where again there were grassy flats and steep, grassy hillsides. A creek drained from the end of the lake. The wagon trail crossed that creek but we didn't, instead keeping the cattle on a saddle horse trail that was a shorter route to Kluskus, along the north side of the fast-moving creek through thick stands of poplar and spruce where the undergrowth was thick with feed. A lot of it was brown from the frost but plenty of green feed grew underneath. The cattle spread out off the trail, anxious to graze. It was early afternoon when we arrived at Kluskus, the ten miles passed easily. The day cleared off and turned hot. We let the cattle go on a dry grass flat below the church where there was plenty of feed.

Staking our horses out on the thick grass we explored the old buildings of the village, which were surprisingly in good condition, and the Catholic church, which was still in fairly good shape. Only a few years before, all the contents of the church had been there: candles and holders, priests' robes, statues, chandeliers, hymn books and benches. Now they were all gone, stolen by city people wanting a souvenir of the country, I suppose. The huge bell that had hung for so many years in the tower had even been taken. As a child I had loved to ring the bell and listen to the sound as it carried across the water of the lake to echo off the Kluskus hills on the south side.

This old settlement had been the home of the Indian people since before Alexander Mackenzie passed through in 1793. It was now abandoned. In the forties, when the people got cattle, the village had moved east six or eight miles to what was called New Kluskus. There they were close to the swamp meadows that were hayed each summer for winter feed, and where the cattle could be fed.

Across the creek from the village, nestled in the pine trees, was the old Kristenuk store. Grass had come up through the cracks on the porch and pine trees had grown up several feet tall around the building. Paul Kristenuk had opened the store around 1920, when the trading of fur was big money. Using teams and wagons in summer and teams and sleighs in winter, Paul did all of the freighting of supplies from Quesnel, over one hundred miles to the east, even travelling on from Kluskus to his store at Ulkatcho village, another seventy miles west towards the Dean River. Alex Paley came to Kluskus in 1925 to run the store for Paul and spent four or five years there. Originally the Hudson's Bay Co. had operated a trading post there in the mid-1800s but the company abandoned it by 1860. The building site of that trading post is unknown to me, and I never knew anyone who did know where it was. It may have been on the same site as the Kristenuk store.

The old graveyard on a small knoll overlooking Kluskus Lake was not used anymore, as funerals and burials were now held on the reserve in Nazko. The hand-carved wooden fences around the individual graves were rotted and falling down, as were the old homemade crosses and the spirit houses. The few granite headstones engraved in Latin or the Carrier language, I've never known which, were now overgrown with grass.

At dusk we ate and then checked the horses, taking them to water and again staking them for the night. The cattle were bedded down where we had left them, below the church. They seemed very content. Gathering dry twigs and pine boughs for fire starter in the morning we crawled into our bedrolls, covering the beds with tarps to keep off the heavy frost.

During the night I awoke to the ringing of cowbells as the cattle ran towards camp and the trail that led to home. I leapt from my bed and pulled on my jeans and boots, all the time yelling for Herb that the cattle were coming. I grabbed my coat from under the sleeping bag and the flashlight, and took off running in the dark, waving the light just in time to turn the cattle off the trail and up the hillside into a tangle of poplar, willows and wild rose bushes. There were a good deal of downed trees, covered in grass. Stumbling over logs and ducking branches I kept up with the cattle till they stopped, coughing and mooing for their calves. We stood with them for a few minutes till they began to graze on the grass. I could hear Herb's teeth chattering in the dark. Turning the light on him I found him clad in nothing but his shorts. I made some remarks that I hoped resembled sympathy while trying to curb my laughter. I asked if he was all right and he said he'd straddled a rather large rose bush in his flight in the dark but thought he'd be okay.

We slowly manoeuvred the cattle back to the open flat and waited till they seemed quiet. Herb went off to camp while I checked our horses — they apparently had not been spooked like the cattle. I then returned to camp and bed. I lay awake the rest of the night lest whatever had spooked the cows returned, but all was quiet. The cowbells tinkled in the distance and occasionally an owl hooted. The stars twinkled in the ebony sky, the loons called on the lake. Slowly the eastern sky began to show signs of the coming day, so I was able to get up and start the campfire and a pot of coffee. While the fire crackled and the water began to steam I went to the creek with a towel to wash. The water was as cold as can be and it definitely woke me up. By the time I returned to camp Herb was up and had added grounds to the blackened coffee pot by the side of the flames. The brown liquid rolled gently within the pot sending out the strong smell of fresh coffee.

It didn't take us long to get on the trail even though it would be our shortest day — about five miles along the side hills and Kluskus Lake. The day was beautiful. We let the cattle graze as they travelled. There was so much feed scattered through the poplar trees: pea vine and vetch and other fine grasses I did not recognize. A lot of fireweed as well, which had gone brown but seemed to have sheltered the grasses underneath as they were still green. When the Indian people raised Hereford cattle and grazed them on these side hills, they were some of the best cattle in the country — and one of the reasons was the feed. My dad had often bought sire bulls at Kluskus, trading horses for them and hauling them home in the winter with team and sleigh before they got too big. During really wet summers, when the swamp meadows were too wet to hay, Lashaway Chantyman, who was no doubt the best cowman on the reserve, cut hay on these hills; this I remember as a child. No cattle were raised here anymore. The older people had passed on or were too old to care for cattle, and the younger people had no interest in the work that went with raising a herd. There would never be cattle on these hills again.

We went through a gate and crossed the stagnant water at the end of Kluskus Lake. We let the cattle go and rode a short distance on to Lashaway Chantyman's small log house and barn. There was no one home so we made camp in the thinly scattered pines in back of the buildings.

We were up early again the next morning; it was hard to sleep past the breaking of day as cattle travel best in the early hours. The morning was cool with snow flurries slowly drifting down. We pushed the cattle along a fence that kept the stock from a hay meadow below. A couple of miles farther we came to the small cluster of log cabins known as New Kluskus, or Clay-Clee (depends who you are talking to . . . some called it "Stink Water") where the Indians from Old Kluskus now lived. There was an assortment of cabins, some small and some a bit larger but none of beauty. A small barn with a small pole corral was down closer to the creek. As we approached, a dozen or so dogs set up their barking while half-naked children ran in and out of the doorways calling excitedly to those inside. The cattle bunched up and milled about till the dogs were hushed. We then worked our way past the little settlement, with greetings exchanged and short conversations, and continued on down the tree-lined trail, with its rocky and rutted path, towards the northeast and the Blackwater River.

On earlier drives we did not come this way, but continued on eastward to the Coglistiko River. I had not been down this trail for many years. Along it the timber was thicker, with very few grassy areas, and we never found anywhere with grass enough to stop and let the cattle feed. The plan was to spend the night at Pan Meadow, which was a swamp meadow once leased by the Frontier Cattle Co.

for haying and wintering cattle. Now Larry and Barb Smith lived there. The actual place was a good mile or better off the main trail. The day seemed long, not knowing where the turn off was. I was concerned that we would run out of daylight, on a trail I was not familiar with, but we arrived before dark. We were made welcome, as was the way with the bush hospitality, even though we arrived unannounced. The cattle were turned into the field to graze on the stubble while hay was forked out of the hayloft of a barn into a corral for the horses. A creek ran under the fence in the corner of the corral, supplying water for them. Barb cooked up a big dinner of moose steak in their small log home. With full stomachs, we sat in the warmth of the crackling fire and the orange glow of the lamplight and enjoyed good company and lively conversation.

After a breakfast of pancakes and fried potatoes we saddled up in the crisp cool morning and gathered up the cattle. Larry gave me directions and advice for the trail ahead. After an hour and a half of pine and spruce forest we dropped down a rather steep hill to the Blackwater River and a small scattering of little meadows, with good feed. We let the cattle graze for awhile before pushing them to the river. Fortunately, in October the river was low. The crossing was very rocky and wide. Back when it was used often with teams and wagons a path had been cleared of rocks, making the crossing easier in high water. It was no doubt done at low water, and the rocks had been thrown downstream, making a noticeable trail in the rock-strewn river. But now it was filling in again, with rocks moved over the years by high water and the shifting of sand. The cattle didn't want to enter the fast-running water. I led the pack horse across and tied him up on the opposite shore, then returned for the cattle. After much coaxing they waded across, tails high in the air and mooing for their calves, which splashed along behind their mothers.

We continued downstream for several hours and made camp along China Lake (now called Kluskoil Lake), pushing the cattle ahead of us to feed through the sparse poplar, where there were areas of good grass. By now there was little fear of them leaving, unless something spooked them during the night. We pitched the tent I had brought along as dark clouds had rolled in and we expected rain or snow. We stacked our saddles and pack gear in a pile and covered it all with a tarp. During the night the rain started and refused to stop. We were reluctant to break camp in the morning, waiting for the rain to let up. Standing around the fire with nothing to do I begin to tease Herb to pass the time while he shaved and then brushed his teeth. I distracted him, and he put shaving cream on his toothbrush instead of toothpaste, so I had my laugh for the day.

The cattle eventually became restless, scattering in different directions, so we packed up camp and pushed on to Poplar Mountain, where the grass was thick and green. At one time the rolling hills along this stretch of the trail had miles of open country with scattered poplars and occasional pockets of spruce in the low areas. Grass fires were set every spring to burn off the old grass and control the second growth and the rose bushes, producing some of the best range in the country. Now the second growth was fast covering the hills, as fires were rare.

It rained all day and we set the tent up in the falling rain and crawled into our damp bedrolls. Morning was no better. From there on we took a side trail off the main trail, one that followed the Blackwater River down to the Nazko River. I had never been down this trail but Herb had, so one of us had some idea where we were going. The trail was less used and had a lot of windfall on it. It was the worst day we had fighting with the cattle, which constantly bunched up and bawled. We lost our tempers and yelled and swore, which was no help at all. The rain fell. Late in the day we finally reached a good camping spot and stopped for the night.

Morning brought clear skies and, surprisingly, a lot of warmth. The damp ground steamed under the warm sun. The trail improved with the miles and the cattle travelled better. We arrived at the Malfait Ranch by mid-afternoon and turned the cattle over to Lloyd. I turned my horses loose to start on their homeward journey. They had nearly a hundred miles to go but I knew they would be home in a few days. There was one closed gate at the end of Kluskus Lake that would stop them but the Indian people there would let them through for me. I took my saddle and pack outfit to Quesnel and the next day flew back to the Blackwater to finish the hunting season.

## CHAPTER 3

# Settling In at Tsetzi Lake

My friend Pat from Quesnel cooked on the first October hunt, while I moved the cows. Pat had never done anything like it before, but seeing as she was nearly six feet tall and a very attractive lady, she could get away with a lot more than I could. Dad fell all over himself to please her, and Rick probably fell in love. She did go out one day on horseback with Rick, on a caribou hunt. The day was miserable, so Rick loaned her a pair of one-piece long johns with the bay window in the back, and she dressed up very warmly with borrowed stuff. The sleet was blowing hard and the frozen crystals stung as they hit, but they did get a caribou high up in the open country above timberline. At one point Pat said nature called. She did not realize the long johns had the flap in back for such purposes so she removed most of her clothes, exposing her bare back to the driving sleet. She said she was stung by the hard, driving frozen rain and nearly froze herself before she got her clothes back on. The guys gave her a teasing about the long johns. Pat said she enjoyed her ten days in the mountains, but was happy to catch the plane back to Quesnel.

We had two more hunts before the season closed. On one of them Rick had a hunter who was after a grizzly bear, as he had bought a tag. Rick took him and his hunting partner by saddle horse into the high country to some old gut piles, and they spotted a huge grizzly. Quickly hobbling the horses, they got within range for a good shot. The hunter, whose name neither one of us can recall, had a 7 mm Magnum rifle and was usually a good shot. However, he only badly wounded the huge bear, which then fled downhill towards thick timber and cover. Tracking him through the scattered balsam trees, all three men were on high alert, as they knew the animal was now very dangerous. The bear had stopped a number of times and bled heavily but continued on when the men got close. Below timberline the blood trail indicated the bear had taken cover in a small patch of thick pine and windfall. The guys circled around the hiding spot and knew without a doubt that the bear lay in that thick cover. Rick refused to go in—the thickness allowed very little chance for a quick shot at a charging bear—and strongly advised the hunter not to either. He ignored Rick's advice and followed the bear into the pines. He was a lucky man: as the bear was charging he was able get off a killing shot. This grizzly became number four in the Boone and Crocket Club record book at that time.

After the last hunt of the season, which turned out to be a very

*Grizzly hunt in the Ilgachuz—Rick Boland with hunter and a trophy bear.*

successful one, Dad decided he would throw a party to celebrate. We had had four hunters who had taken two trophies each and were happy guys. Everyone in the area was invited. One of the hunters flew into town for everything we needed for the party, including a very good supply of alcohol. The local Indians all arrived and set up camp south of the lodge in the spruce by Tsetzi Creek. A lot of the meat we had brought down from the mountains was barbequed. I am not sure what we had for music, but it started out as a great evening, with everyone having a good time. But as the night progressed, things began to get out of hand. A couple of the local girls got into a fight in the kitchen. Dad had hold of one and Toby Cave, who had flown in for the evening from Quesnel, held the other, but there was still some hitting and scratching going on. Finally they were put outside and they drifted off towards camp. In the meantime one of our intoxicated guests fell onto the huge table laden with food, which broke in half, landing the drunk and all the food in a heap on the floor. Rick hauled him outside for a talking to as more fights started up among the locals.

I decided it was best I left. Grabbing my sleeping bag, I walked down the creek a ways and found a spot to bed down. The sound effects were still loud, though, and went on well into the morning. I awoke hours later to glass bottles being thrown into the tin garbage can — it was the only sound from the lodge I heard. I was in no hurry to get up; I thought this was one mess the men could clean up. When I did get up the worst of the mess was gone but there was a lot of damage. There was broken glass embedded in the floor and blood splattered up the walls. At least the big picture window had survived the wild night. It was the last time my father invited the whole neighbourhood to a party.

At the end of the season we pulled all the shoes off the horses and let them go to winter range. Dad had Rick dig a big pit in the ground at the lodge and all the canned goods were buried in wooden pack boxes and then covered with three or four feet of dirt. Everything else was left where it was and all the buildings were padlocked. Then we left for town for the winter, as there was very little sense of anyone sitting out there for the long cold months. We all flew into Quesnel. Dad went to Mom's; Rick and I went to Smithers to look for work for the winter months.

Reluctantly my mom agreed to take my cat, as I couldn't very well leave him behind. He managed the plane ride to town with only an occasional meow. During the car ride from the airport to Mom's he hid under the front seat. He didn't take long to adjust to the house, but whenever the front door was open he hid, not recognizing the surroundings outside. His litter box was in the basement so Mom left the basement door open a bit to allow him free travel. When Dad was there he kept closing the door, so the cat would pee in Dad's shoe. It did not take many times for Dad to remember to leave the door open. After a few months the cat would sit in front of the screen door but still refused to go out. By spring he would eventually go out on the step and the lawn. I didn't take him back to the lodge in the spring, but left him with Mom. Then one day he ventured out of the yard and onto the street, where he was hit by probably the first car he had ever seen. So ended Jimmie's life.

Someone drove by my mom's place one very cold morning and said that my mother was outside, scraping the frost off the windows of the car while it warmed up, the exhaust sending out plumes of smog. My father stood just inside the glass door with his heavy winter coat on, waiting for Mom to get the car ready. They were apparently going somewhere, and seeing as Mom drove it was up to her to get the car defrosted and ready to go.

When spring came, for some reason Lloyd was unable to keep my cows as we had arranged, so before I returned to the Blackwater I had to hire a truck and have the cows hauled to Williams Lake and sold. It broke my heart to part with my cattle, but I had no choice.

I applied to do the 1971 census for the Blackwater area for Statistics Canada, taking my training in Williams Lake in early June, then flying home from Quesnel to the fishing camp. From there, I travelled around on saddle horse and did the census. My area was fairly large but with very few people. The Indian people were pretty well all at Blue Lake doing a fencing contract at the time. The Vannoy family, who lived to the west of us on Cottonwood Creek, were the only white people in my area besides whoever was at the Home Ranch and us. Murray Vannoy did not believe in putting anything on paper. He did not believe in banks, either, and any money he had was kept in cash. They had no radio, and didn't get any newspapers or magazines. Murray went to Anahim on occasion and did visit a little with a few neighbours; on rare occasions he took his two sons with him, but the missus and the two daughters stayed home. People were not encouraged to visit. Murray sometimes visited when we still lived on the Home Ranch and my mother always sent a few jars of canning home to Murray's wife as a neighbourly gesture when he left. Mom always wrapped the jars in as many of the most recent newspapers she could find — although our mail service was not good and they might have been several months old. I think she sent letters inside the papers too, but nothing was ever said. So when I arrived at their little ranch in the early afternoon one day the family was very happy to have company. But I could not say the same for Murray, especially under the circumstances. However, I finally convinced him that anything he told me, within reason, I would take for an answer. The forms were eventually filled out.

After that, I rode to the Cassams' place, on an Indian reserve close to Blue Lake and just north of Tsetzi Lake, where the Indians were fencing. There were a number of cabins there, plus a barn and a hayfield that was being fenced. The old Cassams, Mary and Francis, lived in a cabin back a bit on a hillside. The largest cabin, close to the creek, was the home of William Cassam and his wife Rose. The third cabin belonged to the older son, Wilfred. The Indians from the neighbouring area had pitched their tents about the yard, with each tent having its own campfire for cooking and heat during the cool evenings.

When I arrived, it was obvious that a celebration of some sort had happened. Although it was late morning, there was very little activity. The odd campfire was smoking and a few of the women were making some effort to prepare meals. Most were sleeping in the shade of wagons or trees, and the cabin doors were open, with the children racing in and out, their laughter carried over the campground. A number of children were down by the small creek and appeared to be fishing. I reined my horse in to watch what they were doing. They had five puppies whose eyes had not yet opened, and strings had been tied about their necks. The puppies were tossed into the water to float down a short distance and then pulled back up through the current to be picked up and tossed out again, to float down on the ripples once more. It was not something I enjoyed watching, but I didn't want to scold the children and take a chance of getting on the bad side of anyone when I needed their cooperation for the census.

When I tied up my horse up in some poplars a short distance from the tents and joined a few of the men in the shade, the children abandoned the puppies and came running over to see what I was up to. I spent all day gathering my information and filling out forms, in between numerous cups of pre-sweetened tea and eating bannock, which was delicious. I didn't have any of the dried meat I was offered but later I took more bannock, which was offered the second time with strawberry jam. Doing the forms was made much easier by the fact I knew these people and who belonged to whom.

Dad and Rick spent a lot of the summer of 1971 hauling lumber from Anahim Lake with teams and wagons, as a great deal was needed to build the lodge and cabins. It took a week to make just one round trip. Meanwhile the rest of us kept busy at the lodge. My sister Gayle was out from Terrace for the summer with her two daughters, Becky and Wanda. Dave Helkenberg, a friend of Rick's and mine from Smithers, was with us for most of the summer and my brother Rob was too. And the weather was hot. Gayle and I often wore just our swimsuits all day long. Dad disapproved, but we ignored his grumbling. The flies were really bad through July but that didn't faze us. Several times Gayle and I rode saddle horse over to Tsacha Lake Lodge (now called Mackenzie Trail Lodge), about twelve miles away, to visit the cook, Pearl, who had a fondness for afternoon cocktails. In a letter Gayle wrote to her husband Tom in August of 1971, she said, "We could have been picked up for drunken horseback riding."

Many years later I sat by an old vet from World War II at a social following a Remembrance Day ceremony. He turned to me and said, "My wife and I flew into Tsetzi Lake nearly forty years ago and spent the night with your father. You were at a party next door." I nearly laughed, because in that country there is no such thing as next door. He continued by saying that I came home in my bare feet. I asked him how was I travelling and he replied, "Oh, saddle horse." I am not sure why I had no shoes but it must have been one of the forays Gayle and I made down to Pearl's.

The year before, the manager of the Tsacha Lake Lodge had had a marijuana grow-op—or plantation, as it was called then—back in the swamps and it had been discovered. There had been a raid and a big flutter about it. Things like that were rare in the 1970s, especially in the Blackwater, but I guess there's a first time for

*Becky, my niece, sits (carefully) astride the not-so-gentle paint pony that my dad liked so much.*

everything. Gayle once visited the marijuana plantation on the way back from Tsacha Lake Lodge. Some guy at the lodge had told her that there was still pot growing there, and that it had yellow flowers. So she picked a bunch of the flowers and dried them. Rick, Dave and Rob decided to smoke some after it was dried, but Dave came to the conclusion it was buttercups. Everyone had a good laugh.

Gayle had a poodle called Shimmy at that time. It fell into Tsetzi Creek and if not for Rick it would have drowned, as it could not swim. After that, Dave took it into the creek and gave it swimming lessons, until it learned how. Life must have been awfully boring to spend one's evening teaching a dog to swim.

That second summer at Tsetzi Lake I bought my nieces Becky and Wanda, Gayle's daughters, a red-and-white paint Welsh pony. Becky, who by then was fourteen, was able to handle her; Wanda was too young. Becky rode her some, but she had an attitude typical of ponies. Dad was the one who thought she was the nicest little

*Here's me at Tsetzi Lake shocking loose hay in the 1970s.* VANCE HANNA

horse. She was also a source of entertainment for him. When a person would get her trotting while riding her bareback, Squaw, which was her name, would suddenly turn so fast they would lose their seat, causing Dad to laugh his head off. He was forever saying, "Try this pony out, she is so smooth and easy to ride. Just ride her bareback. Oh, she is gentle, just trot her a bit." When she was trotted she quite often bucked, and generally dumped whomever she pleased, which caused Dad to laugh and smirk for some time to come. It was a wonder he wasn't sued by some of his guests.

While Dad was feeding horses at Sleepy Hollow earlier that spring, before I had returned for the season, one of my mares had had a colt. Because of the pack of wolves that was hanging about, Dad put a bell on the unbroken mare with a very strong bell strap, then turned her on the range. About a month later, after I had returned home, we were told by some Indian people who had been hunting east of Naglico Lake that they'd found a mare hung by her bell strap. She had apparently been rubbing on the trunk of a large fallen pine tree with huge roots exposed and had caught the bell strap on a strong root. She could have walked ahead and probably set herself free, but because she was not halter broken, she had pulled back and choked herself. The colt was still alive and had stayed by the mare. We took the team and wagon as near as we could and caught the colt, which by then was quite weak and offered very little resistance. We were able to walk him to the wagon where we tied his legs together and bedded him in hay. He received a bumpy wagon ride back to Tsetzi Lake. It was not hard to teach him to drink warm canned milk from a pail. As soon as I could I ordered several bags of milk replacer and taught him to eat grain. The paint pony I had bought for my nieces right away acted as his mother, protecting him from the other horses so he was able to run loose in the pasture. He would come running for his three-times-a-day milk and grain. It did not take long for him to fill out from the scruffy bag of bones he once was.

Before returning to the lodge I had bought a large picture window. It was from a renovation somewhere. I had it all crated up and packed with hay to make sure it didn't break, as I had to haul it to Anahim Lake in the back of my pickup and the road from Williams Lake to Anahim was still pretty rough back then. From there it was hauled over the mountains with team and wagon, as there was no way it would have fit into a plane. When the window was removed from the crate, Dad was disgusted because the hay I packed around it was old brown hay. He said it could have at least been something the horses would have eaten! The window was a great addition—it made the lodge bright and gave us a good view of the lake. We also put in a fireplace. Elmer, a pilot from Vancouver, Washington, was a regular customer and also very good with rock work. On one of his fishing trips to the lodge he brought all the stuff he needed to put in a fireplace, and he set one day aside to build it. The novelty for the rest of the summer's rainy days was to light the fireplace and sit around watching the flames and visiting.

D'Arcy Christensen, who had A.C. Christensen General Store in Anahim Lake, would deliver groceries and mail to the lodge once a week, so we started calling it the "Dog Patch Deliveries." It was soon after he got his pilot licence and he was still a little rough on his landings. To distract him even more, Gayle and I and whoever else we could get would grab chairs when he was on his final approach and run out and sit by the runway, to watch his landing and count his touch downs. For most of that summer he would touch down and bounce in the air, sometimes several times, before smoothing out on the runway.

In July, my brother Ken was married in Williams Lake to Andrea Moss. It was a big church wedding and I was one of the bridesmaids, in a long gown and big floppy hat. Rob, then fifteen, was an usher and looked quite handsome all dressed up. I think this was probably the first and only time I saw my father in a suit and tie! But it was also the only wedding of one of his children that he attended. After the church ceremony and the dinner, the band started up with a good country type of dance music. Being a country girl, I found the long dress and heels rather hampered my good time so I went up to my room and changed into jeans and boots, and then let the dancing

*Mom and Dad at Ken and Andrea's wedding—the only time I ever saw my dad in a suit. But then it was the only wedding of one of his kids he attended.*

begin. I wasn't sure it was the proper thing to do, but then I was not one to follow rules.

Rick and Dave were at the lodge while we were away for the wedding, and Eileen Chapman from Smithers was visiting. The guys decided one moonlit night that they were going up along the lake to dig in old hogans, as we called them. Many years before the Indian people had actually lived in them, as pit houses—at the time of the smallpox outbreak they had lived there—but they were now just deep depressions in the ground. The guys thought they might find an arrowhead or two, but I really think they were more intent on scaring Eileen. She was scared to go with them but didn't want to stay at the lodge alone either, so she ended up going along. After digging for some time they found an actual skull in one of the holes. Rick chased Eileen around with it while clacking the jawbones together, as she screamed bloody murder. Finally they buried it again and the trio returned to the lodge and bed.

In August I went to Vancouver to see my mom, who was in Vancouver General having hip replacement. It was so hot in the hospital my mom said, "Wouldn't a cold beer be nice." My mom was not one to drink much. The next time I went up to see her I took a case of beer. She nearly fell out of the bed, and the look on her face was priceless. She told me in a very harsh whisper, "You can't bring that in here!" We could hear a nurse coming down the hall and Mom was making all kinds of signals with her hands for me to hide the beer. The nurse came in and noticed the beer right away, and asked Mom if she wanted the beer put in the refrigerator to keep it cool.

When fall came, we continued our hunts into the Ilgachuz Mountains. On one of the hunts I had a fellow who sat on his horse but made no attempt to control it. The mare did pretty well as she chose but was good about staying with my horse and keeping up. While we were following a game trail through some heavy spruce, we came upon a large dry spruce that had fallen over the trail and hung up on another tree. It was just high enough off the trail for a horse to pass underneath, but not the rider. I turned my horse and went around the trunk of the leaning tree, watching the hunter behind me. His mare seemed to turn after mine so I sat back in the saddle. Then there came a awful crash and the hunter yelling, "Whoa, whoa!" I spun my horse around to see what was happening. The mare had decided to go under the tree after all, and while the hunter had enough sense to try to get out of the saddle he had no sense to try to stop the horse. The saddle horn had caught on the tree, but the mare kept trying to get under it. The hunter had landed behind the saddle and wasn't able to get his big boots out of the stirrups, so he had fallen backwards over the horse's rump. He hung upside down over the rump with his head jerking as the mare lunged forward. At this point I started laughing—it did look funny. By about the fourth lunge the mare made, the hunter's feet came out of the stirrups and he fell on his head in the thick moss and skiff of snow. About the same time, the mare got under the tree with a rather roughed-up saddle horn.

On another trip I had a young guy who had never hunted and had never seen a moose, let alone killed one. We had ridden for a couple days without seeing much and on the third day got into a spruce swamp. Tying up our horses we walked the edge of the swamp for some time. I noted a number of cow moose, some with calves, in the area, and told him that there would be a bull around there somewhere. There were too many cows to be without a bull. We stood for awhile in a grassy area that allowed us a good view through the scattered spruce, listening for some indication of the bull. Suddenly one stepped out of the trees about forty feet in front of us and turned his rump to us, slowly walking away. Apparently he neither saw nor smelt us—his attention was on the cows. I touched the hunter's shoulder and pointed at the bull. Without hesitation he threw his gun to his shoulder and emptied the gun into the bull's rear end.

When everything was being shut down for the winter, I took the orphan colt to the Home Ranch. Ed was wintering there with Barry Rempel, a young guy from Quesnel, feeding the cows, as the Anthony family had moved to Williams Lake for the winter. One winter in the Blackwater had been enough for them, I guess. Ed and Barry said they would look after the colt for me. It was a good thing I took him there, as the winter had a lot of snow.

In a letter Ed wrote Gayle in February of 1972, he said they had had over a hundred inches of snow with a lot of wind. The wind had blown the stovepipe off the house. The team of horses had a hard time even pulling an empty sleigh through the snow. A plane had been in at Christmas with the mail and they had not seen anyone since. Cless Pocket Ranch had lost sixty-seven head of cattle, which fell through the ice somewhere on the ranch. He said the Anthonys had six cats, and they ate the same as two men. Barry shot an old bull moose, but it was so tough they roasted it in the oven on a board, then threw away the meat and ate the board. Barry had also made a batch of home brew from black figs. Ed went on to say that they had lots of flour, sugar, toilet paper, toothpicks and pepper, so Gayle could see they were living off the fat of the land—and he would be damn glad to see bare ground!

# CHAPTER 4

# From Tsetzi Lake
# Back to the Home Ranch

Before returning to Tsetzi Lake in the spring of 1972 I bought a big raw-boned palomino gelding in Vanderhoof, which I named Sadsack. Rick and Dad had bought a number of horses at the Vanderhoof horse sale. Rob, Dave Helkenberg and Frank, a fellow from Vanderhoof, were to trail the horses in to Tsetzi Lake. We trucked the horses out to Big Bend, south of Vanderhoof, and I think we went down Kenney Dam Road, then took a very narrow trail (which today is a logging road) and followed it till we came to a trapping cabin of Bert Irvine's. We unloaded the horses there. Rob had a German shepherd puppy he called Wetzel; he was going to take the pup along in a gunnysack tied to the saddle horn. After packing up a couple of pack horses, they started out. The puppy's head was showing and it seemed content to sit there in the gunnysack sling, looking around. After dropping down an incline from where we had unloaded the horses, the trail crossed a meadow towards the creek. Something spooked Sadsack, the palomino Rob was riding, and it took to bucking. Both Rob and the puppy went flying. From the hill I could follow the progress of the pup by the waves of the grass as it proceeded to leave the area as fast as its fat little legs would carry it.

When it came up the hill I caught it and called to Rob, who was now on his feet and had caught his horse, saying that maybe I would take the puppy with me in the plane, as I was flying home the next day. Rob agreed, and Wetzel was somehow always partly mine after that. I sold Sadsack soon after getting him home, to Barry at the Home Ranch; he named him Hank and put him in the harness, which he was much better suited for.

In early summer, Rob, Mickey Dorsey and Mrs. Paul St. Pierre, and I believe one of the St. Pierre girls, canoed the Blackwater River from William Cassam's place to Nazko. I am not saying they were the first to canoe the river, but they may have been the first to start as far upriver as they did. Dad hauled the canoes there from Anahim Lake with team and wagon and the ladies flew in. Canoeing had become a popular sport in the area and over the years more and more people did it—not only Canadians, but also Americans and Europeans. Everyone chose different starting points, but many started as far west as Eliguk Lake, flying their canoes into the lake strapped to the pontoons of float planes. Some canoes were hauled in with team and wagon. They would start down Ulgako Creek, which drains from Eliguk Lake and runs east to meet up with Carnlick Creek, but is often very shallow. When Ulgako Creek joins Carnlick Creek, from there eastward the water is called the Blackwater River. I have never learnt who named it. Back when Alexander Mackenzie passed through on his trip to the Pacific Ocean he travelled up the Blackwater River west from the Fraser River, and he called it the West River, but the name was changed at some point. (On some maps the trail following the Blackwater River is still referred to as West River Road.) One party of canoes flown in by a pilot who was not familiar with the area unloaded them at Basalt Lake, west of Eliguk Lake. Too late they discovered the tiny creek out of the lake ran west to the Dean River. They had believed the creek ran east to Eliguk Lake.

For a couple of summers a small group of students from Humber College in Toronto would come out with one of the professors and spend eight or ten days working about the lodge. Generally that meant helping with the haying, and getting firewood or peeling logs for a new cabin. In return for this Dad would take them on a short trail ride to the mountains. I never went on those trips, but Gayle and Rick would go.

My Dad loved to play tricks but he hated to have the tables turned on him. During the busy season at the fishing camp, in the evenings it was common for us and the fishermen to sit around the firepit on the benches built there and tell stories. My dad had purchased an ATV three-wheeler bike and it was his pride and joy. He even rode it to the outhouse. One evening he rode it from the front door of the lodge around back to the firepit, parking it by one of the benches. Some one took a rope and tied the three-wheeler to a bench post, which was set into the ground. It was dark and the grass was fairly high, so Dad didn't notice. When he decided to retire to his cabin some forty feet away, he got on the bike, started it and with a grin headed off—for about five feet. The bike came to an abrupt stop, throwing Dad over the handlebars. Everyone howled with laugher. Dad went off to his cabin grumbling and left the bike where it was.

Another time, one of the fishermen was showing Dad how to do wheelies with his three-wheeler, as the man apparently had experience on an ATV. Dad decided he wanted to try it but went out of sight from everyone for his little experiment, then came back crippled up, favouring his hand. He refused to discuss the matter.

Gayle came for a number of summers to Tsetzi Lake to cook for Dad, bringing Becky and Wanda along, and returned to Terrace when school started in the fall. At that time Pierre Elliott Trudeau was the prime minister, and Gayle was a strong Liberal supporter. She and Dad would get into very heated arguments about Trudeau's party. Dad said they were nothing but a bunch of frogs. He knew he could get her all haired up, and then he would have someone to argue with. One day Wanda was down by the creek and found a small frog, which she proudly carried to her mother. She may have had some coaching, but as she held it out she said, "Here is Trudeau." Well, there was some frizzy hair over that one!

One trick Dad liked to play on his guests was to dash out and call to one of them, usually when they were halfway to the lake to go fishing, saying that they were wanted on the telephone. Of course there was no phone at the lodge but nine out of ten people would hurry back to find Dad laughing at them. I always meant to get an old phone and set it up in the lodge somewhere, so it would look authentic for Dad's pranks, but I never did.

I don't know how Gayle managed to cook for Dad as he was constantly telling her what to cook, and not to waste anything. He caught her one day trimming the mould off a block of cheese, and told her it wouldn't hurt to just use it the way it was. She trimmed all the mould off after he left the kitchen and neatly stacked it on a dish, serving it only to him at mealtime. He did a lot of grumbling about that.

Another time Dad had a bottle of Crown Royal stashed in a cupboard for a special occasion. Gayle and I decided one evening when he was away to drink his stash. We carefully cut the label with a razor blade and over a long evening consumed the rye. The following morning we made a pot of tea and refilled the bottle, but we had a bit of a problem deciding just what shade the rye had been. After several attempts we both agreed it looked pretty authentic. A few weeks later, Dad was sitting around the table in the lodge with some guests and said he had a bottle of Crown Royal, and would buy them a drink. Gayle and I were both in the kitchen preparing supper. We stopped and stared at each other. The hour had arrived! Dad dug through the cupboard, found the bottle and returned to the table. Putting it down he returned to the kitchen for some glasses and a pitcher of water, all the time keeping up a stream of conversation. Gayle and I stopped our work and watched through the opening between the kitchen and the dining area, waiting for the explosion we knew was coming. Dad picked up the bottle and studied it for a moment, then said, "Would be a joke if it was tea, ha, ha." He then removed the cap and poured the amber liquid into several glasses. Picking up a glass he took a taste. With a bellow he said, "Jesus Christ, it is tea!" Gayle and I couldn't help laughing as Dad stormed around, angry that he was on the wrong end of the joke. We did in time replace his rye, and after that he kept his stash in his bunkhouse.

Dad stashed a lot of things in his bunkhouse. He always said some of the best inventions were things like chainsaws and mosquito dope. Whenever he came across a can of bug dope he hid it for his own use, even though it may have belonged to one of his paying guests or one of his kids. It didn't matter. I guess it came from too many years without it and dealing with the flies in the country. Whenever we could not find our mosquito dope we'd slip into his bunkhouse and help ourselves to his large stash. I often wondered how many times a can of bug dope went back and forth. Another thing he liked to pick up was Bic lighters. When he thought he wasn't being watched he'd hold up his newest lighter and check the amount of fuel. If it was a new one or reasonably new, it was well hidden, but if it was just about out of fuel he would place it in the top drawer of his desk in the dining area. When someone was looking for a light he would give him or her a lighter from the drawer. Most of the time grinning like the Cheshire cat, because he had no doubt taken their new one twenty minutes earlier.

But Dad wasn't the only one to play tricks around the camp. Wanda, who was nine that summer, spent a lot of her time following Rick and Dave Helkenberg about and getting in the way of progress. She was wearing her two-piece swimsuit the day Rick and Dave were putting the roofing paper on the roof of a cabin. Wanda was watching from the bottom. Dave asked her if she wanted to come up on the roof. She gladly crawled up the ladder. Once up on the roof the guys smeared her with tar. No feathers were available or she no doubt would have had them too. When we discovered what the guys had done to her, we weren't happy. Taking her to the creek, Gayle and I used rags soaked in gas (from the jug of gas kept there for the water pump) to clean her off. By the time we finished she was red as a lobster and no doubt burning all over, but she never complained. Years later she told me she burnt and burnt and was scared to go near an open flame for a week for fear she would burst into flames.

On another day Wanda was fishing at the creek and while casting caught the three-pronged fishhook in her back. She came into the lodge for help. There was no way of pulling the hook out as one of the barbs had gone through the skin and back out. Dad got a wooden spoon and a razor blade and told Wanda to bite on the spoon while he cut the hook out of her back with the razor blade. He must have forgotten about turpentine (on the ranch everything got turpentine), because she didn't get a dose of that, but she didn't cry either.

The water system at the lodge was pretty primitive but it did serve the purpose. At the crown of the roof of Dad's cabin next to the lodge, two forty-five-gallon metal barrels were placed side by side on a platform. Water was pumped from the creek with a small gas water pump. A hose ran along on the ground to the cabin then up the wall to the roof, and into the top bunghole of one of the barrels. Pipe ran from the small bottom bunghole of one barrel over to the next barrel with a tee. From the tee a line came down the side of the cabin and ran under ground to the lodge, where it was connected to the sink and the hot water tank, which stood behind the kitchen range and had water lines running into the firebox. Whoever was pumping water shut the pump off when the water began trickling out of the top bunghole, where the hose was inserted. Around that hose was a cloth jammed tightly into the hole to keep dust and flies out, but if the water was not shut off soon enough the water pressure sometimes washed that cloth out of the opening.

It was during a busy season when we began to notice an odd taste to the water that didn't seem right, as the water was pumped almost daily and some times twice a day. Dad sent Rick up to look in the barrel. It was discovered that a bird had gotten into the barrel and had drowned, and was floating in our drinking water. Dad walked around swearing his usual "Jesus Christ." No one had any ill effects from it, or none of us that lived there all the time, anyway. But then our immune systems were used to all sorts of contaminated water. We drank the murky water in spring runoff, and while riding we drank from sloughs or whatever happened to be handy.

It was decided one morning that Dad, Dave and I would go over to Sleepy Hollow to get some horses—we kept spare horses in the pasture there. On our return trip from Sleepy Hollow Dave and I were both mounted on unbroken three- or four-year-old horses that had next to nothing for groundwork. This must have been Dad's plan all along. Fortunately they were pretty good-natured. My dad was riding my gentle saddle mare and in high glee was literally driving our horses like cows with a stout willow stick. Dave and I were kept busy trying to keep our mounts turned in the right direction, while dad trotted back and forth hitting the rumps of our horses with the willow stick to keep them moving, often at a run and in the wrong direction. We were both very vocal in our protests, but that only made Dad laugh harder. About halfway back to Tsetzi Lake the young horses got the idea to stay on the trail and ahead of Dad, and from then on things went better. Dave and I had pine needles in our hair and twigs down our necks and in our boots. Our hands and faces were scratched from the brush and branches we had come in contact with while taking side tours along the trail. For the next month, whenever we went for a horse it had to be one of the colts. That was how Dad broke horses.

When Rick Boland had first arrived at the ranch at the age of fourteen wanting to be a cowboy, he was just the type of person Dad liked to have around. Dad told him that he knew nothing and neither did the horse, so

*A young Rick Boland at the Anahim Lake Stampede—Rick had arrived at the ranch at the age of fourteen with the dream of becoming cowboy and, over the years, became like family.*

they were going to get along great together. Rick rode every horse that Dad gave him. Rick learned to cowboy the rough way.

One time Doug, a friend of Dad's from the coast, was up visiting and they had been out riding for a few days. At the end of the last day the saddles were removed from the horses. Dad told Doug to take the horse he had been riding out to the gate and turn it loose so the horse could go down to Sleepy Hollow. When Doug returned Dad asked him where the halter and rope were. Doug looked at him in surprise and said, "You told me to turn the horse loose. You never said anything about taking off the halter." A long lecture ensued about the dangers of a horse loose in the bush with a halter on, let alone dragging a long lead rope.

At the Home Ranch, just before haying time, we had to bring the horses off the range to get the teams together for the summer haying season. Then at the lodge we had to do so for hunting season. I loved to chase horses. It might take hours and sometimes days to locate the bunch but the chase was well worth the hours of riding the country. It was best if you were riding a fast horse that could get out and run hard in rugged ground if you had to turn the bunch. And it was a good idea to ride a well-broken one. Getting bucked off while chasing horses usually meant your saddle horse stayed with

*Young horses on open range.*

the bunch and you walked home, unless you could manage to hang on to the bridle reins when you fell off.

A horse that reined well was also a plus in thick timber. When the horses were found and started for home they would start out running hard, nostrils flaring, and their shoulders would soon be soaked with sweat and their flanks heaving, their hooves pounding over the rocky ground as they raced through the timber leaping downfall and breaking branches. As the herd crossed a soft area the mud and sod flew from their hooves and the pounding rhythm changed. Then hard ground would be gained and the pace would quicken again, with more breaking branches as the horses crowded each other off the trail and into the trees, still running hard. You might hear the shrill cry of a colt as it lost its mother's flank, and the return call of the mare as she switched direction in mid-stride to catch up to her colt, running alongside the foal till it was once more running against her flank. The pair would speed away, running hard again on the edge of the bunch. After several miles the pace would slow to a fast run for another mile or so, then a trot. But a lot depended on the day. If it was hot they slowed sooner; if it was a cool day they ran harder and farther. The horses would be streaked wet with sweat and dust. Some quickly dropped down on the trail for a quick roll and then got onto their feet to gallop away. After the pace slowed the biting and kicking would start, as the horses fought for their pecking order. The mares with colts held top spot, then the older geldings and mares. The young horses ran this way and that, crashing off through the thick growth when faced with the bared teeth of an older horse, or vicious flying hooves from some mare.

At the end of the season when the lodge was being closed down after the last hunt, I decided to spend the winter at the Home Ranch with Barry and Ed. It had been a long time since I had spent a winter in the bush, and I was getting tired of town life.

It was early November when we received a radio message from one of the Chantymans at Kluskus that a yearling steer lost during Bob Anthony's cattle drive in October had shown up on the reserve at Kluskus. Creeks were freezing or already frozen and there was about six inches of snow on the ground. Daylight was precious and the temperature was hovering about zero in the day and dropping down to fifteen below at night. But the steer had to be brought home, so Barry and I prepared to ride to Kluskus to get the stray.

We left the next morning as soon as we could, but still later than we wanted. It was *cold*; we could see our breath clearly. On cold mornings horses always seem to have a hump in their backs, and ours were a bit frisky. We took a pack horse for sleeping bags and some grub, and hoped to make the Kluskus Reserve, which was about forty miles to the east on the old wagon trail to Nazko, by late that night. The miles passed by. We crossed through the Cassams' place at Blue Lake, then passed their summer cabin on Tsacha Lake, where rarely anyone stayed. There would have been no one at Tsacha Lake Lodge so we didn't even stop; it was off the main trail anyway. The next place we passed was Antoine Baptiste's. There was no one at home there either. It was by then late afternoon and we had only an hour at most till darkness fell. The air was cooling fast and the ground fog was beginning to rise on the meadows like pure white fluff. The horses were slowing down and needed to be pushed, and their disappointment showed when we passed the buildings and turned them back on the trail to the crossing on Kushya Creek, about half a mile farther. The creek crossing was completely frozen over, and standing on the other side was the white-faced yearling steer. Barry urged his horse out on the snow-covered ice and it gingerly walked across, smelling the ice before putting each foot ahead. On the other side it hurried up the bank onto solid ground. Now that there was a track to follow in the snow, the steer quietly stepped around the horse and out onto the ice, moving slowly across, then past me and down the trail of fresh horse tracks towards home.

Barry and I returned to the buildings at Antoine's. There was edible hay in the mangers of the barn so we unsaddled our horses and tied them up in the barn. Taking our sleeping bags and grub box we went up to the house. The door was locked but we found a window that slid open just enough for us to crawl in. The night promised to be another cold one, and we were not prepared to spend it outside. I had with me the German shepherd dog I had inherited from my brother Rob, so we boosted him in as well. The place smelt strongly of pack rat and Wetzel wasted no time in searching out the rats. There was crashing and banging as he tore about the house, digging under things and leaping over others. We started the fire—luckily there was a stack of wood inside—and quickly heated up a bit to eat, and by then it was dark. We could find no light so we sat around the crackling fire and listened to the dog patrol for pack rats before retiring. In the morning the horses were anxious for home so we travelled fast, but the steer still beat us there.

*Ed Adams, retired dairy farmer and occasional art critic, shoots the picture on the wall at the Home Ranch.*

Christmas of 1972 at the Home Ranch was quiet, just Ed, Barry, me and Stuart Garner, a school friend of Barry's who flew in to spend the holidays with us. Dorthea had left a large reproduction of a painting on the living room wall. Now I can't remember the entire picture, but there was a horse or two—not genuine horses but ones done into the swirls of paint. It had a lot of red and bright colours, too. I am not sure as to what type of art it was, but it was certainly not Western, and it did not fit into the rough décor of the ranch house. On Christmas day, as we sat around inhaling the smells of roasting turkey, Ed leapt from his chair and said he had always hated the picture and wanted to shoot a hole in it. Off to the bunkhouse he went, returning with his Winchester lever action .22. Throwing a shell into the barrel he stepped back and took aim, hitting one of the horses in the head. "There," he said with satisfaction. Stuart jumped up and took a shot, followed by Barry. How many shots were actually fired I can't recall but I later took the remains of the picture to the burn pile out back of the cache.

When the days became longer and warmer we often rode saddle horse to Tsetzi Lake and ice-fished at the end of the lake, where the mouth of the lake opened. We would chop our holes back from the open water a bit. The fish were not big but they were great for pan-frying. Some days we caught only a couple of fish, and other days they seemed to line up to be caught. On one of these days in late March my dad rode over from Sleepy Hollow, where he was feeding horses, and between three of us we caught so many it took several days to eat them. So then we didn't want to eat any more fish, but it was a change from moose meat anyway.

Once the ice broke up on the creeks we would go beaver hunting on moonlit nights, sitting on the creek banks near a dam or feed house till a beaver came swimming about. We'd shoot it with the shotgun and birdshot. With only the head above water the shot didn't damage any other part of the beaver. After fishing it from the creek we had to pack it home, which was not a problem, but if it was a large one a lot of stops had to be made.

It would have been that spring that Bob Anthony sold the ranch to a couple of guys from California. Barry, Ed and I were about the only ones there on the ranch steady, but people came and went.

In May, Ed and I had to go to Quesnel so we arranged for a plane to pick us up at Tsetzi Lake and fly us to Anahim, where I had my pickup parked. The day we were to be picked up there were no planes available so the scheduled flight from Bella Coola to Williams Lake with a stop in Anahim came for us, leaving its passengers waiting at Anahim Lake Airport. The plane landed, then the pilot walked the strip to check the wet spots before he took off, as the frost was coming out of the ground. I was always nervous about flying, especially with pilots I had never flown with before. This one really worried me as I had expected a uniformed pilot on a three-times-weekly scheduled flight. He wore running shoes with no laces and the tongues of the shoes flopped about as he walked. His sweatshirt was full of holes and frayed at the cuffs, and he needed a shave. When he said to climb in we did, although my stomach was full of butterflies. Everything went without a hitch but I was glad to reach Anahim Lake and get in my pickup to drive to Quesnel.

On the return to Anahim, Barry's folks, Jake and Leona, drove to Anahim as well for a visit with Barry, who had come out to Anahim with Dad and the team and wagon. We had rooms at a local motel that had a sloped parking lot. Barry had brought my dog, Wetzel, out with him. So after an evening of visiting about the town I put the dog in the cab of the truck and we retired to bed. Early in the morning we all woke to an automobile horn honking furiously. Running to the window I saw with horror my truck rolling across the sloping parking lot towards the road and the side ditch, and Wetzel with both front paws on the steering wheel. He had somehow knocked it out of park. And sometime the previous evening an Indian lady had decided to sleep in the back of the truck, and she woke up about that moment, to find the truck rolling and a dog at the wheel. The truck came to an abrupt stop in the ditch. I pulled on some clothes and reached the truck and opened the door. The dog leaped down, and used the tire for his much-needed pit stop. I am quite sure our overnight guest never chose that bed again, as she wandered off very bewildered.

We spent a few days in Anahim and Dad was always asking me to drive him here and there. I finally said, "You just take the truck and do your thing." He said he had not driven for many years and wouldn't remember how. I explained that the truck was an automatic and very easy to drive. They had no such things as automatics in the days when he drove, so then I got a lecture about how it probably was not any good. Finally I talked him into trying it, and down the road he went, at a snail's pace. Hours later he wasn't back so I started out to look for him—after all, Anahim was pretty small. As I walked along the road he passed me driving very fast, with a grin on his face, and didn't even stop to pick me up.

Stuart Garner bought a little bay gelding off me that I had started riding, and I agreed to ride him awhile longer, till he was better broken. He was in need of shoes in the spring and I was putting them on with no cooperation from the horse at all. An hour and a half later I had only one shoe on and I was tired, sweaty and had the beginnings of a headache. I had the hammer in my hand and had walked away from the horse a bit, trying to control my anger, and then I turned to look at him. He was watching me and I swear he was laughing, if horses can be amused. Without thinking I fired the hammer at his head. I struck him right on the forehead and he dropped like he had been shot. He got up in a few seconds though, swishing his tail and licking his lips, with just a small trickle of blood on his head where the hammer had made a cut. But I think we had come to an understanding, because the next three shoes were no problem at all.

Haying was in process but it must have rained because Barry, Billy Hayward (who was working there that summer), my niece Wanda and I decided to take a ride and do some grouse hunting, because the hay was wet. It was a nice day. We rode down toward Tsilbekuz Lake as there was good Franklin grouse hunting in the thick timber nearby. There had been an early hatch and that hatch was a good size. We were only hunting with .22 rifles but they are very stupid birds so no one had to be in a hurry. If they were on the ground, sometimes they stayed there, or else they'd fly onto a tree branch and sit there, with a look of "here I am." I had put a bunch of loose wooden matches in the front pocket of my tight Levis before we left and while we rode along they must have rubbed together, as they caught fire. I didn't know what happened but I knew I was hurting. I leapt from my horse and started tearing off my jeans, and while everyone was looking up in the trees for grouse I was able to get my jeans loosened and get behind my horse to extinguish the fire. It caused a good laugh, anyway.

We had a number of guys working that summer in haying. Back then we were still haying with teams and loose hay, but our town help had very little experience with teams. And it seemed that every day there was a runaway and more harness was torn up. There were some good horses ruined as well. The driving lines had so much riveting done on them that they were getting mighty short. One day when a team got away and the horses were running as hard as they could, with the double trees smacking them in the backsides, they were headed straight for a plane parked on the airstrip. The horses were arguing with each other about which way to go. They were trying to separate but the checks of the reins kept them together. But they did miss the plane, much to the relief of the pilot, who was running around waving his arms and nearly got run over himself. After circling part of the field, the team finally stopped near the gate to the corrals.

It was after haying that Barry and I flew into Quesnel to visit Mom and his parents, leaving my German shepherd at the ranch with whoever was there. While we were gone, Wetzel got after the sheep and killed several. He received a severe beating, but it was only a few days before he was back after the sheep again, killing some more, and was shot for it. Once he started, there was no way he would stop the killing.

My mom was still living in the Gunson house in Quesnel. One night Barry, Rob and I all went out on the town and arrived home just as Mom was cooking her breakfast. She was not very happy with

*Mom in Quesnel—for the first time in her life she had some nice things and time to pursue interests of her own.*

the condition of us, so we were tip-toeing about the house when there was a knock on the door. It was one of the neighbours, who was known for frequently drinking a drop or two too many. Mom opened the screen door and told him he may as well come in, as all the other drunks had. I think she got her point across to all of us, loud and clear.

In late November we were in Quesnel visiting Mom and Barry's folks again before winter set in, and when we got to Anahim Lake it began to snow. Before it had stopped we had about sixteen inches of snow. Barry helped Floyd Vaughan put skis on his Super Cub two-seater so he could fly us home, and he took Barry on the first flight. Before landing Barry asked Floyd if it was any different landing on skis than on wheels. Floyd's reply was he didn't know, as this was his first landing with skis, but the landing went off okay anyway.

In the fall of that year we bought Elan snow machines from Barry's dad, Jake, who was the Ski-Doo dealer in Quesnel at the time. Jake let us have them at cost plus freight, which ended up costing us in the neighbourhood of seven hundred and fifty dollars each, brand new. These Elans were sort of the Shetland ponies of the Ski-Doo line, but they got us many miles. Most of those miles were spent kneeling on one knee or standing on the running boards, as they were very tippy if you sat on them. Gas was fairly cheap so we could afford to run about; Barry chased coyotes and did some trapping.

When we first got our snow machines, we went out looking for a pack of wolves that were in the area. We went down onto Styvie

Lake. Before we hit the ice we had to cross a very rough swamp, where—unknown to us—the rifle came out of the scabbard that was tied to Barry's machine. On the lake we drove right into a pack of ten wolves. They were not familiar with snow machines and we were able to get right up to them. Barry reached for his rifle only to discover it was gone. We had to watch the wolves lope away from us and could do nothing. They never let us do that again.

At that time poison was still available to us so we baited for them on the lake. Wolves are not loved by the ranching community because of the damage they can do to livestock. Their method of killing is what gets me: tearing the flesh off a frightened, fleeing animal. Then, when it is down, eating it alive, till it dies of shock or blood loss or some vital organ is torn from it. Animals that do escape generally die later from their injuries.

The day after we put the poison out the Alexis family came up to visit and spend the night, bringing about half a dozen dogs. We asked them to tie the dogs up because of the poison baits, but they felt the dogs would not go the two miles to the lake. During the night the dogs did, and in the morning we had gotten every dog. I felt bad about two especially, which were good lynx dogs, but what could we do then.

Barry caught two wolves out on a lake one day. Because they had just fed on a kill and were so heavy with meat they had eaten, they could not outrun even his little snow machine. He didn't have a rifle with him, only a .22 handgun, but he was able to pull up right beside one of the wolves and shoot it behind the ear.

During the winter, when Floyd was flying by he would quite often stop in to drop off the mail and visit over coffee. On several occasions he told me that my coffee was weak. One time, for some reason we had not had coffee for several days and there was half a pot of old coffee on the back of the stove that had been heating and cooling there for days. I poured him a steaming cup of the bitter black coffee and we visited. When his cup was empty I asked if he wanted another, to which he replied he'd just have a couple cups of hot water. He never complained about my weak coffee again!

In March, Wilfred Cassam rode up and asked if we could feed his team for the rest of the winter, as there was a hay shortage at Blue Lake. Whatever arrangements were made I can't remember but the team was brought to the ranch in very poor condition. Wilfred was very hard on his horses, and mean, as his father had been too. About a month after the team arrived one of the mares we were feeding cattle with aborted twin colts. Barry asked Wilfred if we could use one of his horses for a week or so, not wanting to use the work mare right away. That was fine with Wilfred. The weather had been warm and the low places in the meadows were filling with water under the snow. It was probably the second or third day that we had Wilfred's gelding hooked with the other mare when it stopped and refused to move, just as we were crossing a low place that was filled with water. The mare couldn't pull the sleigh and him as well. Then the gelding lay down in the water and wouldn't get up. Barry ended up standing on the horse's head hoping that having his head underwater would make him want to get up. In the middle of all this we looked up to find Wilfred sitting on his skinny saddle horse, watching us. We finally unhooked and stripped the harness off the gelding as he lay in the water and walked back to the barn and got the other mare. After half an hour or so the gelding got up, quivering and shaking from the cold, and went back to the corral.

# CHAPTER 5

# Our Move to Sleepy Hollow

In 1974, the new owners of the Home Ranch decided that a lot more cattle were needed on the ranch. This may have been true, but our argument was that cattle should be brought to the ranch in the fall after haying, when it was known how many cattle could be wintered. There was no road to use to move feed in for a large herd of cattle. Once cows were fed for the winter and calved out, they could be put on open range that they didn't know and at least have an idea where home was. Apparently our advice fell on deaf ears. The owners then hired a manager out of Oregon. He arrived in April with his wife and daughter, and three dogs: two border collies that would not hesitate to bite you and a lap dog that got up on the table before and after dinner to check out the food supply. The three Appaloosa horses they brought with them were the least of our worries. It was obvious the people were out of their element in the wilds of BC; ranching in Oregon was quite a bit different than here.

We all lived in one house, so everyone made the best of an uncomfortable situation and tried to get along. The owners accepted the lap dog's bad habit of getting on the table, but it was hard for us to tolerate. Not only did it lick the butter and the plates, it seemed to shake itself while walking around on the table—black hair was very frequently found on the butter dish or in the sugar bowl. I also knew that the dog slept with the Mr. and Mrs. under the covers; the wife had told me that herself.

We stayed on with them and finished out the calving, did the branding and turned the cows on summer range, then Ed, Barry and I moved to Ed's place at Sleepy Hollow. He had a large two-room cabin there. Rick had helped Ed build the new cabin a year or two before. I think Ed enjoyed having me there to cook for him, as he wasn't much of a cook. We took Ed's few cows and his sheep. The day we left the ranch I fed that table climber pooch a whole package of those chocolate laxatives. (There is a saying that life is short, so break the rules, forgive quickly, love truly, laugh uncontrollably and never regret anything that made you smile . . .)

About the time we were getting ready to move from the Home Ranch, Pat (née Lehman) and Jim Chadwell and their daughter Patty, with Audie Murphy, moved from Anahim Lake onto Bill Lampert's place on the Blackwater River with their cows, horses and all their belongings. It took them nearly a week to trail the cows all the way around the mountain. Apparently the agreement they had with Bill did not suit both parties, as it seemed that not more than a month later they were on the move again to Twin Lakes, just south of Tsacha Lake, into an old trapping cabin of Antoine Baptiste's. They set about homesteading on a slough meadow beside the small mud-bottom lake. They improved on the land and built a log house. It was always nice to have people moving into the country, as neighbours were few and far between.

Barry and I flew into Quesnel once the airstrip was dry enough. We were married on May 24, 1974, at the courthouse in Quesnel, with Mom, Barry's folks, his grandmother, his two brothers and my brother Rob present. Rob's girlfriend Sandy was my maid of honour.

Dad had an agriculture lease at Sleepy Hollow on a half section of land. It joined Ed's two quarters of land, on the east side. On the west side of Ed was another quarter section of land, which was Indian reserve land. At one time an old Indian by the name of Kluskus Tommy lived there with his granddaughter and trapped in the winter. One spring in the early fifties a grass fire burnt his cabin down and he never rebuilt it, choosing to live at Kluskus or Nazko instead.

Dad decided that he would never develop the half section of land. Now that we were married, Barry and I wanted the property. So Dad held onto the agriculture lease till the improvements were done, then transferred the deed into our names. To finish improving upon his half section of land so it could be purchased, a certain percentage of the land had to be ready for production. Dad used the little 1010 John Deere crawler to do a great deal of ditching on both the south and north sides of the river. He also put in an irrigation ditch that ran from the Indian reserve down through Ed's main field to the river. This dried out all of the natural meadows in summer so they could be hayed. A year or two later Dad hired Oscar Trudeau to clear the land of its thick willows with a large dozer. I believe the machine belonged to Blackwater Lodge. I can't remember how long Oscar was there but he cleared a lot of the land east of the place on the north and south sides of the river. Later Corky Williams, a rancher from Anahim Lake, came with his tractor and a big rototiller and worked that land up. Then we were able to seed it and have ourselves more hay land; most of the natural hay land in the valley was on the two quarters that Ed owned.

While living with Ed that first summer, Barry and I slept in the old cabin, and each morning Ed would rap on the door, kick it open, hand each of us a cup of coffee and give a brief report on the weather. As I described in my first book, he was a man who rose early, and if you were not up with the sun you were burning daylight. This one morning, as he handed us our coffee, he bypassed the weather report to say that we'd had a visitor during the night. It turned out the visitor was a black bear that had gone through the cooler, which was nailed to the wall on the north side of the cabin. The bear ripped the screen door off and proceeded to eat whatever was in there, including a chunk of cheddar cheese that I had stored in a tin can. He put a number of teeth holes in the can before the lid came off and the cheese was available to him. All the boxes on the porch had been gone through and were scattered about.

*The barn and corrals at Sleepy Hollow, seven miles north of the Home Ranch on the Blackwater River.*

The next night the bear returned and decided to go for bigger and better things, like Ed's ram, which was locked up in a small log corral. Now this was a big ram—but it was no problem for the bear to go over the fence, which was six logs high, and pack the sheep back over and away. We knew then that he would return in a few days to kill again, and Ed's flock of sheep bedded down each night by the barn. A few nights later Ed and Barry with sleeping bags settled down in the hayloft with rifles to await the bear's return. They awoke to the flock of sheep racing madly around the corral with the bear in pursuit. Fortunately it was a bright night and a lucky shot took care of that bear.

That was not the end of bears, unfortunately, as a few weeks later another one happened along. Don White from Quesnel was visiting and bunking in Ed's cabin. The door on the cabin had no latch to close it, unless you remembered to pull the latch that was on the inside. But the door always stayed closed because there was a fairly strong spring attached to the outside of the door. When you opened the door you had to hold it open as you passed through; then it would bang shut. Ed and Don awoke to the door being batted open . . . and then it would just as quickly slam shut. It didn't take them long to figure out there was a bear at the door. Don immediately wanted to know where the rifle was, to which Ed calmly replied that it was hanging above the door. Don then wanted to know if the windows opened, as there was only one door, and Ed told him just as calmly they did not. Fortunately the bear lost interest in the door and proceeded to nose through the other stuff on the porch. This gave the guys a chance to get the rifle, open the door and drop the bear. Barry and I awoke to the rifle shot, turned over and went back to sleep. Only one shot meant it wasn't worth getting up for, as the excitement was over.

On the 320 acres of land that was to be our future home, the best building spot was on the north side of the river, on the highest piece of ground on the west quarter. It was just above the river, with a good view of the mountains and meadows right on the western boundary line. There was a small lily-pond lake straight out from the knoll on the far side of the valley, offering an abundance of waterfowl from early spring through late fall. Dad had a small cabin on this spot, so we chose a spot beside it but just a bit lower and started a cabin of about twenty-four by thirty feet. Throughout the summer, on days when we were not haying, we worked on the cabin. Barry felled the logs and Ed would skid them with his work mare, Ruby. Ed would hook the log onto the singletree and cluck to the old mare, and she would come down to the building site dragging the log. I was there peeling logs so I would unhook her and she would return to the bush. But Ruby was the boss of that show. Within a matter of minutes before twelve, or soon after, she would not come to the building site or the bush but go to Ed's barn, as it was lunchtime—she must have belonged to a horse union. Then we would have to walk back to Ed's, as the mare had called lunch break.

We all pitched in and helped to finish peeling the logs once they were cut and on site. The best time to peel logs is in the late spring when the sap is running well, when the bark can be pulled off in long strips. We had missed that, however, and the logs were now a bit dry, so every bit was taken off with a drawknife. It was hard work. When the logs were all peeled, the building started. Our foundation was a collection of flat rocks under the bottom logs, levelled as best we could by digging them into the ground. It depended on the weather how much building was accomplished. We only worked on it when we were not in the field haying.

We hayed until we felt we had enough hay for Ed's cattle and sheep and team, and then we put up more (and it was fortunate that we did). It was all loose hay, the same as we had always done at the Home Ranch—the only way I had ever hayed. By the time we finished haying, the cabin was ready for the roof. We had only enough lumber for the floor, doors and sills, so the punching had to be done for the roof the old-fashioned way. Logs about eight inches through were cut then split in half, and the flat side laid over the stringers. A layer of heavy plastic was laid next, then numerous loads of dirt till it was about eight inches deep all over. Barry put the roof on the cabin

*Stacking loose hay at Tsetzi Lake with teams in the 1970s.* VANCE HANNA

with Stuart Garner's help, while I went guiding for Dad to make a little cash for the winter ahead. (A couple of years later the roof was covered with shakes split from straight-grain pine trees.)

A lot of windfall and downed trees surrounded the cabin site; we burnt it in big bonfires, salvaging the solid stuff for firewood. There was a good stand of pine trees scattered about the place too. (Every year I raked the entire area of pine needles, so in time grass came in.) Over the next few years we got a shop of sorts built north of the cabin, and a barn, corrals and a henhouse to the east of the cabin. In back of the henhouse was a large outcropping of rock. Later a corral was built around this, and it became a popular spot in the spring for the cows, as the snow melted off the hill early—it was a dry spot to lie down. Unless the wind was blowing its chilly breath down the valley . . . then it could be down right miserable.

Sleepy Hollow is a valley about three miles long, running east to west, and about half a mile wide. The Blackwater River winds through it. The river has a sandy bottom and seems to barely move as it winds back and forth making its lazy way east. The south side of the valley is made up of high pine-covered hills. On the north

*Audie Murphy looks down at the Sleepy Hollow Ranch and fields.* WANDA
SIMPSON

73

side the hills rise up as well but a bit closer to the river, and the land is much more open than on the south side, offering grassy poplar side hills, ravines filled with large spruce, some big stands of cotton-woods and brush draws and small swampy draws where grazing is available. The valley floor is quite flat and not a rock can be found. There's very sandy soil on the high ground and good black soil in the lower areas. At one time, many years ago, I believe the valley was a lake, with the river dammed off by beavers. Perhaps an exceptionally high water year took out the dams and drained the valley; this would explain the deep, rich soil. Large willows cover part of the valley, including the riverbanks. There are a number of water-filled sloughs scattered along the three-mile stretch, plus two small lily-pond lakes. During very dry summers, on one spot of the lowest part of the wild meadow we had to be careful mowing, as what appeared to be a big tree buried in the ground would surface just enough to be hit by the sickle bar. It seemed the arid summers shrunk the soil and meadow moss enough for the log to surface — during wetter years it was never seen. This is another reason I believe that at one time the valley was a lake, and perhaps before that covered with trees; at least one large tree is preserved in the damp soil and sand of the valley bottom.

The Ilgachuz Mountains could be seen to the south-south-west. In the west, the Rainbow Mountains were visible. The Itcha Mountains could not be seen as the hills to the southeast were in the way. On clear days, when the sun rose in the east it hit the tops of the Ilgachuz first. When they were covered with snow they turned rosy pink. Then the Rainbow Mountains turned colour. Slowly the sun's rays crept down as the sun climbed higher, hitting the tops of the hills. It seemed that it hit the river valley long after everything was bright with day, and because of the hill on the east side, the house was the very last place that the sun hit.

With the lily-pond lakes, the river and the many sloughs, a lot of water birds made their home there, with mallards, blue-winged teal and bufflehead all nesting in the valley. The northern pintail, common merganser and common golden eye were seen in the spring, on their flights north, but did not nest in the area. A number of shorebirds nested as well, the killdeer being the most common. Flocks of Canada geese stopped briefly in the spring but rarely nested. Occasionally snow geese were seen, and trumpeter swans could stop for short visits at any given time. It was common to see them even in winter, flying over on their way to the mouths of lakes where there was open water. They no doubt came from their wintering ground at Lonesome Lake. The ruffle grouse chose the north side of the river as their habitat and nested there. I loved to hear them drum in the spring, which was a mating ritual for them. We did not hunt them on the property, but they never seemed to increase— probably due to predators such as the mink following the river, the great horned owl and the bald eagle. All three were often seen in the valley

For some reason the area around the house was a popular spot for crickets in the summer, and we would fall asleep to their singing. Although it annoyed some people, I found it peaceful—like the splashing of the muskrats on the lily-pond lake, the croaking of the frogs in the mud pond next to the river and the throaty call of the common nighthawk as it dove about for insects.

With the hill on the north side of the river being covered with a lot of poplar trees, the fall colours were especially nice, with orange, yellow and gold. The rest of the hillside was covered with big spruce and pockets of cottonwoods.

In the late fall we often had bouts of fog for several days and the frost would be thick on all the trees, willows and fences. Spiderwebs covered with frost were nature's masterpieces. If the snow was on the ground then it was truly a winter wonderland. Everything seemed so clean. On these days it seemed that not even the squirrels chattered or the chickadees moved. Then there were those days after a heavy snow, when whiteness covered everything and the trees would be standing stately in their heavy white coats of snow, waiting for a wind or a warm day to shed them.

It was on the south-facing slopes that the first poplar leaves of spring came out. We always looked for the first tinge of green on those south-facing slopes. First it would be the grass, then the leaves.

On the steeper hills to the north, where there was less grass growing, the wild onions were one of the first things to appear. This was an attraction for the bears in the spring, especially the black bears. They dug up the bulbs and ate them.

The first flowers in the spring were the dandelions, which appeared first on the side hills, then on the high ground in the meadows, and a good number of the pastures would be yellow with them. Dandelions were another favourite food of the bears. They would walk along cropping the yellow heads like a cow grazing. The large corral at Ed's was an ideal place for them, as it seemed the dandelions grew thickest there.

I always enjoyed waking up early on a spring morning, drowsy from sleep, and hearing the sounds about me: the rooster crowing from the henhouse and the quacking of the wild ducks on the pond; the honking of the geese overhead, along with the singing and cries of so many other birds. Some mornings there would be the calls of the sandhill cranes as they migrated north in huge flocks, circling and calling while they either regrouped or looked for a place to land. Sunrises were colourful, the eastern sky turning pale pink then brightening as the sun peeked over the pine-covered hills.

*The ranch house at Sleepy Hollow.*

The colour would fade as the day began. As the morning warmed the mosquitoes became active, and later other flies droned against the sides of the log buildings. Butterflies flitted about and the frogs called from the marshes. In the distance a cow would bawl for her calf; a herd bull would send out his bovine call, then as it faded wait for a challenge, but if none was returned, silence prevailed. The horse bells rang from the side hills as the horses grazed on the new growth. Far off a plane could be faintly heard as it passed by on a flight to some distant lake. The southwesterly wind would ripple the water on the lily-pond lake just out from the house.

Before we moved to Sleepy Hollow, Dad had contracted the local Indians to do some fence building. On the western property line along Ed's property, a buck fence was built from the river on the north side and up the side hill about halfway to where the hill got steep and the spruce was heavy. Dad then had all the property on the north side fenced. Ed had a fence built on the south side between his property and the Indian reserve to the west. The remaining property on the south side had a nature barrier: steep hills thick with pines and windfall.

There was a bridge at Ed's, which had been built in the sixties, but it was some time before we built one at our place. However, the first winter we put three of the longest trees we could find across the river, and they just barely reached. This at least gave us a walkway across the river. A post was put in on both riverbanks and the logs were cabled to them to keep the high water from washing them downstream. Many times I saw them floating in high water. We used them to go to the garden patch we had across the river, and to the fields as well.

The garden there was much like the one at the Home Ranch: the root vegetables grew very well, and sometimes cabbage, but it was too frosty for potatoes, even though we were several hundred feet below the elevation of the Home Ranch. When we built the cabin we built a small storage place under the floor for vegetables. The small carrots I pulled, scrubbed and canned the same day, and when I opened them they were like fresh garden carrots. I also canned a lot of moose meat in the winter, while the moose were still in good shape. Any extra fish from ice fishing I canned as well. When the hens were laying well I put eggs up in "water glass" in five-gallon buckets, for when the old hens moulted and the pullets hadn't started laying yet, so we had eggs most of the time. With the hens, garden, wild meat and later a milk cow we were partially self-sufficient in our little log home.

Driving cattle from the field to the corrals, crossing the bridge over the Blackwater River.

# CHAPTER 6

# Some Drives Were Better Than Others . . .

Midsummer of 1974 two hundred pairs (cows and calves), ten bulls and a milk cow—a total of 411 head—were moved into the Home Ranch. The cows were moved by Ronnie Harrington, boss and teamster, with his wife, Betty, as cook, and their daughter Linda and son Steve cowboying with ten other people. One couple on the drive was married right before leaving on the trip, at the Nazko Ranch. The bride was to ride in the chuckwagon with Ronnie and Betty and help cook. The groom I assume rode saddle horse. The cattle had been trucked to the Nazko Ranch. The cows and calves did not arrive together but several days apart, on separate trucks, causing considerable grief, as there was then a problem getting them to mother up. Then the cattle were trucked from the Nazko Ranch to Moffit Harris's place on the Baezaeko River, the jumping off point for the drive to the Home Ranch, eighty-five or so miles cross-country, following the wagon trails west.

The morning the drive was leaving, Ronnie got the team—one of them a stallion—hooked up, but they were fresh and rambunctious so there was a runaway to start with, after the team was hooked to the wagon. In the process Moffit's log outhouse was knocked off its foundation and scattered about. Ronnie promised Moffit he would fix it, which he never did get done. Once the team settled down the cattle drive was underway.

Two hours out, the Coglistiko River was reached. Ronnie had told the cowboys that whatever they did when the cows started into the river, they couldn't let them turn around and come back—they had to keep pushing them to the opposite shore. Well, that didn't happen, and the cattle started back, some climbing up the banks of the river and bawling for their calves while the rest milled about in the water. The young Holley girl, who was riding a pony behind the wagon on the trip while her mother chased cows, was beside the wagon when the chaos on the river began. Ronnie passed the lines of the team to Betty, grabbed a rope from the wagon and jumped on the pony. Ronnie's legs were barely above the ground as he rode into the river, roped a calf and dragged it to the opposite shore, which got the herd moving across the river. At this point the stallion decided to add some excitement and reared up, then kicked back, just missing Betty's head and knocking the front out of the wagon box, injuring Betty's ankle. There was a bit of a runaway before Betty was able to get them under control and stopped. Betty continued on with the trip in spite of her injury.

Rocky Mountain was reached that night and camp was set up. It was July but the weather turned cold and it froze hard. No one was prepared for the cold weather. They laid over the next day, as a horse had been hurt badly, although no one remembers what exactly happened to it. Dr. Alex Holley rode up from Baezaeko on saddle horse to attend to the injured horse.

The drive continued the next day with the team and wagon leading the way. Betty and the bride made lunches in the wagon while it bounced down the rocky trail. They would hang the lunches in trees along the trail for the riders behind to pick up as they passed by with the cattle.

Several days later the drive reached Kluskus and they decided to lay over another day there, to rest the cattle. On the morning they were to leave, as they were getting ready to move out, a bunch of loose horses that grazed in the area came running down the side hill towards the cattle and the loose horses that were being trailed behind the wagon. Not wanting the two bunches of loose horses to mix, Ronnie passed Betty the lines to the team, telling her to drive them to the nearest stand of timber and tie them up. He then took a saddle horse and went after the invading horses to drive them back in the direction they had come from. But the horses were too fast and circled around, running at full gallop past the team. The stallion, excited by the running horses, took off with his workmate, the wagon and Betty. Betty was frantically trying to turn the team into the timber when Ronnie realized the team was on a runaway and changed course to chase it. Betty said the team by then had such a speed up that even Ronnie, whipping his saddle horse, couldn't catch them. As the team entered the timber they collided with the first tree—a big one. One horse went on each side; the tongue broke from the wagon and the harness ripped. It was a sudden stop: the front of the wagon was against the tree and the two horses faced the wagon from either side of it, inches away from Betty, who sat rather stunned facing the skinned bark of the tree.

There was considerable damage to the wagon and the harness, not to mention Betty's nerves. The team were uninjured. People who spend a lot of time in the bush know how to improvise, so things were soon patched up enough to continue on.

The day the drive was to get to Tsetzi Lake, Betty wanted to look nice, so she washed her hair in a creek along the way and rolled it in curlers while bouncing along in the wagon. When the wagon pulled up to the hitching rack at the fish camp my dad rushed out and scooped Betty from the wagon in his arms and gently set her on the ground, saying, "Just like Hollywood, eh, Betty?" To Ronnie he said, as he glanced at the team, "Good to see you pulled their tails." (There was nothing my dad hated worse than a horse with a long tail.)

Before leaving Tsetzi Lake the next morning, Betty cooked breakfast over the campfire in the pouring rain. She had a very large cast iron fry pan in the coals, into which she had carefully broken a good dozen eggs. As she bent forward with the flipper to separate the eggs so she could turn them over, the accumulation of water on her cowboy hat poured into the fry pan. Without hesitation Betty quickly stirred the eggs together, making scrambled eggs, and no one was any the wiser.

Ronnie was very familiar with the country, had a good crew of cowboys and knew where there was sufficient feed for that big of a herd to overnight and what would feed them for noon stopovers. It made the drive a success, and the animals reached the Home Ranch in good shape and all accounted for. Upon arrival at the Home Ranch they were turned into the hay meadows. None of the hay had been put up yet so there was lots of feed. The new Oregon manager would not leave the sight of the ranch buildings for the range—but then he had no idea where the range even was. He could keep an eye on the new cattle if they were on the hay meadows.

Three months later, in October, Bob Anthony arrived back at the ranch, claiming ownership again. The manager and his family had no choice but to return to Oregon, and a crew from Vanderhoof was sent in to move the new herd of cows and calves back out, as they apparently had not been paid for. Now that the ranch seemed to be under Bob's control once again and there was no hay put up to feed any cattle, the original bunch of cows had to be moved. Barry and I, along with Stuart Garner, Tommy Sill (a local Native) and Ray Jacques, from Quesnel, were hired to take the original herd of cattle to Anahim Lake. It was a fast decision and a rather ill-prepared one. We had been sitting back watching the confusion and commotion going on at the Home Ranch and next thing we knew we were throwing stuff together to drive about a hundred pairs and a bunch of yearlings and bulls to Anahim Lake. The blessing about this was that Bob Anthony owed Barry money, and he never paid unless he had to. Now it was payday, for both the money owed and pay for the drive we were to go on. Barry took payment in cow-calf pairs: the beginnings of our future cattle herd. We were lucky we had put up extra hay. The cows were taken to Sleepy Hollow the day before we left on the drive.

We anticipated the drive would take us four days. We took one pack horse for sleeping bags and food. I believe we also took a couple of tents. In order not to have to take along much for cooking, Barry's uncle Leo, who was working at the Home Ranch, quickly cooked up some stews and canned them. We then needed only one pot and a coffee pot.

We left early, and it was a good thing we did: the cattle fought us all the way. We decided to take a saddle horse trail that follows a tributary of Pan Creek up through a narrow canyon into the pass between the Itcha and Ilgachuz Mountains. This trail is located between the two wagon trails, and it doesn't go high — matter of fact it is the lowest route between the two mountain ranges. It had its drawbacks, though, and one was muskeg. But the beauty of it was the narrow canyon. It was the only place we could hold some 250 head of homesick animals when night came. We chose the narrowest spot and pushed the cattle up the canyon onto some swamp meadows, then set up a hasty camp and staked our horses. We hadn't even had time to eat and the cows were back in camp. They never let us sleep, and continued to try to head home all through the night. The couple of hours before daybreak were the only rest we had. We had set up one tent on either side of the creek. In the morning Stuart was carrying on as his wet boots had frozen with the tops turned over and he had to thaw them by the fire before he could get his feet into them. I don't know if anyone else even took theirs off.

Pushing the cattle up the canyon was no easy job. The trail was hardly noticeable in places. Some areas were covered with extremely swampy ground. To stay out of the bog you had to ride against the steep hillside, where a narrow trail was worn into the dirt. It was meant to be used in single file, which was hard to do with a bunch of cattle. At the end of the canyon was a grassy bowl, followed by a rather steep climb through the rocks onto the open flats above. The cattle spread out in the grassy bowl and as we raced back and forth to keep them moving, one cow fell into a spring hole. They are quite common in that country, where spring water comes to the surface. Most of them are deep, and this one was no exception. Tommy was a big brute of a guy, and not only big but mean. He yelled for help a few times but no one paid much attention, although I was watching to see if one of the guys would help him. He got off his horse, grabbed the cow by the tail and dragged her out onto the green mossy bank of the spring hole, then proceeded to kick her as hard as he could. She was on her feet fast, and running to catch up to the rest.

On the dry flats above the canyon we were finally able to get a count of the herd, the first since counting them out of the gate at the Home Ranch. We were short four head, which we knew without a doubt were two cow-calf pairs lost soon after leaving the ranch.

For the rest of the day the trail followed scattered draws of dry grass and small creeks to Corkscrew Basin, a wide valley with Corkscrew Creek winding its way down through it. All day the cows still tried to turn back. One dry cow was especially bad. Time and time again she would duck back to try to escape, always taking others with her. She had been a problem on the first day as well. By the time darkness came we were well down into Corkscrew Basin and the feed was good, so we hoped they might stay. Our horses were nearly played out and we were exhausted. Again we chose the best possible place to cut off the herd when they started back—as they soon did. We hadn't even gotten camp set up and the bells on a few of the cows were coming around a hill close to camp. Tempers were short, and it was decided that if the cow that had caused so much trouble for two days was in the lead, she had to be shot. The guys grabbed rifles and ran down to the trail on the creek to await the herd as it rounded a large bluff, intending to shoot the problem cow. Only there was a different one in the lead, so no shots were fired. We again pushed the herd down the creek, for a quarter of a mile or so. The feed was good. We were at a lower elevation than the night before and the grass was not as frozen, plus it was more of a dry-ground feed than what the muskegs and swamps had offered. The cows had to be as tired as we were, as they had been on the move for two whole days.

We could not believe our good fortune: the bells, carried on the cool night air, faded away as the herd drifted down the creek, away from camp, and then silence fell. The cattle must have finally decided that they were not going home, and fed and bedded down.

The jars of stew that Leo had canned were opened up and we discovered that they were spoiled beyond being edible. The stews must have been a bit tainted before they were canned, as it had only been a couple of days. This was the planned supper, the only food we had left for an evening meal, so as hungry as we were we proceeded to eat the third day's breakfast and most of its lunch, leaving very little for the next day.

The third day was slow moving. When we caught up to the cattle in the morning, some were feeding, while others were still resting. They had pretty well stopped trying to turn back but they were tired, and would stop as soon as someone wasn't behind them, pushing them along. We probably only had about ten miles to go to Lloyd Norton's place, which was the old Bryant Ranch, but it took most of the day. It was a tired bunch that arrived at the ranch shortly before dark, with very hungry cowboys. The cattle were turned into the hayfields and the horses into the pasture. We were fed and then bedded down in the bunkhouse. It seemed a bit like heaven after the past three days.

On the fourth and final day the cattle had to be pushed hard. They didn't want to turn around but didn't want to go ahead, either. By the afternoon we were on the gravel road out of Anahim Lake and the younger calves were lying down on the road, tired. Cows went off the road with their calves and stood there. When we reached the rodeo grounds it was a relief to turn them into the arena. Bob met us there, and they were his problem, then. We spent the night at the Frontier Inn having dinner at the café and drinks in the bar—we felt we deserved it. Ray caught a ride out to Williams Lake, going back home to Quesnel, and Tommy vanished onto the Ulkatcho Reserve. Stuart, Barry and I went over to 4 Mile Ranch the next day and stayed the night, then rode back over the mountains to home. At least the weather had been good, other than the cold nights.

While we were driving the cattle south over the Ilgachuz Mountains to Anahim Lake, Wilbur Pond, a rancher and the brand inspector from Vanderhoof, and his crew of cowboys started east with the bunch of cattle that had been moved from Nazko to the Home

Ranch earlier in the summer. A Vanderhoof businessman had financed the cattle, and now with the ranch under new management he wanted them out of there. So Wilbur was hired, along with various cowboys, to move these animals out to the old Hobson's River Ranch south of Vanderhoof. Some of the cowboys flew in to the ranch with John Kluber, who had the flying service in Vanderhoof, and others rode in cross-country on saddle horse. Wilbur said he flew to Tsetzi Lake with Kluber, and because he was expected a saddle horse had been left there, tied to the hitching rack, for him to ride the four miles to the Home Ranch.

The first couple days were spent getting things sorted out with Bob Anthony, who at first claimed all the cattle. There was a good deal of drinking on Anthony's part, and joining him were a few of the locals. One of these locals always packed a handgun, which he turned on Anthony at one point, causing considerable excitement in the ranch house. One of the cowboys bolted for the door, doing a somersault out of it and back onto his feet, then ran around behind another building. One onlooker said that the move was good enough for Hollywood! Anthony took the gun away, put it in a vice, bent the barrel around, and then returned it to the fellow.

The first step was getting everything organized for the trip. A lady by the name of Jo was to drive the chuckwagon and cook. Problem was, she had never driven a team before and she had no experience as a camp cook; she was a quick replacement for a cook and chuckwagon driver who backed out at the last minute. They were lucky to get the gentlest team of mares that was on the ranch.

Only three people had their own horses—the rest were to use horses that were there, and I never did learn who actually owned those horses. Only one had shoes on; the rest were bare-footed, and their hooves were in bad condition. Ron Crosby said he laid claim to the only shod horse. Dave Helkenberg arrived the night before the drive left, and he managed to get shoes on a few of the saddle horses. He was the only one there who knew how to shoe a horse.

The morning they started out, Wilbur told me, the best cowboys left with about forty pairs, but after sorting themselves out on the trail about half turned back, because they were not actually pairs. The cowboys pushed the cows to what was believed to be Paul's Meadow and never looked back. When the main bunch never came and hunger set in the cowboys returned, finding the main herd had not gotten very far down the trail, with cattle going in every direction. Dave shod the team of mares that morning and got them going, then caught up to the cattle. No one seemed to want to ride in the bush for cows so whenever cows went off the trail they were left behind. Dave had to ride drag to keep gathering up the strays, although he should have been in the front because he was the only one who knew where they were going. When they reached Paul's Meadow, sixteen miles east of the Home Ranch, the cattle that had been left there earlier had drifted off. They camped there for several days, trying to get the cattle all together. On the first night a snowstorm hit during the darkest hours, covering the ground with six inches of snow. Some of the cowboys were not dressed warmly enough for October temperatures; very few had long johns or rain gear, and some did not even have gloves. There was also a problem with the food not being campfire fare, nor was there enough of it.

When they finally reached Antoine Baptiste's place with all the cattle they had trouble getting them across Kushya Creek. The creek is not very wide or swift but has a mud bottom till it reaches the timber, where there is some gravel. (There are a few crossings with a rock bottom, but they must have crossed near the buildings, where there was mud.) Two new calves had been born at Paul's Meadow and they were hauled in the wagon to Antoine's. Both calves, but only one cow, were left behind there.

At Antoine's they hired on several Indians: George Chantyman, Duncan Harris, Ike Baptiste and Ike's wife. These people were a real asset as they were all good cowboys and knew the country all the way to Walter Erhorn's place. Once the drive reached there, they would return home.

One of the bulls was a herder, getting ahead of the cows and holding them up on the trail. Ron and Ike roped the bull and dragged him to a tree, where he was tied up. Ron got his rope off but

Ike had to leave his behind on the bull. The drive moved on, leaving the bull tied to the tree.

The drive went from Antoine Baptiste's place to Missue Crossing on the Blackwater River, then on to Tatelkuz Lake. From there, Ron, Tim and John Hiebert flew home. They had been seventeen days getting that far. (Talking to Ron later, while writing this book, he asked me how far it was from the Home Ranch to Tatelkuz Lake. "And don't tell me it was only five miles!") I was also told that the total trip took seventeen days. The night before they flew out the last of the food they brought with them, several cans of chicken, was prepared. As it heated by the fire, the pot tipped over and all was lost in the ashes and coals.

Looking back on the trip, John Hiebert says he should never have been on the drive, as he wasn't a cowboy and had never even ridden a horse before. And because he had a lot of energy, he wanted to wrestle with the other guys and fight. This did not sit well with Wilbur, who told him to save his energy for chasing cows. John was so hungry upon reaching the first camp he went straight to the cook fire, looking for something to eat, and was given a lecture by Wilbur: cowboys cared for their horse before they looked after themselves.

John had the least experience, so he became the person to play tricks on. Because he couldn't ride he was given a very old horse that was no longer used for regular ranch work. He was still very scared of the horse; he walked and led it for two days, feeding it sugar to make it like him. When he finally got on the horse a bunch of cattle came running towards him, with Dave trying to get ahead of the cattle to turn them. John's horse started to run ahead of the cows and John dropped his reins and hung on to the saddle horn while the horse loped ahead of the cows. Once Dave got ahead of the cattle and turned them, John's horse stopped. He was amazed he hadn't fallen off. Dave told the rest of the riders not to believe John when he said he couldn't ride, because he could! Things got somewhat better after that.

When Walter Erhorn's place was reached, the wagon trail petered out so the wagon had to be abandoned. Everyone tied their sleeping bags, personal effects and as much food as they could onto their saddles and the drive continued. At this point everyone seemed to be at a loss as to which way to go, except for Dave, who was the only one who knew the trail right through to Big Bend. But Dave could not be everywhere. A couple guys from Vanderhoof had gone into the area before the drive to cut the trail out, so at least they were not fighting windfall, but apparently the trail was still hard to follow. And the cattle were being driven in smaller groups, at different spaces apart. Wilbur was going down a trail with about twenty pairs when he met up with Gary Telford, who had joined the drive at Tatelkuz, coming up the trail with an equal number of cows. Wilbur wanted to know where Gary was going, and Gary had the same question. They joined forces and turned Gary's bunch around and continued along the trail.

Because Big Bend could not be reached in one day, the cattle were pushed out onto a peninsula on Knewstubb Lake for the night, and everyone camped at intervals on the narrow strip of land to hold the cattle back, as there was very little feed. At this camp a food drop was made from the air. The first box, containing canned goods, survived the drop but the second box, holding pancake mix, burst, scattering flour for some distance. They reached Big Bend the next day. From there a chopper flew the ladies—Jo, Marilyn and Jay—to River Ranch and the cowboys—with the exception of Wilbur and a guy named Steve—to Vanderhoof.

The following morning the cattle were scattered up and down Big Bend Creek. While the two guys tried to gather the herd, Wilbur encountered a steep side hill. He got off the mare he was riding for some reason or other and when he went to get back on he decided to mount on the high side. This was not the side the mare was used to, however, and she leapt ahead as he was swinging into the saddle. He fell onto the ground and broke his wrist, yet managed to remount and get the cattle back to Big Bend Meadow. By then some of the cowboys had returned. One removed a bottle of whiskey from inside his jacket and offered Wilbur a drink, which was not turned down. A few minutes later Wilbur was offered another drink of whiskey, this time from a mickey. Wilbur said he took a large drink and put the mickey in his pocket and rode off; it was all he was going to get for the pain in his broken wrist for the rest of the day. That night Wilbur was driven to the hospital in Vanderhoof, where Dr. Mooney put a cast on his wrist. Wilbur said, "He never even washed my arm, and I had not had a bath in three weeks!"

From there the cattle were driven to River Ranch, and no one recalls the last leg of the journey so it must have been uneventful. Once the cattle were delivered, Dave returned to Walter Erhorn's with his two saddle horses to pick up the team and wagon and drive the team back to the Home Ranch, with the saddle horses tied behind the wagon. By this time it was November and the weather was cold, and somewhere between Tatelkuz Lake and Missue Crossing beavers had dammed a small creek, flooding the trail with water — by now it had several inches of ice on it. Dave had to get into the water and break the ice with an axe in order to get the horses and the wagon across. By the time he was through he was soaking wet and very cold. Once he was across, he found a big pitchy stump along the trail and dumped the remainder of the chainsaw gas on it, then lit it on fire. He was able to warm up and dry out.

After returning the team and wagon to the Home Ranch Dave hired Wilfred Cassam and the two of them started for Nazko, picking up cattle that had escaped the drive and started back in the direction they had been driven in earlier in the summer. The temperatures dropped to about thirty below before they reached Nazko Ranch with the cattle they had picked up. Wilfred's saddle horse, being thin and badly overused (Wilfred never looked after his horses), died on the trail when the weather turned cold. Dave sold him his spare horse. (This one made it through the drive but died later in the winter.)

Bill Lampert took the remaining cattle that were at the Home Ranch after Pond's drive; whether they returned there or never left in the first place I don't know. My dad bought the two pairs that returned after our drive to the Home Ranch; we took them to our place at Sleepy Hollow, so Dad again had a few cattle. The cows that

Bill took were mostly black baldies. I cannot remember how many of these cows ended up at the Home Ranch, but I think it would be safe to say a dozen pairs. About Christmas time we went to the Chadwells' by snow machine, down the ice on Tsacha Lake. Near Mackenzie Trail Lodge a black cow and a calf were standing out on the ice at the edge of the lake. We told Jim, who said he would go get the pair, but before he did the wolves killed them both, right out there on the ice.

Eleven or twelve head of these cattle ended up going through the sale ring in Williams Lake, with the proceeds going to the rightful owner, but there were still about thirty pairs unaccounted for. This was the last time the Home Ranch ever had cattle.

# CHAPTER 7

# Early Years at Sleepy Hollow

Our first winter in our cabin, we had only the bare necessities. We did have a kitchen stove and an airtight heater, though. The kitchen stove was secondhand, but in excellent shape. It had been given to us when we went to Nazko in the summer to pick up our wagon. We bought a dresser from the manager who was leaving the Home Ranch, because there was no room for it in the plane when they were hauling their stuff out to Anahim Lake. We also had our wedding presents, including a set of dishes and a lot of linen and towels, and the rocking chair Rob and Sandy had bought us. A rough bed was nailed together and we put foamies on it. We also put together a rough board table, a counter and a few cupboards, and built some benches.

The area where we built had a lot of windfall and dry trees, so we had a huge pile of firewood. We had cut and stacked all the downed wood that was solid, burning the rest. The dry trees were felled and cut and stacked as well. At the corner of the cabin, where there were four trees, we put up a rough woodshed, with a pole roof. It kept the snow off the wood for the kitchen stove, at least. An outhouse was built out back.

A garden had been planted at the Home Ranch that summer, although all that did well were the turnips. They were large and firm.

The weeds seemed to have choked out the rest of the vegetables. Now that no one was living there we pulled all the turnips, hauling them home to be stored in the cubbyhole we built under the floor of the cabin. We had very little money, but the turnips were free, as was wild meat (moose were plentiful), so we would survive. We spent the winter hunting squirrels and doing some trapping; Barry chased coyotes with his snow machine.

Snow machines were very popular then and during the winter everyone was out with them. Of course they were not the machines we have today, but they got you there. It was a time of constant company and a full cabin. Many nights we had wall-to-wall bodies bedded down on the floor. Our cabin wasn't that big, and even with the small amount of furniture there still wasn't a great deal of room. Once, when a large group was over, anything that wasn't used was put out on the porch to give us more floor space. Barry would play his guitar late into the night, not wanting the evenings to end.

When Dad returned to the lodge in the spring we would often gather over there, because the lodge had much more room. As the

*Here's Barry and me, photographed in 1974, with our first snow machines.*

evenings progressed the conversations became louder, as whiskey loosened everybody's tongues. Most people smoked, and the room would fill with cigarette smoke as people drifted in and out. It wasn't uncommon to have several people outside with flashlights working on a snow machine or to have a carburetor taken apart on the kitchen table by the light of the gas lantern hanging from the ceiling. Often a flashlight had to be used as well because the light was poor or someone was standing in the way of it.

One day Barry and I went to Euchiniko Lake, about forty-five miles east of us, to meet a group of people coming from Quesnel. After feeding the cattle we filled our snow machines with gas and in less than three hours we were at Euchiniko Lake. Bunch Trudeau lived there alone. She had several cabins that she rented out for a little extra income. Barry's dad, uncle and aunt were there with a number of others. The trip back home was an all-day affair. It seemed that every couple of miles everything stopped. Someone had to change a belt, or a plug, add gas, retie a load on a skimmer or have a pit stop. I began to think there was no chance we would arrive before dark. Every once in awhile we stopped to count heads and see if everyone was accounted for. Jake Malic was constantly taking side tours and someone would have to wait for him or go look for him. As the day wore on Jake became annoyed and said he was fine, and not to look for him. We arrived home just before dark, minus Jake, who showed up a good hour and a half later—walking, because he had run out of gas. Everyone laughed.

When the days became longer we often took our snow machines and went over the mountain to Mike and Dale Lehman's, who lived about twelve miles east of Anahim Lake. From there Mike usually drove us to town for supplies and the mail. We would spend the night with them and return home the next day. On one of these trips Dale gave me a gas washing machine, as she had gotten a new one. They even put it in their skimmer and hauled it home for us. I was thrilled: washing clothes by hand was not the nicest thing to do.

It was a clear day in March with a bit of a wind when a little plane on skis came out from Quesnel. We stood out in front of the cabin to watch it land. Instead of landing east to west, as all ski-equipped planes normally landed, Al decided he'd land to the north and would stop right on the riverbank by Ed's place rather than taxi after landing. But he forgot that he'd put Teflon on his skis, and they skimmed over the snow with no drag. Al realized he was not going to stop in time so he tried to take off, and he did get airborne before the drop-off at the riverbank but then he was faced with tall trees. When he turned a tight left the wind caught him, and after some very interesting manoeuvres he crashed into the thick willow growth along the river. The sound of the frozen willows breaking was a loud racket, and when it was all over the plane had settled out of sight.

Barry ran to his snow machine and was trying to start it when I told him to take mine, as it started easier. He asked me what I was going to ride, to which I replied that I was not going down there to see all that blood. Ed started walking up the ice towards the crash site, after grabbing an axe from his woodshed in case he had to chop Al out of the aircraft. He met Al coming down the river without a scratch, but a little shaken up. Al said he thought he may have needed some toilet paper but even that turned out okay. The only damage the aircraft suffered was a small tear in the wing fabric. The worst was getting the plane out of the thick tangle of large willows and back onto the meadow. The willows had to be cut, then the plane gently lowered down the riverbank. From there it was taken down the river till a place was found where we could get it back up on the meadow. The torn hole was mended and Al flew off home the next day.

We bought our first milk cow on a trip to Anahim Lake in July of 1975, when we went in for the Anahim Lake rodeo. I was expecting in October, and with a baby we would need milk. The half-Guernsey heifer was a long yearling and already bred. At the same time we bought a yearling Hereford bull, getting them both from Lester Dorsey. We had two teams and wagons at Anahim for hauling freight home. The guys built one of the wagon boxes higher and loaded the two animals into that wagon, and they were hauled to the Blackwater. I wish I'd had a camera for a photo. At night they were unloaded and staked out with the horses, and we'd load up again each morning. The heifer, called Suzie, was a gentle little thing but the bull wasn't, but after two and a half days he was also gentle and halter broken.

Coming down a muddy draw on the north side of the mountain, Barry took a wrong turn on some old wagon tracks. (There were tracks every which way, as people were always looking for a smoother, drier route through the muck and rocks.) The wagon got mired in the mud and against a rock. We had to unload the livestock, backing them off the tailgate into the mud; they actually tried to climb back into the wagon, rather than wade to dry ground. The hour was

*Here's me milking the half Guernsey, our first milk cow at Sleepy Hollow.*
*We bought her in 1975 in Anahim Lake because I was expecting in*
*October, and with a baby we would need milk.* VANCE HANNA

late and the mosquitoes were out in swarms. We decided to camp there for the night, as there was water and horse feed, but we were in a bad spot for picking up wind to drive the flies away. The horses had to be tied up and they thrashed about all night long, breaking branches and pawing the ground, looking for some sort of relief from the droning, biting flies. Lester Dorsey and Tom Mathews had come back with us, both driving team and wagon. The flies didn't seem to bother Lester, but Tom was very vocal on his dislike of the flies, the camp, the trail and the country in general. Back then mosquito-proof tents were rare, so there was no resting. It was an awful night, and I vowed I would never again go back into the mountains in July.

By this time Bob Anthony had sold the Home Ranch again and he was having an auction to sell whatever was left on the ranch that could be moved before the new owners arrived. This included wagons, sleighs, haying equipment, horses, and household items and tack. Everything had to sell, and this was the reason Lester and Tom had come with us to the Blackwater. The auction actually turned out to be well attended, with a fairly large crowd coming by wagon (as Lester and Tom had), saddle horse, airplane, motorbike and helicopter. Barry's uncle Leo (who had been at the ranch off and on with Anthony from the beginning) bought a lot of stuff for Barry and me, since we could not afford to, including a tractor and the sawmill. He also bought a number of the old horses to keep them on the place. For helping out with the sale, Anthony gave me my mother's treadle sewing machine, which Mom had traded to Dorthea when the ranch was sold. I was very happy to have it; not only had it been my mom's, but I had no sewing machine. I still have it to this day.

After the sale the buildings were bare. All that was left were the homemade bunks in the cabins and a few dishes and pots in the old house. The kitchen range was left in the lodge, plus a few foamies, and the barrel heater was left in the ranch house. The tack shed, which was always so full of stuff, was empty but for a few pieces of rotten harness, worn out horseshoes and broken halters. It was very depressing to see the old home place stripped like that.

There were guests booked for a trail ride in August and the party was to be picked up at Titetown, west of Nazko. Dad and Rick were driving wagons loaded with camp gear. A lady friend of Rick's from Smithers and Esther Alexis, Peter's second youngest daughter, were handling the loose horses. It would be a three- or four-day trip with the wagons to reach Titetown. I went with them the first morning to help get the horses on the trail. We were several miles out on the trail when the lady from Smithers couldn't handle her horse and it ran away with her. As they tore by me, with her screaming, I reached out and grabbed the horse's halter without thinking. The horse jerked me from the saddle and I landed on the ground on my stomach. As I was seven months pregnant, this was a concern. Both wagons stopped, and the horses milled around as Rick's friend, who had also fallen off, got to her feet and remounted. We were only a mile or so from Rose Cassam's so I decided to go there. On my arrival I explained to Rose what happened, telling her I would be alone at home; if problems arose I wanted to be with someone who would know what to do. I knew that she had no doubt attended home births, as it was common practice among the Indian people to have their babies at home. She just shook her head and said, "Oh dear, oh dear." We drank tea and visited for several hours, and with no apparent side effects from my fall. Rose felt I was safe to return home. Untying my saddle horse from the hitching rack I swung into the saddle, waved goodbye to Rose and rode a short distance to the Blackwater River. I let my horse drink from the fast-moving water, then crossed over the gravel-bottom river and up the bank and rode upriver with my horse dancing about, anxious to be going home.

We were very fortunate back then as Sister Suzanne from the medical clinic at Anahim Lake held a clinic every month at the Indian reserve at Kluskus, flying there by helicopter. On the way back to Anahim she always had the pilot take a side trip and stopped at Sleepy Hollow for coffee and to deliver our mail, which she would have picked up from the post office before leaving for Kluskus. She kept me in a good supply of antibiotics and vitamins, with enough to pass out to the locals if needed, and a good supply of bandages, burn medication, eardrops and other medical supplies—whatever might be needed in the area between her trips. So I had the sister's good care while I was carrying Jon.

Sister Suzanne wanted me in town a month ahead of my due date, October 10, so I flew into Quesnel in mid-September to await the birth, and stayed with my mom. But I was bored, as I was used to being very active. I walked a lot but it didn't seem to matter where I went, someone always came along and insisted on driving me home, as I shouldn't be out walking in my condition. Jonathan Barry arrived in the early morning hours of October 6, weighing six pounds, four ounces. Barry had arrived in town a few days earlier so he was there when Jon was born. I left the hospital three days later wearing my usual jeans. Jon was a good baby and rarely fussed unless he was hungry. After spending a couple weeks in town with our families we took our little son and went back to the Blackwater.

It is funny how parenthood changes one's thinking; well, for some people. We went to Anahim in late February with Jon, who would have been four-and-a-half months, wrapped up in his snow-suit and a wool blanket on my lap. On our way home, as we were nearing the top of the pass, a storm moved in with heavy snow and wind. We had a hard time finding the trail. Normally it would not have fazed me but I was very scared we might end up lost in the storm and have to spend the night out in a snowy camp, or we would run out of gas if we couldn't find the trail for some time. All kinds of images came to mind as we wandered around in the blowing snow with very little visibility. We did locate the trail in the timber and got home just fine, but that was the end of mountain trips for me with a baby.

I took Jon with me everywhere in a backpack. He spent a great deal of his first two years of life there, while I took care of every-day things like milking the cow, cleaning the barn, splitting wood, haying and fixing fences. I didn't have a dirt bike then, so I rode everywhere on my then-favourite horse, Surf, a big, long-legged bay gelding. I had ridden Surf so much that I trusted him completely.

When Jon was just over a year old I began working part-time as a telephone operator for Hazel Mars, who had the contract with

BC Tel at Anahim Lake. If she needed me she would have Floyd Vaughan fly to Sleepy Hollow and pick me up; he'd also fly me home after the work was done, which might be a week to two weeks later. Usually it was by ski plane, as I worked mostly in the winter. Once when Floyd came it was extremely cold and I had gathered up blankets and extra heavy clothes for Jon and I'd made up extra bottles of milk. Floyd said it was only a twenty-minute flight, to which I replied that if something happened and we went down in the mountains I intended to be prepared. Floyd just shook his head.

It was during one of these trips when I was on the switchboard that I put a call through between two ladies in Anahim. This switchboard was very old. It was the kind for which a person's number might be a long ring and then three short rings; the operator had to manually do the rings. When the call was completed the person was to give a short ring to indicate that the call was over. Well, I never heard any ring so I plugged into the line to see if it was clear. These two ladies were still talking and one was saying, "Barry over

*Jon, at age one, with his babysitter Esther Alexis, taken at the Home Ranch.*

in the Blackwater has finally found the Lord," and I couldn't believe what I was hearing. I knew I should get off the line but couldn't help wanting to hear the rest. The last thing that would ever happen was Barry turning to religion. But how many Barrys were there in the Blackwater? This lady went on to say, "He goes over to the Blackwells' to preach the gospel." Then I knew they had to be talking about the caretaker at Laidman Lake. I had heard that someone was staying there, but did not know his name at the time.

In June it was normal to get high water when the snow packs melted off the mountains. It was one of those years when nothing really happens for weeks, then it turns hot and the snow all melts at once. The river rose till it overflowed its banks and spread over the fields. Each morning there was less field showing, till the whole valley appeared to be a lake. The willows that grew along the banks of the river as it wound this way and that down the valley were the only sign of where the river was. The fences were no more, with only the odd stake sticking out of the water. A lot of times the buck fences began to float, then sections would break free to wash with the current, till they hung up on high ground or a willow clump. Then there was one tangled mess of fence covered with old grass, sticks, pieces of driftwood—whatever had ridden the waters down past that particular spot.

I had decided to go into town to visit Mom, as Barry was gone somewhere and there wasn't much I could do at home anyway, till the water dropped. Someone was flying into Dad's and I knew I could catch a ride to town. So with Jon, who then would have been twenty months, on my back in his backpack and a duffel bag full of clothes for us tied to the saddle I rode up to Ed's. He met us at the gate and opened it, then ran ahead of the horse, wading nearly knee deep in water with his gumboots, to reach the bridge and open the gate on it. Both approaches to the bridge were partly under water. With the horse walking on it the water squished up between the cracks to splash back on the dry planks. We clumped across the plank bridge and rode out onto the high ground of the field, where the water was belly deep to the horse; we wound around, sticking to the higher ground till there was no avoiding the low part of the field, where the water was flowing with a stronger current. I knew there was an irrigation ditch there so I had to try to hit the crossing of the ditch, where the horse wouldn't stumble on the piled-up soil. The west wind was by then sweeping down the valley, causing whitecaps on the water, which the horse decided he didn't like. He was snorting and shying, one way then the other, and I began to get concerned, as I couldn't swim. I finally kicked him into the deep water, which got deeper and deeper till the horse was swimming. Then I was scared that he might roll, but fortunately it was only a short distance and his feet soon touched bottom. The water gradually lessened as we approached the timber, till it was just sloshing and then squishing underfoot, and soon we were on dry ground.

After a couple years of renting the Gunson house, my Mom bought herself a mobile home on North Fraser Drive in Quesnel. Although she was in a mobile park it was still her own home and she took pride in her yard and her flowers. She would start plants early in the windows of the mobile, to be planted outside once the danger of frost had passed. She had always had flowers at the Home Ranch but due to the short growing season she was limited in what flowers she could grow. In Quesnel she was able to grow most plants, and even had rose bushes. One day she was proudly showing me her plants she had started indoors, explaining that the marigolds were nearly ready to be put outside. One plant in particular was growing much better than the others: it was a good inch or two taller then the rest. Mom commented that it was odd that it grew so much faster. I was as dumb as her, but Barry (who had shown up in Quesnel) laughed and told me it was a pot plant that my brother Rob had put in with her plants for her to tend to. After thinking about it for awhile I decided I had better tell her what it was. She carried on about the plant and then took it outside and put it in the garbage can. After half an hour or so she said that maybe the garbage man would see it in there, so she'd better get it out of the garbage can. In the end I think she flushed it down the toilet, so no one would come across it and think she was growing "dope"!

That summer was an extremely wet one. It rained heavily all spring and into summer. By haying time the fields were still too wet to get out on. Bill Lampert and the Alexis family upriver had the same problem. Barry and I decided after checking that the now abandoned Home Ranch meadows showed more promise than anything along the Blackwater River. We moved to the Home Ranch for the long haul, because if we hayed there then we would have to winter there as well. The ranch house was still livable, as it still contained stoves and spare furnishings and had a roof, even if it was leaky. It needed a good cleaning and for us to get rid of the mice that were living there. Barry mowed hay with the tractor on days it wasn't raining and I raked hay with the team when it was dry. The Alexis family also moved up and set up camp down the creek from the house. I was then able to have Esther Alexis, who was sixteen or seventeen, babysit Jon. She was very good with him, which eased my mind when I went off to the field. Peter Alexis and his family were going to stack the hay. It was a very discouraging job, as it was hard to get the hay dry and into the stack. We turned the hay in the windrows and in the shocks trying to dry it, while it became browner and browner, and the rain continued to fall.

There was a young white couple with Peter's family—I am not sure if they had been invited, or if they had just come along anyway. They had their own team and wagon and several small children. I believe they originated from Vancouver. At that time, these types of people were referred to as hippies: back-to-the-land people who knew very little but could be told nothing. Their attitude was that everything belonged to everyone, and they used Peter's horses as freely as if they were their own. One day the lady caught a saddle horse of Peter's and saddled it up, cinching the horse till it groaned and its movements were hampered by the tight cinch. She then asked me to help her strap her baby onto her back in the backpack she had. I jumped at this, as it had a strap around her middle, which I pulled as tight as I could till she complained. I then told her that was how the poor horse felt. She ignored the dig, mounted up, whipped the horse into a gallop and headed for the field.

We did finally manage to get what we hoped was enough hay up for the cattle we had, including Ed's, Peter's and Bill Lampert's. None of us had very many but together they made a fairly large bunch. Bill Lampert butchered all the cows he had taken from the Home Ranch after the Pond drive. Using the airstrip on the ranch he hauled the meat to Williams Lake with his plane. With that much butchering the gut pile was rather large, and it was bear paradise for a couple weeks. There were several grizzlies that came in at night to eat. We would stand outside after dark and listen to the growls and roars from down by the corrals as they fought among themselves. One very dark night, while the bears were feeding and fighting, I went out to use the outdoor bathroom, which was situated fifty yards or so from the house towards the corrals. I settled down with the door open and listened to the bears, and then I heard something right behind the bathroom, which sounded just like a bear growling. I leapt to my feet, grabbing the door, slamming it shut and frantically trying to pull my pants up. My mouth went totally dry with fright. Then Barry started laughing outside.

Fortunately, it turned out to be one of the mildest winters I had ever seen. Not only was the hay of poor quality, but the house was no longer very warm, with Dorthea having had the dirt taken off the roof. The coldest we had was ten below, for one night. We did not have that much snow, either. At Christmas it rained hard for two days causing a major flood; we spent the first night moving things around the house as the water dripped down onto the floor and ran down the walls. The meadow flooded then slowly froze, leaving a very large skating rink. Barry sharp-shod the team in order to get out to the haystacks to get hay to haul to the cattle. It took the horses awhile to feel comfortable on the slick ice but once they realized they were safe with the sharp shoes they walked right along, with the sleigh sliding around behind them.

When we moved out of the Home Ranch in the spring, George Chantyman from the Kluskus Reserve, who was married to Peter's oldest daughter, helped me move the cattle. Separating Alexis's and Lampert's cows, I helped George get started for their place on the

Blackwater. Lampert still had the black calves off the cows he had butchered. My father would never have had a black cow. George asked me if the black animals had black blood. I was rather surprised, then realized he was serious. I told him no, that his skin was dark compared to mine but our blood was the same colour, and the same applied to the cows, and meat. He seemed a lot happier to know that.

When Jon got too big for the backpack he was carried in front of my saddle, tied to me around my waist, but he would soon fall asleep and I would have to hold him up with one arm. How he could sleep that way was beyond me, but he did, and usually most of the time.

Through June and July of that summer I started helping Marilou Blackwell with the cooking on the weekends at Moose Lake Lodge, taking Jon with me. I would ride over to Tsetzi Lake and John Blackwell would pick me up with his float plane and fly me to Moose Lake. When the weekend was over, I would be flown back to Tsetzi Lake. Money was short and the weekend job came in real handy.

For a wedding present Rick had given us a little bay quarter horse mare he called Daisy. She had somewhat of a sour disposition, so I never rode her much. She was nice when she wanted to be, but other times she would bunch her muscles and I would tense, waiting for the worst, and then she would relax and step right along— then do it again. She would do this sometimes all day. Then the odd time she would buck! One day I was taking friends back to Tsetzi Lake to the airstrip to catch a plane out that Barry was coming in on. I gave Daisy to one of the guests to ride, and she was so good with him. When we were leaving Tsetzi Lake to head back home, Barry got on the mare and I had just begun to tell him how good she had been that morning, when she started to buck straight towards the creek, and dumped Barry over her head. He crashed through the alder bushes into the water and the mare trotted off. There was no need to finish my sentence. Yet Barry really liked the mare, so mostly he rode her. Then one summer she disappeared, along with a grey gelding of Dad's, and we never saw either horse again.

William and Rose Cassam often went to town in winter and stayed for several weeks. They would send a radio message, asking one of us to feed their cattle. Barry was home with Jon, so I took the snow machine one day and went to the Cassams' to feed the cows. William's parents were still alive then, but they were also away. Mary, William's mother, had a bitch dog that had been left at home. She was out in the meadow following the horses, eating their manure and looking nearly starved. I fed the cattle from the haystack in the meadow then decided to throw some hay out from the stack at the corrals as well. In the haystack were three small puppies so weak from hunger they could hardy move. I had a .22 rifle on the snow machine for hunting squirrels. I shot all three puppies, and found a gunnysack in the barn to put them in. I then took them to Dad's. By that time I was crying, upset about the starving puppies and knowing I should not have shot someone else's dogs. My Dad took the gunnysack, saying he would get rid of them, and assured me I had done the right thing. I went home feeling somewhat better. Nothing was ever said, so the family must have just assumed the puppies died of starvation.

# CHAPTER 8

# Around the Ranch

In the summer of 1977, Barry wanted to move back to town. We left our animals in Ed's care and went to Quesnel. We lived for awhile in the basement of Barry's folks' place and Barry went to work at one of the local sawmills. Later we got an apartment and I started work at the Dunrovin, a facility for the elderly, as a housekeeper. Karman, a cousin of Barry's, babysat for me. I would drop Jon off in the morning and as I backed down the driveway he would stand at the big picture window crying his heart out. I would cry all the way to work then phone Karman, who assured me that as soon as I was out of sight Jon went to play.

This was the first summer in my entire life that I spent away from the Blackwater country, and I was homesick. I hated living in a ground-floor apartment, and Barry was off most evenings and weekends with friends. I felt like I was suffocating, living in the noise of the city and the city smells. I missed the fresh air, the silence and the birds. In late October I quit my job, packed up my belongings and drove to Anahim Lake with Jon and my mother. From there my mother flew back to Quesnel. I bought what groceries I needed or could afford and got Floyd to fly me back to Tsetzi Lake. I had sent a radio message to Ed as my dad had already left for the winter. Ed met me at the airstrip with team and wagon and took Jon and me home. Jon did not seem fazed by the fact he was taken from bright lights and constant relatives and grandparents' attention to a little log cabin with propane and kerosene lights and a wood stove. At that time of year only Ed was about. The cabin was cold after having no fire on for so long, and the mice had taken over for awhile—their droppings were everywhere. The worst was a weasel that had moved in, and because I had left the top drawer of the dresser open a crack, this became its toilet facility. Everything in the top drawer had to be thrown out, but the weasel had cleaned the mice out of the house at least. Barry came home a month or so later.

We had a cat when Jon was little, a grey female named Maui, who was an excellent mouser. Females were the best hunters I found, and because of the distance between neighbours there was little fear of a tomcat finding our place—but somehow one did. It was in the coldest part of winter and Maui was inside the cabin when she decided to have her kittens. She was rolling around meowing, which attracted Jon's attention. I explained she was having her kitten, and I wanted it understood there was only going to be one! Well, one arrived, and Jon peered under our bed as the mother washed her new

*Jon with his cat Tiger, a useless mouser but a good companion.*

baby. I waited for more to arrive, planning to get rid of them without Jon seeing, but nothing happened. I had to go milk the cow. While I was milking Jon came running to the barn and exclaimed, "Maui now has two babies!" Oh well, he got a lot of enjoyment from those two kittens. One I gave away when it was grown and the other I had a neighbour neuter. What happened to Maui I can't remember, but we ended up with only the neutered cat, Tiger, who was totally useless as a hunter. He was Jon's cat and slept on his bed for years. I had to get another cat to do the hunting.

One time, I had a horse in the corral at Ed's place that I wanted to halter break. Jon was about three, just the age at which he could travel quite fast. A friend was staying with us so she was keeping an eye on Jon in a grassy area at the back of the corral. I had just gotten hold of the horse and along came Ed's tom turkey, with feathers all puffed out and his head bright red. He did look rather menacing. Sandy was scared of him so I had to climb over the fence, get a stick and run the turkey back up towards the cabin, where his mate pecked at grasshoppers or whatever was on the menu that day. I then crawled back over the fence and got back to the horse. The turkey returned almost immediately, not once, not twice, but three more times. I was getting tired of the fence climbing. Then Ed came along and I remarked that his turkey was a nuisance, as it wouldn't leave Jon and Sandy alone. With his calm, quiet manner Ed waited for the turkey to return, grabbed him by the neck with both hands and swung him around a number of times—while the turkey squawked and flopped and feathers flew—then flung him back over the fence. The bird hit the ground hard, tried to stand and fell a number of times, then finally got his balance and toddled off in the direction that his mate gone in. He never returned to bother us again. Jon found the whole thing funny and talked about it for the rest of the day.

Jon was a very well-behaved-boy, but like all boys he liked to get into some trouble. At one point, Jon was not very old, but old enough to want a knife. He must have said something to a group of men who had spent the night with us on their way to the mountains.

While they were packing their horses up in the morning, one of the guys gave Jon a knife, with which he soon cut himself. I noticed blood dripping between his fingers as he stood out in the yard with his hands clenched together over the knife. I asked him what happened, and he said one of the horses had bit him. Apparently he thought if he told me he had a knife I would take it away. Another time, we had company and Jon was out in the yard when I called him to come into the house. He must have been about four. He grabbed onto a tree and said, "Don't beat me mommy!" Then he began to giggle, much to my relief, because by that point there were raised eyebrows among our visitors.

On the Home Ranch Dad had always raised Hereford cattle. In the forties he had shorthorn bulls for awhile but he went back to Herefords and felt they were the only beef cattle to raise. So the tradition continued, with us raising Herefords as well. Our cow herd started with the cows Barry had gotten from Anthony, the original Home Ranch cattle. Dad had bought the two pair of Herefords that had returned to the Home Ranch after our drive, so he had a few cows, which we kept at our place. We decided to try cross-breeding and purchased a Simmental bull one year. Dad had a fit and said we were ruining the herd, but then he couldn't be outdone so he bought a Charolais bull. That was the beginning of our crossbreeding program. Different people told us that we would have a lot of calving problems, but it was a lot less, and our weigh gain on the calves really made a difference.

We had a deep snow winter in the late seventies. I am not sure what winter it was, but the snow was deep. Then came a thaw and it crusted, which spelled disaster to the wildlife as well as our rather large herd of horses rustling out in the snow. We had very little extra hay so we had to decide which horses were to be saved and which had to be shot. Fortunately I was home with Jon, and Dad and Barry had to make the choices. All the older horses that were not used much, or not used at all, had to go. As did the young ones that were not old enough to be useful and a couple of the young broken ones that were considered rather worthless. It was a sad time. One of those horses was Whitey, a white gelding my dad rode for many years. He had been born in the mid-forties and was about thirty-three years old then. He was still very active and had more than likely spent every winter of his life pawing for his feed in the snowy swamps, surviving them all. We left the horses as long as we could with hopes for a thaw, but it never came. Once we had a smaller number, we bought tons of high-protein pellets and had Floyd fly them in to Tsetzi Lake with the ski-equipped Beaver. These were fed daily to the remaining horses, and they were able to survive the rest of the winter.

Barry, Jon and I went to Rainbow Lake, about thirty-five miles west of us, on our snow machines to visit John and Sandy Zigler, who lived at the end of the lake in a cozy log house with their two boys. From there we decided to go to Moose Lake to visit the Blackwells. It wasn't a fast trip in those days, as snow machines were a lot slower than they are now. We had one Elan and another Ski-doo a bit bigger. John had an old twin track with one ski in front, and I think Sandy had the best machine of the tour, a reasonably new Arctic Cat. She was packing her two boys and I had Jon in front of me. We came to a very steep hill and there was a good amount of snow with no trail. We stopped at the bottom of the hill, and then John went up the hill as fast as he could but got stuck just before the top. He had gotten off the machine and had gone around to the back of it when Sandy started up the hill going as fast as she could. She never let off the throttle but ran into John and his machine. I thought at the time she may have broken his legs. As he lay in the snow moaning and swearing in pain he asked her what she thought she was doing, to which she replied, "But you told me never to stop on a hill."

About 1977 or 1978 Walt and Nora Lampert and their three kids, Laurie, Billy and Henry, moved onto the Lampert property that Bill Lampert had bought back in the sixties when we were still living on the Home Ranch. The place once belonged to Shag Thompson and before that it had been one of the Frontier Cattle Co. holdings, where hay was put up and cattle were fed. Bill, Walt's dad, had been running it for a number of years with a few head of cattle and a hired hand. It was nice to have a family move in, especially one with small children only a few years older than Jon.

In 1977 Dad and Rick sold the hunting area to a German fellow by the name of Gus Abel, as Rick was getting married and planned on making his home in Smithers. One hunting season, however, was apparently all Gus wanted, as the business was soon for sale again.

We had no road into Blackwater country till the mid-1970s, when the Kluskus Forest Service Road (shortened to the Kluskus Road by the locals) coming south from Vanderhoof finally reached the area. At that time the good road ended at Matthew Creek, north of us at 157 km on the Kluskus Road (157 kilometres south of Vanderhoof). There was a winter haul road, which came south another six miles (to 167 km) but was impassable in summer for a number of years till the mud finally set up to allow a hard surface. So in order to use the road we had to go out to 157 km with team and wagon, following a trail that Murray Vannoy had cut a few years before when he decided to move his family to a meadow over on Matthew Creek. He had originally settled on Cottonwood Creek, which was about fourteen miles west of Sleepy Hollow. After a number of years there he wanted to move farther back, as he felt there was too much of a population where he was. His closest neighbour was some six miles away, and he more than likely got company once a month. But he built the trail and was in the process of moving his family and all their belongings back there when the small tractor he was using to tow a heavily loaded wagon overturned on him and he was killed. His wife and children returned to Montana, where they had come from. The trail he cut wound around swamps and bogs and had its fair share of mud and rock. But that wasn't any different from any of the other wagon trails in that country.

Plateau Mill (now owned by Canfor and called Canfor Mill) built a logging camp at 157 km. This was handy for us, as there was always someone around so it was safe to leave a vehicle there. Walt Lampert and Ed Adams built a corral and a loading chute there, for hauling cattle when we started driving our cattle to the end of the road and trucking them to Vanderhoof for the sales at the Vanderhoof Auction Mart. If a person had to leave a team overnight, while they ran into town for supplies, there was now a corral to leave them in.

Dave and Jane Rozak bought the Vannoy meadow a few miles up the creek from the camp after Murray Vannoy died. When the camp was not in operation the Rozaks were the caretakers there. Since the camp was only used for logging in the winter months, the Rozaks lived at the camp more than they did at their small cabin up the creek. Dave built more corrals for his cattle. Hay was stored there and the cattle were calved out there. The extra corrals were very handy for us, as well as the Lamperts.Our first couple of years at Sleepy Hollow, the few cattle we had to sell, plus what Ed and Dad had, were driven to Anahim Lake and sold locally there. I did not go on these drives, as Jon was a baby. When the Lamperts moved in they also had a few cattle, so that was when the chute was built at 157 km and we started driving the cattle there and having them trucked to Vanderhoof. Up to this time we had sold yearlings, and we still did for awhile. It must have been in the early 1980s that we started to sell the calves.

It took time to increase our herd, as we didn't have many to start. Rose and William Cassam also had a few cattle. For a number of years Rose and I drove the cattle to the end of the road, spending the night camped at the corrals as we waited for the truck the following morning, then rode back home. This was easiest when the kids were small. When the haul road became passable with the pickup and we could get right in to the ranch, often Barry would come in the morning, and we'd turn my horse loose or send it with Rose back to the ranch, then go on into town. Once the kids got a bit older we all went to take the cattle out and camped at the corrals. Often we had friends help us. It was around then that William rather then Rose started to help, and he would go on into town with us.

The last six miles of the Kluskus Forest Service Road had no gravel on it so it still had mudholes, even when it finally set up enough to be passable in summer. But we were able to get closer to home, at least. Walt Lampert improved the trail into his place, so with a 4 x 4 and chains and a lot of savvy for driving in the mud we could get within three miles of Sleepy Hollow. We slowly improved the remaining trail to the ranch but it was a two-and-a-half-hour drive from the forest road to the ranch. Stretches of it were solid rock—and I mean rock, you were driving on rocks. It took skill to manoeuvre around them with a truck. If you were not careful it was easy to high centre, and then it was out with the jack-all. You'd have to jack up the high-centred side, and with the chainsaw (you always packed a chainsaw) cut a log to put under a tire to get moving again. There was the odd smooth spot—not many, but a person could appreciate them—where you could let your breath out and stopped clenching your teeth. The mudholes were the worst. We corduroyed the very worst spot and other places, if there was room; we just made new ruts around them. The secret was to stay out of the ruts if at all possible. Spring and fall were the most treacherous. Summer was the only time you might not get stuck, unless it had rained a lot. The truck always had a shovel, a jack-all, chains, a come-a-long and an axe in it. Usually the chainsaw was taken along as well. Winter we were snowed in if the snow got too deep. Walt would plow his road to the Kluskus Road so we could leave our vehicle at the Y where our roads met. We used a snow machine to get to our pickup if we wanted to take our vehicle into town, but I seldom left the ranch in the winter.

When Audie Murphy (who came into the country with the Chadwells) got a 4 x 4 pickup and started driving back into the Blackwater, he made a sign and put it up on a tree on the worst stretch of rocky trail. The sign read, "Watch for *Rock* on Road." Every other sign would be shot full of holes but no one ever shot at that sign. In the nineties a road was build around that part of the trail. The sign remained there for years till the tree it was nailed to was attacked by the mountain pine beetle and died. It later fell down with the sign still on it, in a tangle with other fallen trees. One year, Alex and Gertrude Fraser and Art Kelly and his wife from Quesnel decided to drive in to see my dad. They got stuck in a mudhole

*Come spring and fall, the drive to the ranch was very treacherous. As evidence, here's our grey Ford truck in spring.*

between 157 km and 167 km. Barry rescued them with team and wagon and took them to Tsetzi Lake. Alex at that time was the minister of highways. He was furious that that section of the road had no gravel, so soon after he returned to Quesnel that part of the road received some gravel—not a lot, but it did help the worst of the mudholes.

In appreciation of being rescued, Art built us a round table with a lazy Susan in the centre. The table was five feet across on a large stand. It was the nicest piece of furniture in the house for years to come.

In the late eighties, when our boys were big enough to reach the foot pedals of the pickup and see out the windshield, they were allowed to drive—once we were past all logging activity, so no logging trucks were met. They became good drivers on the poor roads. Coming home once with James driving he said, "Mom, now I know why a lot of people are drunk when they get to our place, it is the road!"

The late seventies was an eventful time for us, with lots of changes. Ed wrote Gayle a letter during the winter of 1977–78, saying that Jon was growing like a weed and talked really well; that Jon had two kittens, and one had used Barry's slipper for a litter box; that Gus Abel had sold the hunting area to two men, one from Williams Lake and the other from Vancouver. He also noted that Floyd had brought me a radio. It was a marine band radio of sorts, but I could talk to the Vaughans at Nimpo Lake with it, and Mrs. Edwards at Lonesome Lake, as she had one too. It may seem like a minor thing, but it wasn't. It was our first communication to the outside world. It was a great comfort to me to know that if Jon was to get hurt or real sick I could get help.

Clint Thompson from Bella Coola spent the fall of 1977 with us and helped out, as Barry had had back surgery. Clint was very

*Here's Jon and I, taken in 1977.*

good with Jon, spending hours with him. A couple of years earlier Dad had bought a half-Welsh paint mare, which my nieces were able to ride. When she was around a year or two she had had a cute paint foal and my Dad gave it to Wanda. I'm not sure how old the colt was when we figured out she had a mean streak; it was three or four years old when Clint was staying with us. He messed around with her for awhile but she wanted to strike at him all the time. He felt she was not worth the time spent with her. I'm not sure how long

Clint stayed with us but he left before Christmas. The winter was cold, and on one occasion Ed froze his chin and nose while out feeding

In 1978 Ed sold his two quarters of land to Wes and Jorja Carter from Amboy, Washington. Ed was given estate for life in the sale agreement, so he was able to remain in his cabin and keep his horses and cows. The Carters then built a short distance upriver from Ed, on an opening on the hillside, among some very large pine and poplar trees. They contracted the building of a small log cabin the first summer, and the second summer they built another log cabin and got a start on a log house, which was never finished. Jim Chadwell started an airstrip farther up on the hillside but that was never finished either. The Carters did not spend very much time there. Wes usually flew up, landing at the Tsetzi Lake strip, and would come over on his three-wheeled ATV, which he stored at Tsetzi Lake. Jorja did come up in the summers some, when the kids were out of school, but not that often.

The summer of 1978 we met Bob Slater, or "Dune Buggy Bob" as he was fondly called. He arrived one day in the summer doing the back roads with his dune buggy; I believe he was headed for the Arctic Circle on that trip. He had left his home in Surrey, driven through Squamish and up through the Gang Ranch and the Chilcotin, then arrived at our place. Painted on the hood of the dune buggy by hand was a map of North America, and the routes of different trips he had taken with his vehicle were marked in red. After spending several days with us he moved on, but he returned for a number of summers to spend time with us. When Jon was about six

*Bob Slater's dune buggy, with which he travelled around North America. For a few years, Slater often visited in the summer.*

*The Carter house on the ranch. The Carters, from Amboy, Washington, bought property from Ed in 1978 and used it mainly when the kids were out of school.*

Bob took him to Vancouver for a week to see Stanley Park and other sights of the big city. I was in a panic—my baby going off to the big city for his first time away from Mom—but he left with a big smile on his face and apparently never missed me.

During one of Bob's visits he got in the habit of coming in, removing his boots and stepping into Barry's slippers. One day Barry came in ahead of Bob with a hammer and two five-inch nails, and nailed the slippers to the floor. Bob came in shortly afterwards, kicked off his boots and stepped into the slippers—nearly falling on his face when he tried to move. There followed an awkward silence. Bob never again used Barry's slippers. I think the message was received loud and clear.

In October of 1978 a bunch of the guys had a major poker game at Dad's. The biggest pot was $9,280. I think Wes Carter was the big winner. The party carried over to our house. I remember that it was Jon's third birthday, and he got a lot of toys and clothes, but also forty dollars and half a gallon of whiskey.

It was about that time that CB radios were discovered, and soon everyone in the Blackwater country had them. Our first communications had been with the marine band radio, and not that long before. I don't know who got the first CB but they sure caught on. We had a gas generator and chargers so we were able to charge our battery, and we used to charge the neighbours' as well. Later on we used a small solar panel to keep the batteries charged. Our call sign was "Sleepy Hollow," Tsetzi Lake was "Tsetzi Lake" and then there was "Blue Lake"—that was the Cassams—and the Lamperts were "Carnlick." The Alexis family had "Blackwater,"and so on. In the mornings and evenings everyone was usually on it listening in on everyone's conversations. If a snow machine went by and didn't stop and you wanted to know who it was, you called someone else, as they usually stopped somewhere. Cold mornings it was, "How cold is it at your place?" Then everyone would comment on the temperature and the weather and pass on any little bit of news they had. It was something to look forward to, to break the monotony of the long, cold winters. It was especially nice for the women, who were alone so much. I used to think of how nice it would have been for my mother, who lived so many years in isolation with no outside communication of any sort. I felt very fortunate. I think when people live in an isolated area with none of the modern facilities every little thing that makes life easier or brings great pleasure is appreciated so much more! I know that's how it was for me.

# CHAPTER 9

# New Additions to the Family

I awoke early one morning to hear the food cooler being ripped off the back of the cabin. Sitting up in bed, right under the window, I was startled to find a very large black bear looking in at me. Our noses were only a foot or so apart, and that pane of glass was very thin. I awoke Barry and told him. He got up and went after the bear with the rifle, as I ran to different windows trying to locate it. It was one of those mornings in September when there was heavy but patchy ground fog; I would catch glimpses of Barry moving about, then the bear. As the fog drifted by the corner of the cabin I caught sight of a tent, and realized my niece Wanda, who spent a lot of each summer with us, was sleeping in it. I opened the door and told her to come inside, as there was a bear out there. She was out of the tent and into the cabin in about three leaps, her nightgown trailing out behind her. Lucky for the bear the fog gave it cover and it got away.

When I learnt in my seventh month of pregnancy in 1979 that I was having twins, it took a bit getting used to. That was the last thing I had expected. Jon could still ride in front of me, and with a baby in a backpack on my back I knew I could still get about on my saddle horse. But that was not going to happen now.

One day I went over to Tsetzi Lake to see if someone would take me in to Quesnel, as I had an appointment with my doctor. There were several planes there and the bunch of guys said they would take me in. Dad needed to go to town as well, as he had some things to do there. So it ended up that three planes flew into town. I was to meet the guys back at the airport a few hours later. Mom picked me up and we kept my appointment. Then we did some grocery shopping and went back to the airport. One of the guys suggested I fly back with him rather than the fellow who had brought me in. I said no, I wanted to fly back the way I came in, and he made a face and walked off. On the hour flight back there was very little conversation, but we flew very low, gaining altitude to climb over little hills then dropping down again. A lot of the time we were just skimming over the treetops. I had Jon on my lap. When we reached Tsetzi Lake the pilot said he wanted to circle around and get the feel of the wind. I asked if he could just land as I was beginning to feel nauseous. So we went straight in for a landing. He cut power too soon and the plane came down short of the runway, landing in the swampy area. From there it seemed to bounce in the air and the second landing was on the runway, but we hit so hard both the doors flew open. I had a seat belt on but Jon was only sitting on me. It was a good thing I was hanging on to him for dear life! The pilot did get the plane under control and we taxied to a stop. I was a bit shaken up and made a remark about it to the other guys after they landed. The fellow who had wanted to fly me on the return flight said the guy I flew with was drunk; he had spent the afternoon in the bar. I was very thankful that things had ended up okay.

The Carters spent more of that summer at Sleepy Hollow and had brought up with them a young fellow from Amboy, Washington, by the name of Jimmie Williams, who was about seventeen. Jimmie couldn't do enough for me. After working at the Carters' all day he would come over to make sure I had wood and water packed in and do any other things that needed doing. He made the summer a lot easier for me. I decided then that one of the babies would be called James.

Sister Suzanne still had the helicopter pilot stop by at our place to check on me after her clinic at Kluskus each month. She wanted me in Quesnel a good six weeks before my due date of mid-Nov-ember. Jon and I moved in with my mom in late September. In the early hours of October 15, I woke my mom and told her I had called a cab and was leaving for the hospital. I put Jon in bed with her and went out to the taxi. On the drive to the hospital the cab driver told me he had taken a lady to the hospital the night before and she had had twins! When I told him that I was also having twins he stomped on the gas pedal and careened around the corners, actually scaring me. When we got to the hospital, he grabbed my arm and half dragged me to the emergency door, and rang the bell furiously. When the nurse opened the door he was gone, without even getting paid.

The twins, being a month early, weighed only four pounds, ten ounces and five pounds, four ounces. Unlike Jon, who was very fair when he was born, they were dark, with a lot of black hair. My mom and my mother-in-law, Leona, were at the hospital and both were crying when they were allowed in to see me. George, who owned my dad's old hunting area at the time, was my second visitor. He stopped and saw the babies first, then came in my room laughing, saying that with all that black hair the babies looked a lot like Peter Alexis, the Indian guide.

Because Barry and I could not agree on names, he named one and I named the other. So we had James Floyd, named for Jimmie Williams and my dad, whose legal name was Floyd, and Wesley Jacob, named for Wes Carter and Barry's dad. James was released from the hospital after five days but Wesley was kept for a good ten days, till his weigh got over five pounds. Mom, Leona and I took turns going to the hospital to feed and cuddle him. Because of their size they had to be fed often—and having two babies was a whole lot different than one. It was decided that when one woke to eat, the other was woken up and fed as well, so we could get a couple hours of sleep in between.

I was given a shower at Maggie Smith's place—she was a good friend of my mother's—and I received so much stuff I cried. The best was a pickup load of Pampers; they ended up lasting me a year. That had been a big concern for me: how to wash and dry diapers for two babies. We couldn't afford Pampers. When the twins were nearly a month old we went home, driving to Vanderhoof then down to the Y. Stuart Garner drove home with us, just to haul the shower stuff.

We still couldn't get right into home then, so Ed met us with the team and wagon. The twins slept the whole wagon trip home, bounced this way and that, and seemed to find the rough ride soothing, tucked into little baskets. This allowed me to hang onto Jon so he wouldn't fall off the wagon.

That first winter when the babies were small, I never went very far. Steve and Dee Dee Lyons and their little daughter, who was a few years older than Jon, spent part of the winter at the Home Ranch. They were friends of the Carters. They came to stay once and looked after the babies while Barry and I went to Vanderhoof overnight. That was the only place I went all winter.

Jon at four was very serious and a good child. He was such help with the twins and became so responsible for his brothers. But in

*Here's me hauling loose hay at Tsetzi Lake with the team, Baldy and Polly.*
VANCE HANNA

*The twins, James and Wesley, on the porch of the ranch house in their walkers in the summer of 1980.*

raising kids one should have even numbers. Three was an odd number, and one child was usually left out—and it always seemed to be Jon. The twins it seemed to me would gang up on him, tormenting him to no end. It was probably made worse by the fact that twins are so especially close. James learnt to sit up and crawl before Wesley, but he was the bigger of the two so that was expected. Later on, what happened to one happened to the other. If one got a tooth, the other did within days. When one got hurt, more often than not the other got hurt. One chipped a front tooth; within days the other chipped the same tooth. The similarities were endless.

Barry's Uncle Leo gave us a three-wheeled ATV, and since I was unable to pack the three children on a saddle horse, it was a godsend. Leo had built a box for the twins on the back, and padded it with vinyl-covered cushions. This was handy for their protection, while bouncing about in the box. The back cushion for some reason

*Dad and I with the three boys at Tsetzi Lake. The twins are in the box on the back of the three-wheeler.*

*My niece Wanda at Sleepy Hollow looking west. Ed's place is to her right.*

125

was not attached like the others, but that didn't matter. One afternoon in the spring just after the snow melted I noticed the cattle
had gotten a gate open and were going into another field, where I
didn't want them. Getting the twins into their snowsuits and Jon into
his coat and boots, I took all three out to the three-wheeler; I put
the twins into their box and Jon in front of me. At that time we had
no bridge at our place and had to go up to Ed's and use the bridge
there. I always drove fairly fast, and as I was tearing down the field
towards the opened gate I glanced into the back to see how the twins
were doing—lo and behold, one was gone! Forgetting the cows, I
turned the bike and raced back across the field, retracing my steps
to the bridge, where I found James in his snowsuit, sound asleep on
the bridge approach where he'd bounced out. As I picked him up
and put him back on the bike, he never woke up.

Dad felt the paint horse of Wanda's that Clint Thompson had
worked with, the one that had shown a mean side, was not a good
horse for Wanda, so he traded it to Peter Alexis for a steer calf. At
that time the Indians still had cattle. The mare had been picked
up and taken to the reserve; the calf we were to pick up when it
was old enough to wean. Victor, who was Peter's youngest son, rode
the paint mare to Sleepy Hollow one day in May and it looked like
a horse with its spirit broken. Her head hung down and she was
scruffy and very thin. Victor said the only way they finally were able
to start riding her was using a method some people call "post-hay,"
where the horse was tied to a tree and not fed or watered till it became too weak to fight back; then they rode her for many miles every
day. Victor said that she was gentle now, and maybe he'd turn her
loose for awhile. About a month later Victor stopped by again. The
Blackwater River was in high water with mountain snow runoff. He
asked if I had seen the paint mare coming down the river. I asked
what side of the river she was supposed to be on and he laughed and
said no, in the river. He then told me that after his last visit he had
turned the mare loose on green feed for a month till she fattened
up, then he went to ride her again. He couldn't get her saddled so
he tied a hind leg up. She kept fighting and got away from him,

jumping into the river that was just out front of their corrals. With her leg tied up she was unable to swim and had drowned. William Cassam told me a week or so later he had seen a paint horse floating in Tsacha Lake. I am sure a bear fished her carcass from the water before it drifted too far.

After the twins were born the small cabin hardly had room for the five of us. It wasn't bad while the twins were still in their little baskets, but when they outgrew their baskets and went into cribs the space became more crowded, even with them pushed side by side. When the twins got big enough to go in Jolly Jumpers they had to be hung over the bed, as there wasn't available floor space. So during the spring and summer of 1980, with help from Ed and whoever stopped by, we added on to the back of the cabin. The addition was the same size as the original cabin but with an upstairs, which in time became three bedrooms. The downstairs of the addition was not well planned, so for a long time it was just one big room; I had a cot in there for company, and there was a lot of floor space so I built a large cupboard to use as a pantry. The building was often referred to as "Noah's Ark." Barry made the back door wider than a normal door and our snow machines, which were not as wide as new ones today, could be turned sideways and brought in. They could then be torn apart and worked on in the warmth of the back room. It was also used for the dirt bikes, and our large back porch seemed to become the shop, as more stuff was moved to it from the shop itself.

One evening in the fall when the Carters were at their cabin, Olin, who worked for them, came over and offered to sit with the kids if I wanted to go visit with Jorja and Wes for the evening. This offer I could not refuse, as babysitters were few and far between. After I put the boys down for the night and Olin was settled with a book and a pot of coffee, I grabbed my jacket and went out to the three-wheeler. It took me six or eight minutes to reach the Carters' cabin, which was about a mile away. I can't remember whether we passed the evening drinking wine or rye, but there was a lot of laughter and conversation. Along about midnight the talk turned to UFOs and other stories that spooked me. When I left some time later it was pitch black out. I started the bike, called goodnight to Jorja and Wes and roared off through the dark with my head full of spooks and feeling something was right behind me and might get me. I passed Ed's dark cabin and went around the barn, along the corral fence, then down a short, steep hill to cross the gravel-bottomed spring that ran across the road. While I bounced down the hill something bumped against my back. Well, I knew then that there was something behind me, and I was too scared to look back. I squeezed the throttle as hard as I could and the three-wheeler flew along—I don't think all three wheels were ever on the ground at once. When I reached the gate at home I didn't let off the throttle but hit the gate, hoping the latch would break. Well, it didn't. The bike stopped quite suddenly, killing the motor, and the lights went out and I was thrown into the poles of the gate. I scrambled to my feet, crawled through the gate and ran for the house, hitting the door at a run, and landed inside with a crash. Olin leapt up off the couch with a look of panic on his face. Suddenly I felt somewhat foolish, so I mumbled a goodnight and ran up the stairs. When I awoke in the morning and thought of my hasty flight I realized it was the unattached cushion that had flipped forward and touched my back, not some alien from outer space.

On the morning of May 18, 1980, Mount St. Helens in Washington state erupted, causing a lot of devastation. We heard about it from the radio. My dad insisted he had heard the explosion, although no one else heard anything. I suppose it gave him something to add to the conversation about the subject.

I think it was Ed who put up the money for a New Holland round baler that summer, and we bought a wheel rake. Somehow we ended up with a side delivery rake as well but that didn't work very well on the rough fields—we were constantly breaking teeth and bending things. We had always put up loose hay at the Home Ranch and Sleepy Hollow, as well as at Tsetzi Lake. The wheel rake was much better as the wheels rode up and down on the uneven ground. Up to that point all the haying had been done with horses, and a set of derrick poles and slings stacking loose hay. Ed had still done the mowing with a team-and-horse mower and used a team to rake as well. So when Wes brought up a big tractor from the States, and with our small one with a three-point hitch mower, haying suddenly became much easier. Ed found himself with nothing to do as the team was suddenly eliminated. He refused to drive a tractor: they were "a curse to mankind." So he took his wagon with the hayrack and followed the haying crew, picking up any hay left on the ground with a pitchfork. When the hayrack was full he took it to his barn and filled the loft. When that loft was crammed full of hay, he filled ours.

It would have been late in the fall when Wes came over and there was the disagreement over the range boundaries. The Ministry of Forests range officer had been out that summer looking at range. Ed's range had been a five-mile radius of Sleepy Hollow, which was what Wes got when he bought the place. When we applied for range the boundaries were changed and our range ran from our property east to Tsacha Lake, and Wes's went west from his place to Naglico Lake. Wes had been gloating that we would have to go five miles before a cow could be turned loose. When the Ministry of Forests notified him of the boundary changes he was not happy. He had been up at his cabin drinking, and then drove down to our place in his pickup to voice his displeasure. He finally called Barry outside and hit him, breaking several ribs. Barry tore into the house nearly flattening me and grabbed the shotgun from the gun rack and was out the door, firing one shot at Wes's fleeing back as he ran around the house. Thank God Barry stopped there. Wes leapt into his truck and took off with the motor screaming and drove right through the gate. The latch held and the gate broke.

The following morning we saw Wes going across his field with his dirt bike, heading for Tsetzi Lake. We bundled up the kids and started for town—we'd had to wait till he left home as the road went right in front of his cabin. We went to the police and explained what happened. Since Wes had come uninvited and had been asked to leave, then had struck Barry, the officer said that no charges could be laid. We went back home and Wes had left, flying back to the

States. Now it seemed that war was on, and there were other problems. We had hayed together and the greater share of the hay had been stored on Wes's place, but we knew better than to go onto his property. We did have hay, but not enough to get our cattle through the whole winter. Luckily there was an old stack of brown hay at the Home Ranch, left over from the winter we had stayed there. Dad had the little 1010 John Deere crawler, so we ploughed the trail to the Home Ranch and moved our cattle up there till calving time. The big stack of rotten hay lasted them about a month but by then we had enough hay left at our place to finish out the season. Even with the hay of ours, Wes ran short and had to move his cattle all the way to Anahim Lake in late March, just as the cows were starting to calve. Wes and D'Arcy Christensen had gone in together and bought a ranch in the Anahim area. My dad bought the Sleepy Hollow property from Wes a few months later and gave it to my brothers, Ken and Rob.

# CHAPTER 10

# The Three Boys

At the beginning of the 1980s, Blackwater Lodge was just being developed. It was located about seven or eight miles down the river from us, where the Blackwater River drained into Tsacha Lake; the property was only a lease of lakeshore, adjacent to Tom Baptiste's cabin on the lake. The lodge had been started in the 1970s, but not developed to the point where it catered to any paying guests. A couple guys, Bill Warrington and Mark Headley, both from Portland, Oregon, started it up, and Mark had lived there for a number of years. It seemed that he was more interested in wilderness living than in developing a business. He had bought a number of horses from Anthony's auction sale and rode them about in the summer, and had a dog team he used in the winter. He grew a Grizzly Adams beard and for a number of years seemed content to spend his time alone. One summer after a visit to Portland he returned with a wife and within a few months moved to Alaska.

After Mark left the construction at Blackwater Lodge started in a big way. There were a lot of young people from the Portland area there, building cabins and sawing lumber using a small mill they had. Some of these young people were without work permits so they came and went, and occasionally one would get deported back to the States. At that time their transportation back and forth to

Vanderhoof was four-wheel-drive pickup, so we saw a lot of them. If the road was bad getting to our place, it was worse downriver. Barry helped them get out of mudholes when they were nearby; otherwise they were on their own.

At some point a 6 x 6 was purchased, and was used to haul in building materials. It was not uncommon to wake up in the morning to several of them sleeping on the couch and floor, as they had reached our place in the early hours of the morning and quietly come in and bedded down for a few hours. We enjoyed having these young people around—they were just a great bunch of kids out for a summer of wilderness experience. They were also very good to the boys, bringing them treats from town. When summer was over they would all return to the States, and in the spring most came back for the next season. About the same time as all the building was taking place there, Bill Warrington bought the Tsacha Lake Lodge from Harold Lionberger and changed the name to Mackenzie Trail Lodge.

Before we got the water system in we used to start the water pump and fill plastic garbage cans with water, and store them in the back room. It must have been about November, as it was fairly cold, and it was about dark, that Bill came up and brought his wife, Jean, with him. I had never met her before. She was a city lady, and we had a hard time finding something to talk about while Bill and Barry visited. I had poured coffee and we were sitting around the table when there came a splashing sound from the back room. I was mortified—I was sure a mouse had fallen into the water. I was so embarrassed and remarked to Jean that it must be a mouse, and I hated mice. She jumped up, took the flashlight Bill had placed on the table and trotted into the back room, and said, "Oh Bill, what a big mouse!" If I could have disappeared I would have, because at that point I knew it was a rat!

My biggest fear when my boys were small was that they would wander off into the bush and never be seen again, or they would die of hypothermia before they could be found. Around that time there were a couple other cases, one near Houston, in which that had happened, and it sent new waves of fear over me. Yet I wanted my boys to enjoy the outdoors and the freedom that went with it, as I had. With the workload I had it was impossible to be with them every time they played outside. They were taught young to answer me when I called, but they didn't always. Once, when Jon was maybe two and a half, he was playing outside, dressed in his snowsuit and felt packs. I went out on the porch and called him repeatedly, getting no answer. I pulled on a jacket and boots and ran around the yard calling his name, then spotted him under the porch, playing in the dirt with his toys. By this time my heart was racing and I felt physically sick from fright. Another time I was washing clothes in the winter and went out to hang clothes on the line, and saw Jon (who would have been about three) disappearing around a bend on the river with the dog, following a snow machine trail on the ice. He was about a quarter of a mile away by then. I don't remember if I ran and caught up to him or took a snow machine, but at least that time I knew where he was.

James disappeared once in the summer at about the age of three. Wesley and Jon were playing close by, unaware that James had vanished, and I called and called. I circled the building and corrals and followed the riverbank with fear in my heart that he had gone to the river and fallen in. I tried to think of whether he would wash downstream or float in a back eddy. By then everyone in the area had CB radios. I ran to the house and called Tsetzi Lake, as Barry had gone over there, but could not get an answer. Then I called Tsacha Lake Lodge, and they answered immediately. I told them James was gone, and I needed help. They got in the plane and flew to Tsetzi Lake to tell Barry to come home. All of this took probably took another forty-five minutes. I was heading back out to search some more when I saw James coming down the trail that led from Ed's, strolling along—a happy child, unaware of the crisis he had caused. I just sat down in the yard and cried in relief.

When Wesley was about four, his dad was going somewhere with the dirt bike and Wesley begged to go along but Barry wouldn't take him, and left him crying in the yard. Shortly afterward the twins came in and asked if they could go to Ed's to play, which was half a mile up the trail. I told them that they could and I would come up soon to get them. Where Jon was then I can't recall—he may have been over at my dad's. I finished whatever I was doing an hour or so later and walked up to Ed's to get the boys. James was playing in front of Ed's cabin but there was no sign of Wesley. Neither Ed nor James seemed to know where he had gone. I knew he was upset that his dad had left him behind, so I went to check the trail, which was muddy in spots from a recent rain. There in the mud were his little footprints, following the dirt bike.

Fear gripped me as I frantically tried to decide what to do. I had no bike and by the time I found a horse and caught it, it could be an hour or more. I asked Ed not to let James out of his sight and took off running, slowing up to catch my breath and praying as I ran that he would not leave the trail. I must have covered more than a mile and a half when on a straight stretch of the trail, where it came out of some second growth, there was a little boy running towards me. We met and collapsed on the trail, both crying and holding each other. In his hand was a scrap of paper I had remembered seeing at the Y another mile and a half farther up the trail. He had decided at the Y to return home. Perhaps the two trails confused him, not knowing which way his dad had gone. I picked up the exhausted child in my arms and carried him to Ed's. I then discovered that James was no longer there. I asked Ed where he had gone, and Ed replied, "Oh, he is around here somewhere." Making Wesley run with me I hurried home to find James playing in the yard, unconcerned that he was all alone. I am sure we all slept dead to the world that night.

I left Ed with the kids during the winter once as I had to go somewhere on the snow machine and didn't want to take them for whatever reason. Jon was about eight and the twins were four. I thought that with both Jon and Ed watching the younger boys, they would be okay. Jon was very good with them and usually very responsible. When I returned the boys were racing around the house with knives. I said to Ed that they shouldn't be doing that, to which he replied, "They said you let them do it all the time."

Another time, the twins were out cutting willow bushes and I wasn't paying much attention to what they were doing till one of them came in crying and could not explain to me what had happened. I stepped out the door to see where the other one was to find him standing outside, crying quietly. His whole face was covered with blood. He had been wiping his eyes so his face was smeared and his hands were bloody as well. I was scared to go to him, fearing what I would find, but I knew I had to. To my relief I found a small cut on his forehead, which was bleeding profusely but was the only injury. Apparently one of them had been using the meat cleaver to cut bushes and had struck the other on the forehead.

When Wesley was just learning to walk he went behind the heater and bumped his forehead against the stovepipe, which caused a rather bad burn. I had no idea what to put on it as I was out of the medication the nurse usually left me, but I had vitamin E, which I kept putting on it. Fortunately the burn healed without leaving a scar. When he was about nine or ten we had a whole houseful of snowmobilers and Wesley was making a pot of coffee with the drip coffee pot we had when somehow the boiling water spilled over his lower arm and wrist. Jon was the quick-thinking one and got Wes's arm under the cold water tap and then into a jar of cold water. We were snowed in at the time but phoned a friend in Vanderhoof, who drove out and met us at 167 km. Wrapping Wesley's arm in wet towels we took snow machines the fourteen kilometres to 167, then getting in with our friend drove to the hospital. They dressed Wesley's burn then released him, but he had to go to the hospital every day to have the dressing changed till the danger of infection passed. We had to leave him in town and go back home, as Jon and James were home feeding by themselves. I can't remember how long Wes was in town but it must have been ten days to two weeks. He will always have scars from that burn.

One nice day the boys and I had gone to the Lamperts' for the afternoon on the snow machine. The boys enjoyed spending time with the kids there, and it gave Nora and me a chance to visit and drink tea. On the way home we were following a team and sleigh trail made by the local Indians. Coming up the sleigh track was a muskrat that had obviously been frozen out of some pond and was looking for a new home. I stopped the snow machine to one side as the muskrat came scurrying along, wanting the kids to see it. The muskrat came right up to us, showing no fear. It paused, rose up on its hind legs to peer at us for a few seconds, then dropped on all fours and continued on its way to whatever fate had in store for it. I felt helpless, knowing nothing short of a miracle would save the creature, but I assured my small boys he would somehow find a home.

When he was maybe five or six, not very old, Jon told us he wanted to ride bulls. At the time, we had a black calf that Jon had named Beulah, which was about three hundred pounds. Barry put a helmet on Jon, then caught the calf and put on a bull rope, then Jon. When the calf was let go I think Jon stayed on for three jumps — not that he wanted to, but it worked out that way. As he picked himself up off the ground, trying not to cry, he told us he no longer wanted to be a bull rider.

*My dad on his three wheeler with the three boys at Tsetzi Lake.* HALLE FLYGARE

One year I got a Honda 185 dirt bike, which all four of us rode on. Jon would ride behind, hanging on to me, and the twins rode in front, held on by a long wool scarf tied tightly around them and my waist. I think of the trails we rode over, the rock and mud and having no brakes on the bike at all. I always had to remember to gear down to first before starting down steep hills, or we no doubt would have had a terrible wreck. But it got us away from the house, and over to my dad's. We would also go to the Lamperts' so the kids could play together.

During the winter, we had friends from Quesnel out visiting between Christmas and New Year's. They had left their trucks out at 164 on the Kluskus Road, as the strip of road along a big clearcut had drifted full. The weather turned bitterly cold but they wanted to return to Quesnel to celebrate New Year's. One of their snow machines had blown a motor and needed to be towed out to their trucks. Since Barry had been snowmobiling with them and I hadn't had an opportunity to go out, I went along to tow the machine back to 164. It was only about ten miles out to the trucks but there were problems on the way. The days were short and by the time all the trucks were running and the machines loaded it was early afternoon, with the temperature at about thirty-five below. By the time I left them and started back the sun had dropped behind the mountains and the cold had intensified. My face was exposed to the cold even while I was ducking down behind the windshield. I did not have such a thing as a face shield — I never even had a helmet back then. I found the slower I drove, the better it was. My eyes watered, icing up my lashes, and I knew my face was freezing. I would stop often and rub my face till it began to sting. When I came out of the timber at the west end of the valley to the open hillside, the cold was worse. I seriously considered leaving the machine and walking, as moving the air made it bitterly cold. I finally drove up to the house and stumbled in the back door. My nose and both cheeks had frostbite and later peeled. The temperature was fifty-five below. It was one of the few times that I saw Barry really concerned.

And I am not sure what Barry was doing on the day he ran a

large splinter into the top of his hand and it then broke off, leaving nothing to get hold of to pull it out. The splinter was probably two inches long and the size of a pencil. If we lived near town it would have been off to the hospital, but out there we had to deal with it on our own. He told me I would have to cut the flesh a bit to enable me to get hold of the splinter, which I didn't want to do, but had to. I poured some turpentine on the back of his hand and tried to cut using a scalpel, my hands shaking badly. It wouldn't cut and I said so. Barry replied calmly that I was trying to cut with the back of the blade, and had to turn it over. Amazing how it then cut through the flesh, leaving a trail of blood and making a hole big enough to pull the splinter out.

Audie Murphy, who was then working at Blackwater Lodge, came up on his dirt bike with a lady friend named Jane one day and we decided that we would all go up on the Fawnie Mountains with our dirt bikes—Barry and I each had one by then. We took the kids over to Tsetzi Lake for the day. The Fawnies were north of us, and there had been a lot of exploration going on so a narrow road had been pushed into the timberline from the Malaput Road, a logging road off the Kluskus Forest Service Road. It was twenty-five or thirty miles from home to the top of the mountains. The Fawnies are not high but they do have some areas high enough to be bare of trees. The road up there came out of the timber onto the open country. Right there on the edge of the timber was an SUV, belonging to the geologist who had parked it there by the side of the road. The geologist was off somewhere hunting rock samples. We continued on up some steeper slopes till we came across an old abandoned camp— clearly the large camp had been set up while drilling had been going on, as there were still a lot of ore samples in large wooden boxes and long lengths of pipe there. The wooden tent frames that the tents had been erected on were still standing.

North from the camp the land dropped away to a small valley and a little lake. Down towards the lake was the camp's garbage dump, and digging in the dump was a small grizzly bear. Barry and Audie got on their bikes and roared off towards the bear, leaving

Jane and me at the campsite. Jane had doubled with Audie, as she had no bike, and I had left my bike farther down the mountain for whatever reason and had walked the last bit, so we both were on foot. Barry would roar by the bear, then Audie would come in from the other way and roar past. It didn't take long for the bear to be on the fight, and it was not far to where we were—without a tree anywhere. Jane and I climbed up one rather shaky tent frame, which didn't offer much protection. Finally the guys came up to where we were and picked us up and we left in a hurry, as the grizzly was mad. We stopped only long enough for me to get my bike, and got off the mountain. We found out later that the bear followed us off the mountain and when he got to where the SUV was parked, he took his anger out on it by jumping up and down on the roof, partially caving it in, and breaking some windows.

When the twins were about four years old Esther Alexis came over one day wanting to find the range horses—Ed was sending a horse or two over to the Alexis family to break, and Esther had been sent down for them. But she had a problem: she had a small baby, Dean Peter, who was probably only four months old. She was packing him on her back in a blanket, Indian style, but didn't want to pack him that way on a horse chase and asked if I could watch him for a few hours. This I did, and I had the baby on a blanket on the floor when the twins came in. They stood looking at the small baby for a short time, then one said, with a bit of panic in his voice, "You're not going to keep him, are you, Mom?"

The round table that Art Kelly had built us turned out to be a source of entertainment for the kids. When they were alone in the house one or two would sit in the centre as the other one spun the lazy Susan, giving them rides. They were not allowed to do this when Barry or I were around, but they were alone a lot so got to do it anyway. And one day, a young fellow rode in on a saddle horse—I am not sure where he was going or where he had come from—so I invited him in for coffee. He accepted but seemed very uncomfortable as he sat at the table while I made the coffee. One of the kids wanted to show him that the centre of the table turned and spun it so hard the pitcher of cream slid off the lazy Susan, across the table, and landed in the young man's lap. It broke the ice a bit, and we both ended up laughing after our embarrassment passed. It was a good thing he'd left his chaps on, so he at least kept reasonably dry!

Another source of entertainment for the kids was the piano that Barry got from Blackwater Lodge. I think he traded a saddle for it. Barry played it a little, but when the kids were alone in the house they would make a terrible racket on it, which could be heard all the way to the barn. Both twins would hit as many keys as they could at one time. The boys also liked when planes going by buzzed the house. Because our house was above the field on the hill, the planes would come down or up the valley flying low over the fields, passing the house at nearly eye level, then pull up after they passed the house to gain altitude and fly off to their destination. When the kids were little they would sometimes line up side by side on the hill and moon planes as they roared by, with their three little bare bottoms stuck in the air.

My mother and Barry did not see eye to eye—or rather, to put it plainly, did not like one another. When the kids were little Mom came and spent time with us at least once a year, if not twice, and also flew out several times to have Christmas with us, since we couldn't leave the ranch that time of year with the feeding we had to do, and in the seventies and eighties we were more than likely snowed in anyway. Mom quite often did shopping for me when she was coming out, picking up stuff that came on sale or things I really needed. Once she brought out two straw brooms, since they were on sale. Barry, who was never in a good mood if Mom was there, asked if my mom had had to bring a spare vehicle.

It seemed every day brought something new with the boys. Jon must have been about eight or so when he was very upset one day. I cannot recall now what it was about, but he ran up to his room, shouting that he was going to run away. I went up after him, knocked on the bedroom door and went in. I said, "Jon, if you're running away, wait, as Mommy wants to go with you." He just said, "Oh, Mom!" He never said he was going to run away again.

CHAPTER 11

# A *Legend Passes*

In the summer of 1982, at the age of seventy-two, my Dad suddenly seemed to start aging fast. I had not noticed it much before then, even though he had not been in great health. For one thing he would not eat properly. His heart was not good either; he'd had his first heart attack back in the sixties and several since. But we could only do so much about his diet; after all, he was a grown man. He was now getting a bit frail, too, which was hard for me to accept, seeing as my father was always so strong. He had also mellowed a lot from the loud, domineering guy he used to be, and was very fond of his grandsons—he called the twins the "little mice."

Dad had spent several winters in Arizona with his brother Fred and sister-in-law Pauline, coming back to the lodge in the spring. While Alex Fraser was minister of highways, Dad would spend time with him and his wife in Victoria. While Alex was at work, Dad would just tag along with Gertrude. He had a very serious heart attack in San Francisco airport once, while down there with Alex and Gertrude. I can't recall the year but it must have been about 1980. He was attended by the best doctors and did pull through, but it took a lot out of him. Mom and Ken flew to San Francisco and brought him home. Yet he still tried to keep up with the work at the lodge. Gayle no longer came out summers, so he would hire someone about the end of May to help out for the busy season.

But my dad certainly hadn't lost his sense of humour. I am not sure why Dad sold one of the propane refrigerators he had to John Blackwell, but he did. John came to pick it up with Wayne Escott in a Beaver aircraft. The fridge was packed out of the lodge and loaded on the wagon that Dad towed behind his three-wheeler. He carefully drove down to Tsetzi Lake, where the airplane was tied to the somewhat weathered wharf. John and Wayne proceeded to lift and carry the heavy fridge along the wharf to the airplane. About then the wharf collapsed into the cold water of the lake, submerging the guys to waist deep, while the fridge bobbed about on the surface. Dad had already been paid for the refrigerator so he found it very funny and laughed about it for weeks. And I heard that the fridge never ran after that soaking.

While visiting with Dad one day we got on the subject of poison. We'd probably had a problem with a predator or something. I knew he had a new can of 1080 poison; he had told me he had buried it. I asked him where it was and he said, "What, do you think I'm going to die?"

It was only a few days later, towards the end of May 1983, that I took the kids and drove into town. Barry stayed at home. There was a forest fire burning east of the lodge, and the forest service guys were staying at the lodge with a couple of fire crews and a chopper while they were fighting the fire. Dad would have been in his glory, not only having an audience to entertain but his cabins would all be rented out, bringing in an income. They had a cook so meals were prepared and on the table. At that time the Quesnel radio station still had its twice-daily message time for the outlying areas. Dad never missed a broadcast—not only because he received messages, but also so he could keep up with what the neighbours were doing too, by the messages that they sent and received. There were a number of men in the lodge at the time so there were conversations going. Dad was sitting on top of his desk, so he could be close to the battery-operated radio that was on a shelf above it. He once told the guys to keep their conversation down, as he couldn't hear, but they continued to talk in lower tones. No one was paying much attention to Dad—till they heard a thump, as he fell from the desk to the floor. Apparently someone told him to quit kidding around, then realized that he was not. Dad was given CPR without success. The helicopter pilot took off and went to Sleepy Hollow to get Barry, radioing for additional help from the air. But no amount of help would have saved my dad on that twenty-eighth day of May. Barry flew into town with the body and came and told my Mom and me.

We knew that a large crowd of people would be attending the service. Since the weather was beautiful, we planned to hold the memorial in LeBourdais Park, in Quesnel. The funeral home made most of the arrangements. Even with all the chairs there were still not enough seats for the record crowd that attended that day, coming from all over. Dad's sister Hazel and his brother Joe came up from Illinois. I asked Milt Rutherford to give the service. For many years Milt had been a pastor at Anahim Lake, and he was well-acquainted with the family. Alex Fraser or Toby Cave gave the eulogy—I can't remember now, but they both spoke for some time. A number of other people spoke as well. My sister Gayle wanted the song "Green, Green Grass of Home" to be sung, and even now, whenever I hear the song it reminds me of that day. The wake that followed in the evening would have made Dad happy, to see so many of his friends having such a good time. There was guitar music and singing, good whiskey and loud laughter. Toby had flown out to the lodge and picked up Ed, who was thoroughly enjoying himself, as he seldom went out. He had somehow put his riding boots on the wrong feet at some point, but he didn't seem to notice.

Dad had mentioned a number of times that he wanted his ashes scattered over the Indian village of Kluskus. In July the family gathered at the lodge at Tsetzi Lake and Floyd Vaughn came with his Beaver aircraft, taking as many family members as he could on our dad's last flight over Kluskus. Rob opened the window and spilled Dad's ashes out, to drift over the village. Floyd refused payment for that flight.

After Dad's death, someone was needed at the lodge. Rob, who worked in the bush logging but was shut down for spring breakup, was able to move out there. Jon, who was eight at the time, went with Rob back to Tsetzi Lake and we followed a few days later. I guess the cupboards were fairly bare of food, and after their long drive Rob and Jon were looking for something fast to eat. They came across a small box of raisins only to discover that Dad had filled it with deer droppings, no doubt so he could catch someone and be able to laugh at them. Well, he missed that laugh.

Rob began cleaning up the place, as a number of things had been let go with Dad's failing health. One task that needed to be done right away was digging new holes for the outhouses. Rob dug very deep holes, and later Ed took his team of horses over to drag the outhouses to their new locations. Ruby and Sundown made up the team Ed was using then. Sundown seemed to be half asleep most of the time and that day was no exception. He spent a great deal of the time trying to eat and not paying attention to what he was doing. While the team was dragging one of the small log structures to its new spot, Sundown walked right into the deep hole and down he went. Ruby was unhooked from Sundown, and Rob took the halter

*Ed Adams with his unruly team, Sundown and Ruby.*

shank and tried to make the horse jump out of the hole. But first Sundown had to eat whatever grass he could reach while standing in the hole. Argyle, Ed's dog, ran in circles about the hole, stirring up grass and dirt, emitting the odd sharp bark and gathering speed. Finally the horse did scramble out and order was restored.

On one of my trips to the Home Ranch to check cows that ranged up there I took the kids all to Rob's on the dirt bike and left them there while I went to the ranch. The twins were hard to tell apart at that age. When I returned several hours later Rob had taken a black marking pen and put a J on James's forehead and a W on Wesley's. All four of them seemed to find it quite funny but it took awhile to scrub the marks off.

Rob would often walk to our place in the afternoon, picking rocks off the trail and cutting the new growth back off the sides. He would then stay for supper and walk back. By the end of summer it was a much better trail, wide and minus a lot of rocks. When winter came Rob closed up the lodge and went out to log till the following season.

It was probably late April or early May of 1984, when the ground was bare of snow and the bears were out, that Barry took the rifle and

*The twins sitting on the milk cow, Soupy.*

went deer hunting. There may have been some deer around but it was unlikely that early in the spring, as it seemed most of deer that left in the fall returned in early June. We had no fresh meat at the time so the idea seemed like a good one. Barry came back several hours later carrying on his shoulders a skinned carcass of meat. He laid this on the porch railing and left again. I examined the carcass. The meat seemed awfully dark for deer meat, and the legs were short. On closer examination it seemed there were dark hairs on the meat. Suspicion began to sink in. I got a knife and cut a piece and gave it to the dog, which was lying on the far end of the porch. He jumped up with his tail between his legs and ran under the porch. So then I knew it was bear meat. I cut a front shoulder off and took it to the henhouse, laying it down just inside the door. The hens approached it cautiously, heads bobbing, talking to each other. One hen turned her head each way as if one eye saw things differently than the other, then let out a squawk and ran to the corner. The rest followed her, all piling up, feathers flying, squawking in fright. I wondered how something as dumb as a hen could detect the smell of bear, but apparently they could. I removed the quarter of meat and the pitch of noise lowered in the henhouse. I put the meat up on the log fence and found the crows were not nearly as fussy.

For a joke, Barry then decided he would barbecue the meat and invite our neighbours. He took his dirt bike and went around to all the neighbours he could, then came home and prepared for the barbecue. He had a makeshift spit and kept turning the meat as it slowly cooked. I prepared a big potato salad and fresh bread. A large number of people showed up and apparently they liked the meat. I didn't eat any, not that I never ate bear, but this bear was just out of the den and didn't appeal to me. After everyone ate Barry went and got a bear paw and threw it down by the fire. Linda Alexis realized she had eaten bear, which most of those Indian people just won't eat. She chased Barry about, swearing at him. George Chantyman, who was a Kluskus Indian, laughed and laughed. He knew he had eaten bear, as the people at Kluskus ate bear on occasion; he was probably enjoying the joke as much as Barry was.

One time, the dog woke me in the middle of the night with its barking. I knew by the bark that it was upset—it never barked just to bark. Getting up and going to the twins' room I looked out the window into the yard bathed in moonlight to see a very large black bear headed for the house, with the dog backing up from it, keeping up the vicious barking. The bear paid no attention to the dog but continued on towards the house. I woke Barry and ran downstairs and turned on the propane light, which awoke Don White, who was sleeping in the back room. He and Barry both joined me. The dog continued to bark, but now from the safety of the porch. Barry was loading the rifle as Don looked out of the east window only to leap back. He said the bear was sitting right under the window. Barry opened the door and stepped around the corner of the house to shoot the bear at about ten feet, but it was not a killing shot and the bear ran. More shots were fired but then Barry came in to say that he didn't dare shoot again in the dark as the bear was in line with the tractor, welder, fuel barrels and pickup out by the shop. He wasn't sure if he had hit him after the first shot. The following morning the guys located the bear at the back of the barn where he had dug a hole and lain down. The carcass was cold and stiff.

It was in the winter when an Indian couple we were friends with showed up with their two little kids on their snow machine. The guy had been celebrating something and still had some of his gallon of wine left. He proceeded to finish it off, all the time becoming more quarrelsome, while his wife tried to get him to go home. Barry got up and went to bed. Audie Murphy was with us at the time, but he remained in the background, not saying anything. The five kids were playing in the back room with toys scattered about. When the wine was gone the fellow decided it was his wife's fault that the bottle was empty and stood over her as she quietly sat on a chair and threatened her with the bottle. About this time I interfered, asking him to give me the bottle. After talking for some time he passed me the empty jug. As soon as I had it in my hands, Audie pounced on the guy like a whirlwind, taking him to the floor and starting to beat him severely. The children began screaming and fled upstairs as the blood flew. Finally I said that was enough, and Audie let him up. He then pulled a knife on Audie, who ran out the back door in his sock feet and went up to Ed's, where he stayed for the rest of the night.

I sent the kids to the river with a bucket to chop some ice to put on the man's face and finally got the blood stopped. Then I insisted that he go home alone and I would bring his wife and children home the next day. All he seemed concerned about at that point was that he might have black eyes, but I assured him he wouldn't. Getting his coat and boots on I led him out to his snow machine, which I managed to get started, and sent him on his way. The next morning I took the wife and kids home with our machine and skimmer. I walked in the door of the cabin to find my friend sitting at the table, and he slowly lowered a huge pair of sunglasses to show swollen black eyes! I gave a little wave with my hand, said a quick goodbye to the rest of the family and took off for home.

The 1980s were lean years, and there never was much money. We had food on the table, but there was nothing for extras or emergencies. But I swear, there was always someone above looking out for us. Once, while I was in Quesnel visiting family, I wanted to return to the ranch in the worst way, but did not have enough gas money, and didn't want to ask Mom for money. I went to the bank and there was four hundred dollars in our account where the day before there had been none. I took the money from the account, bought groceries and filled the truck with fuel. Then, taking my babies, I drove the 240-odd miles home. Another time the hay mower had worn out and a new one was badly needed, but how was it to be paid for? Driving to Vanderhoof, we found a used three-point hitch mower for eight hundred dollars. And there just happened to be that amount of money in our account. I know they were probably bank mistakes but the best part was it always happened when the money was needed and nothing was ever said about it. So I called them my little miracles! Of course, the next time a mower was needed there wasn't the money, but good friends loaned me the money and said to repay it when the calves were shipped in the fall.

For a number of years Barry would go mushroom picking in the spring with friends. It might be for a few weeks or a month and a half, depending on the mushroom crop and the weather. It was his spring holiday. That was when the kids and I would usually go to Quesnel to visit Mom and the in-laws for a week or ten days.

Keeping the horses within the boundaries of the pasture was a challenge when the river served as a fenceline. The horses eventually began making crossings of their own in low water, which caused problems. Whenever they made a crossing, a fence would have to be built to keep them out of the river. One year we invested in an electric fence that ran off a twelve-volt battery, which we charged with the tractor; the charger clicked every couple of seconds when the battery was charged up. But the battery went dead quite often. The horses would go to the electric fence and stand there. If it was clicking they went away, but if it was quiet they went right through it.

We had a dapple-grey workhorse named Andy who was always finding ways across the river into the hayfield and taking the other horses with him. I put a halter on him with a long lead rope that I ran between his front legs, over his girth and back between his front legs, where I tied it tight enough to keep his head down but not low enough to be uncomfortable. I missed seeing him next try to cross the river but saw the results. He was soaking wet and covered with sand, with his ears hanging down and probably full of water. My guess was he tried to cross the river somewhere deep enough that his nose went under water, and when he couldn't get his nose out of the water he ended up flipping over. He stayed in the pasture and away from the river for a long time after that.

And then there was the rooster; well, several over the years, mean ones, but this one not only guarded the hens but the whole barnyard as well. Barry was in the corral with a young horse he was trying to catch. He had a lariat rope in his hand but was trying to corner the horse to catch it rather than rope it. The rooster came running across the corral and flew at Barry, who kind of kicked him aside several times. The rooster was very persistent, which was getting the horse excited. Finally Barry started whaling on the rooster with the coiled-up lariat. Feathers were flying and the rooster was squawking rather loudly. About this time the horse had enough of all this strange behaviour and leapt the fence to gallop off to parts unknown. Barry threw the rope down in disgust and the rooster returned to his flock, short a great deal of feathers.

In the spring while mating, the flicker birds liked to make as much noise as possible when they were pecking on something. They discovered that the aluminium pole that the CB antenna was mounted on could really send out a loud ring. Their pecking on the pole would have been accepted if it had been during the day, but they liked to do it about daylight, and the pole was mounted on the roof right close to our bedroom. So the noise would start about four in the morning. One morning it was worse than usual, and Barry finally leapt from the bed, got the shotgun and blew the bird to kingdom come. He no sooner got back into bed than the racket started again. I remarked that he shot the wrong bird. What he said couldn't be found in any dictionary.

# CHAPTER 12

# Ed Adams

Ed Adams always liked sheep. When he arrived at the Home Ranch from the States in 1960 he soon talked Dad into having sheep at the Home Ranch, but only a few. When he left the Home Ranch in 1974 and moved to his place at Sleepy Hollow he bought the sheep from the ranch and hauled them to Sleepy Hollow with team and wagon. He tied their legs together and put them in the wagon box of the rubber-tired wagon; two and a half hours later they would arrive at their new home. I cannot recall how many trips Ed took to haul them all, but probably four or five. Ed always did his own shearing and butchering, but in later years, as he got older, we would help him. More for the sheep than for Ed, as it began to look more like a butcher job than a shearing job, with big bloody gashes here and there from the sharp shears.

When time came to shear, we'd put the sheep in the round pen in front of Ed's barn. As we needed one we would catch them, dragging the sheep outside the gate into a much larger corral, where the shearing would take place. For those who have never seen a sheep sheared, the fleece comes off in one piece. The sheep is set up on its rear end and the shearing is started at the head. Ed had his ewe about half sheared and I was working on another when he must have cut his. She began to fight and her and Ed ended up rolling over and

*Ed Adams, a good friend and helper on the ranch, in the doorway of his cabin with his cat Lashaway.* VANCE HANNA

over through the grass down a small incline. She managed to escape and raced off with her half-sheared fleece flowing out around her. In her panic to escape the frightening mass of wool behind her, she ran into the log fence time and time again till she fell exhausted onto the ground. I then glanced over at Ed to see how he had fared. He was sitting up in some fairly tall grass with a large tuft of wool sitting on his head, and he was also watching the ewe. He then said, "Well looky there, she is bound and determined to kill herself."

The coyotes took a lamb or ewe occasionally while they were out grazing. Ed kept bells on the ewes, so when they were running it was a lot of noise, which may have discouraged the predators. The worst was one night when a number of dogs out running the country got into the flock while they were bedded in the corral. Ed came over early in the morning, saying the sheep were all torn up, and he was nearly crying. I went back over with him and could not believe what had been done. One ewe was all but skinned, her sides showing only exposed meat. Ed got his .22 rifle and we shot at least half a dozen others that were badly torn up; we felt the rest would recover from their wounds.

We were hauling rails in the spring with team and sleigh for some rail fence. Ed loved to drive a team so his team was the one kept in for the winter. Ed was perched up on the top of the big load of rails. The team was going up a steep little hill at the back of Ed's barn where the cows had been fed earlier in the winter and there was a lot of manure. The weather was warm so the packed snow had become more like ice. It was melting and the water trickled down the hill, making miniature creeks. The team was really digging for traction to pull the heavy load, and Ed was encouraging them with words like "Come on boys, get into the collars," when one of the horses threw back a gob of manure with its hoof while Ed had his mouth open. Well, he got a mouthful and began spitting and gagging, spitting out onto the ground not only the manure, but both his upper and lower sets of teeth as well.

During the spring thaw one year Jim Chadwell had his bulldozer parked at Ed's place. Why it was there I don't recall, but it had broken down. Mike Lehman and Roger Williams came over from Anahim Lake by snow machine to help him get it running. When it was fixed Jim started for home with it, first having to cross the Blackwater River to the south side. The ice on the river had begun to thaw. Halfway across the dozer broke through the first layer of ice to the layer below. Jim must have thought he was going right to the bottom. The guys were on the riverbank with Ed watching him cross when this happened. Ed remarked, "Why, you could have knocked that man's eyeballs off with a stick."

Ed had the sheep, and also always had hens. He then went through having turkeys; in time the coyotes got them. The hen turkey was nesting near the cabin in a clump of willows and was taken from her nest early in the morning. The hen tasted so good it was only a matter of days before the tom was taken. Then from somewhere he got guinea hens. The grey-and-white-spotted West African bird was like a watchdog, and their shrill cries were loud even at our place, half a mile away. The pair followed the hens and watched out for predators such as eagles, hawks, coyotes and the Indian dogs. They did nest, but I cannot remember the eggs ever hatching. One finally disappeared and the other was around for another year before it vanished. Then some of Ed's friends from New York bought him a pair of peacocks, which he kept in the barn. He was afraid to let them out but one day a young Indian lad was curious about the noises in the barn and opened the door while his parents visited in the cabin, releasing the birds. After that Ed let them out but the coyotes got them too.

Then Ed wanted pigeons. He rarely went to town so I agreed to get him a pair of pigeons. On one of my trips to Quesnel I talked on the phone to a fellow who had lots of birds and agreed to give me a pair. I was not sure where he lived, but while driving in a settled area on the outskirts of town I saw pigeons flying about. I stopped and told him I was there for the pigeons. He looked a bit surprised but went to some cages and while removing a pair he explained their pedigrees. I knew then I was in the wrong place. The guy put them in a cardboard box and then told me they were thirty dollars a pair. The other birds had been free! Well, thirty dollars was a lot of money but I was so embarrassed at my mistake I paid the man and took the birds. Ed just grinned when I told him there were purebred pigeons. They did well for awhile and increased in the barn. But their droppings covered everything, including Ed's harness and collars. I hated to help him harness up because of that. Then the hawks got after them and it wasn't long before they were cleaned out.

Ed bought some turkey chicks one year but was having trouble keeping them alive, so I volunteered to look after them. There were four left when I took them to my house, keeping them inside in a cardboard box, behind the wood stove. I lost one but the remaining three seemed to thrive and were growing. Then I had to go away for a couple days and Rob stayed at the house to do chores. When I came back I checked the turkeys to find only two in the box. I asked Rob if one died; he said there had been three earlier in the day, although they were trying to fly out of the box. I looked around the kitchen to find one had flown out of the box only to land in a pail of water sitting by the stove. Needless to say it had not survived. So out of a dozen birds we were then down to two. Those finally got big enough to move to the barn and range freely. Their favourite place was by the porch. Once, it was pouring rain and they were standing in the rain looking bedraggled and too stupid to go to the barn, or seek any dry shelter. Taking the broom I herded them to the barn. A few days later one more died, probably from getting so wet and cold. So as soon as the last one got a little size we ate it—not that it was ready to be eaten, but if it had been left much longer it would have surely found a way to die. No one out there ever tried to raise turkeys again.

Soon after we moved to Sleepy Hollow, Ed had wanted goats and got a billy and a couple of nannies from someone. I believe Al Reinsdorf may have flown them in from Quesnel in his plane. The kid goats were so cute (but then they became goats!), the nannies were curious and the billy stunk, as he constantly urinated on himself. If you were downwind you could smell him a long ways away. The goats started coming to our place to visit. Once they got in the woodshed and knocked the woodpile down. Another time they pulled most of the clothes off the line. The final straw was the day we were not home and they spent the afternoon on the porch. They ate up the lower half of the screen door and then chewed up the line from the marine band radio that ran up the side of the wall to the antenna. This was our only means of communication at that time. We finally convinced Ed the goats had to stay home or he had to get rid of them, so he gave them away to Sandy and John Zigler at Rainbow Lake. They did not last there much longer, as eating clothes from the line became a favourite pastime. Sandy shot at them one day with the shotgun, only meaning to scare them, but forgot I guess about the spread of the pellets and did a fair amount of damage to some of the goats.

In the late 1980s Ed began to show signs of Alzheimer's disease, although at the time we didn't realize what he had. We just knew there was something wrong and so did he. On more than one occasion he said to me that something was wrong but he could not really describe the symptoms. We began to help him more, and one day he wanted what was referred to as the "old cabin" cleaned. This cabin had been built in the late thirties when the Frontier Cattle Co. had a pre-emption on the valley and hayed and fed cattle there. In the seventies, about ten years after Ed had purchased the place, he built a bigger cabin on the hill above the old one with Richard Boland's help. Now he just used the old cabin for storage. Like all old log buildings in that era there was no foundation, one corner being put on a hummock and the other on a horse bun type of foundation. So the cabin had settled badly, and several bottom rounds of logs had rotted away. The two windows were about twenty inches off the ground with several panes of glass broken. The roughly built wooden door had already been sawn off several times and still dragged badly. It only opened about two thirds of the way unless forced. The interior of the cabin was dark and dusty. Old bits of harness hung from nails on the rafters, as well as old lanterns and horse collars. The floor was covered with old oil jugs, grease pails, doubletrees and singletrees, old bedsprings and cardboard boxes full of wide mouth Mason canning jars. Several wooden boxes against the wall contained Ed's tools. There were also boxes of *National Geographic*, as Ed had started subscribing to the magazine when he first arrived at the Home Ranch in 1960. Handsaws and a crosscut saw hung on nails on the wall with a lot of other stuff. Against the back wall was a large wooden box from Happy Thompson's day, when he owned the place. In it were a lot of old gunnysacks and pieces of hardwood, but also an old case of dynamite. Not knowing what to do with the dynamite and scared to move it, we left that be.

Behind the door was an old wood heater someone had given Ed, but it had been in poor shape when it had arrived and Ed had never used it. We thought we'd start with it first, loading it into the wagon to go to the dump. Barry and I started working it towards the door. Under the stove was Ed's cat Fluffy, who had disappeared the year before. She apparently had died under the stove, and because nothing had disturbed the body, it then had become rather flat and

*Ed in 1989, shortly before his death. Ed had been a part of our lives for almost three decades and he was like family.*

mummified. Barry grabbed the skeleton complete with all the hair and passed it to Ed, saying, "Here is your cat, Fluffy!" Ed took the body and put it under his arm and began stroking the hair, murmuring to it. It was then we knew that Ed was having serious problems.

As time progressed Ed became worse. I took to cleaning his cabin whenever I had a bit of extra time and doing his laundry. As I went through a bunch of empty boxes while cleaning I found a Christmas cake that my sister Gayle had sent him. She baked the best Christmas cakes in the world—we always looked forward to them as the holidays neared. I gave it to Ed, who said he thought I had taken it, as he couldn't find it. The following day I went back to his place with the clean laundry, and when I opened the door I could smell something burning. There was a mist of smoke circulating in the kitchen area. On the middle of the wood range was a tin pie plate and in it was the Christmas cake, charred about halfway up. I told Ed he had ruined his treat and after peering at it for some time he said he'd thought it was a roast of moose meat. Another time one of us arrived at the cabin to find it full of smoke and Ed hunched over in his cowhide chair he kept near the stove. He had built a fire on top of the kitchen stove and watched it flame and smoke while waiting for the kettle to boil for tea.

Ed must have thought he was back in New York state the day he came over in a panic because his team was out on the railroad track and would get hit by a train. I had learnt it was best to humour him, so I calmly remarked that I had seen them there and had put them back in the pasture. He was happy to learn that and hurried off home.

At last it was decided he could not be alone anymore. We were lucky to find a fellow who had moved from Oliver to Quesnel and was looking for something to do. So Joe Whittitt came and stayed with Ed. Joe didn't mind cooking, so Ed was fed on a regular basis and we knew the place wouldn't burn down. I continued to do the grocery shopping whenever I went to town as well as the laundry.

Ed continued to deteriorate and a year or so after Joe moved in he began his wanderings. He would just take off, without Joe knowing where he went. Joe would then come get us and the search would begin. Joe and the kids would be on foot, and Barry and I on our dirt bikes. Once Barry found Ed a good mile down our fenceline with an armload of split wood he had been packing since he left home. He was then confused as to why he had to leave the wood on the side of the trail and come home with us. Another time he fell in the river but managed to crawl out on the opposite bank, thus putting him across the river from where we were searching, but luckily one of us spotted him. These walkabouts continued, but when he started doing so at night it was real cause for concern. Joe would wake to find him gone; so then we had to look with the snow machines, because by then it was winter. Fortunately Ed would stay on the well-travelled trails but he was usually in his long johns and sock feet, so if he wasn't located right away he could freeze.

It was then we knew we could no longer keep this man safe. Ed had been a part of our lives for so many years; he was like a family member. But at this point he no longer knew us and thought we were people from his past. We had known for some time the day would come when we could no longer keep him, but the decision was made partly due to the fact that he no longer knew us and safety was an issue. But just try to find somewhere for him to go—no one wants the responsibility for these people if they can help it. I phoned different agencies and doctors for months before I finally found a sympathetic lady in Prince George who made arrangements for Ed to go to St. John's Hospital in Vanderhoof. From there she said they would find him a home.

It was a sad day when we loaded Ed up in the pickup and Barry and I drove him into town. I left him sitting in the waiting room of the hospital with his suitcase by his feet after doing the paperwork for him. The next morning I went to see him before leaving town. He was sitting up in a hospital bed, shiny clean, very sedated and totally unaware I was even there. From there he was placed for a time in the Omineca Lodge (Riverside Place) but because of his constant wandering he had to be put back in the hospital. He continued his wandering there as well. The ambulance attendants were to keep an eye on him when they were not out on call. Still, one day Ed ended up in the operating room looking over Dr. Rummel's shoulder as the doctor performed surgery. I was visiting Mom in Quesnel shortly after that when the hospital called to say Ed was worse. Mom and I went to see him one last time, spending the afternoon sitting by his bedside. He died a few days later. He was eighty years old. It had been a mere six weeks since we had moved him from the ranch. I am sure if we could have kept him there he would have been with us longer.

# CHAPTER 13

# A Variety of Events

It was in a very heavy snowstorm in March, sometime in the mid-eighties, when George and Cecilia Chantyman, George's sister Bella and several small children were going back to Kluskus on two snow machines and a couple skimmers after visiting the Alexis family up-river from us. When they got out onto Tsacha Lake the heavy falling snow confused them and instead of turning right out on the lake they turned left and went up the lake to where the Blackwater River empties into it. The water stays open there year-round. With the blinding snow they could not see landmarks to tell where they were, and before they realized it they were on the thin ice at the water's edge. How they managed to all get out is a miracle, as they lost both snow machines and the skimmers into the water. They then figured out where they were and walked across the lake to Blackwater Lodge (which was closed up for the season) and got into a cabin, where they were able to get a fire going and dry out. In one of the buildings they found a CB radio and got hold of Ted Williams at Euchiniko Lakes Ranch, who along with another fellow came to rescue them with snow machines and skimmers.

One day we took snow machines over to Anahim with the kids, to spend the night with Linda and Ken Karran at their ranch on the Dean River, at the foot of Anahim Peak. At that time they did not have indoor plumbing either, but it was my introduction to Styrofoam seats in the outhouses. It was pitch black out and I had not taken a flashlight but found my way down to the little log building below the house by staying on the path shovelled through the snow. Upon reaching the door I grabbed the latch but I couldn't seem to pull the door open. I did a mental head count: yes, everyone was accounted for; there couldn't be anyone inside. I gave the latch a violent jerk and the door came open. I stepped inside and felt around to locate the seat and sat down. It was probably minus eighteen or so outside, cold enough to know the seat would be freezing—except it was instantly warm. Then I was positive that someone was in that little building with me. I held my breath as long as I could but couldn't detect a single sound. I finally reached out and felt my way around the walls with my hand but came in contact with no other living soul. With a sigh of relief I realized I was truly alone!

The next day we had to return home, although Barry did not want to. Ken and Linda decided to come with us on their machines and spend the night at our house. On the way back Barry was in front with Wesley and towing the skimmer, driving much too fast. I tried to keep up but found it hard to do so as I had the other two boys with me. Along the trail we found a gas jug, which Barry had apparently lost out of the skimmer he was towing. Ken picked it up, tying it onto his machine. Farther along it was our duffle bag lying beside the trail. That Ken picked up as well. By then I was really concerned for Wesley. As we came out on the brushy flat where we could look out on Geese Lake I could see Barry and Wesley standing by the machine, across the small lake. Barry had been driving too fast and the machine had flipped. Barry hit the ice so hard he lost both his boots. Lucky neither one was seriously hurt, and the snow machine had not suffered any damage. After that it was a slower trip.

In the winter I most often had a snow machine so it was quite easy for all of us to pile on it and go visiting on nice days after our chores were done. We visited Rose and William Cassam a lot, as they were very close. We would take the river, travelling on the ice to the rapids about a mile and a half below the house, then jump up the bank and run down the trail to their house. This was only a winter trail, however. In the summer the road to their place on the north side of the river was not something I did with four of us on the dirt bike, as there were a lot of rocks and mudholes, where the bike would sink then spin on some smooth rock a foot under the mud or high centre on a rock I couldn't see or some log buried in the black muck. I would do it alone, but it was too difficult with the kids. Later on, when Jon started home correspondence, our visiting was only done on the weekends. I tried to keep the teaching to five days a week in the morning and early afternoon, and take the weekends off. But it was time consuming.

I never did like flying much, as I've said, but I did a lot of it over the years. Once we had built an airstrip at the Home Ranch in the 1960s we usually flew back and forth to Quesnel and Anahim Lake, as it was a fast way to travel, and in those days it was reasonably cheap. I guess a lot depended on the aircraft and on the pilot. But again, I was more comfortable with some pilots than others. Once, I had to fly into Quesnel in winter and caught a ride with a ski plane that brought Rose Cassam into Blue Lake. Barry took me over there with the snow machine and then took Rose down to her place and hurried home as the kids had been left alone. It was thawing that day and the snow was sticky. The plane was a Beaver aircraft and the pilot had taken the back seats out for whatever reason. I sat in the back on a plastic milk carton while the pilot and his son, who he was teaching to fly, occupied the two front seats. We ran up and down the lake a number of times trying to get off. About then I told them to let me out, as the engine seemed to be heating up and the fumes of the hot motor were strong. They ignored me and continued to run up and down the lake, packing the snow down. We still couldn't get off. Then the pilot stopped the plane and got out and pulled big plastic garbage bags over the skis. The plastic bags stopped the metal of the skis from sticking to the wet snow and we were able to then get airborne. As we levelled off the young fellow nodded to a gauge— apparently it was not working or something was wrong. The pilot looked over and flipped his hand in an offhand manner, as if to say it was okay. That didn't make me feel any better. I started praying and continued to do so the rest of the flight. As we neared Quesnel and began our descent into the airport the pilot reached around and under my feet into a tangle of stuff, and came up with a headset, which he put on his head and used to call the airport to say we would be landing on the snow alongside the tarmac. I was so happy to be on the ground I wanted to kiss it.

The bridge we built across the river at our place in the late 1970s made it so much easier to get across, instead of having to go up to Ed's. But it didn't last more then ten years and the logs started to rot, although we were unaware of it. Barry was taking the tractor and wheel rake across the bridge one day and was halfway across when the stringers broke. It was fortunate that they all broke at once, letting the log structure fall evenly onto the water, although it must have been an interesting ride as the bridge was quite high above the water. The tractor and rake stayed on the bridge as it went down so Barry was able to drive the tractor up the very steep angle of the broken bridge and reach the field on the other side. I thought it would tip over backwards but it stayed on all four tires. We then had to make a decent river crossing for the tractor till we could get another bridge built. (By then the bridge that had been at Ed's had gotten old and unsafe, so had been removed.) The bank farther up the river was blasted with dynamite to make an accessible entrance into the river on the north side, and there was a sandbar on the south side, so we had a crossing to use till the bridge could be replaced. During the following winter, when we could get out on the ice, the bridge was replaced with four stringers of doubled logs banded together. Barry made sure this one was not going to break.

In 1985 we got our first radiophone. It was so nice to be able to talk to our families—especially Mom, who by then was pretty well wheelchair bound. For machinery breakdowns we were able to order parts and have them available when we ran into town, or with company coming in we could phone for them to bring things we needed, as well as the mail. When we finally got the radiophone and antenna we were anxious to get it set up. The morning after we arrived home with it we put the antenna together, and with the radiophone sitting on the porch Barry began moving about the yard with the antenna, while I keyed the mike waiting for a response from the operator. Because we only had fifty feet of wire between the phone and antenna he was limited in how far he could go. We were also forty-five miles from the repeater so the antenna had to be in a good spot for the thing to work. It was very discouraging when other people got on the air and we were not able to get a response. We would then have to wait till the channel was clear to start again. We could only hear one side of the conversation—those on the landline—as the radiophone was private. A young couple in Anahim were getting married that afternoon and would not stay off the phone. She was on the landline and he was on the radiophone. Apparently they were both nervous and needed to keep reassuring each other. They would hang up and we would once again search for a good spot for the antenna, and then they would phone each other again. We learnt all about their upcoming nuptials by the time she had to leave for the church. And once that happened the channel was quiet. We finally found a spot up on the roof where the operator heard our signal and was able to hear us clearly.

We wanted the boys to learn to ride, as it was natural that they should, living on a ranch. Even with the large number of horses we had, we really never had a horse that would have been considered a reliable kids' horse when they got old enough to start riding, so we were looking for something suitable. We first bought a black-and-white pony for them. It was gentle, no doubt about that, but definitely had a

*Here are James, Jon and Wesley in about 1985.*

mind of its own. We finally gave up on it, and I traded it off for a roll of fencing wire and two lengths of insulated stovepipe. We then got lucky and came across a sorrel Welsh pony in Quesnel called Buttons, and it was the best little horse anyone could want. Jon used him first, then the twins started riding him. The twins seemed more interested in riding than Jon. The kids could do whatever they wanted and Buttons obeyed. Once, I was coming back from the Home Ranch with the team and wagon and the twins, who then were about six, followed behind on the pony. One had gotten off for something and was trying to get back on. Buttons just stood with his head turned to watch. When they both were finally on his back, only then did he move, trotting to catch up to the wagon.

One day when James must have been about five or six—it was just before we got Buttons—he rode with me to Tsetzi Lake. I had given him a big bay gelding called Sundown that was a du-al-purpose horse: he could be worked or ridden. He was also very gentle. Halfway up the hill from Sleepy Hollow James started yelling. I turned in my saddle and there was Sundown right behind my horse—but with an empty saddle. James was hanging from a branch of a pine tree. The horse had taken a shortcut to catch up and gone under a tree with a large branch that threatened to sweep James from the saddle, so he grabbed the branch and hung on while the horse passed underneath.

When the hunting area changed hands the new owner brought into the country a paint mare that was fairly small for mountain use. She was very gentle with a sweet nature. We traded a draft type of horse we had for the mare, and finally had a decent saddle horse for Jon.

We sometimes got very strong winds; most of the prevailing winds were from the southwest, and got a good sweep down the valley before hitting our house up on the hill. It was a day late in the spring when the wind became so violent it was not safe to be outside. The branches on the trees were breaking, as the trees bent under the strong wind. Then the rain started as well. All we could do was stay inside and be sure the kids stayed back from the windows, which

rattled with the force of the wind as rain with pine needles, pine
cones and fine grit splattered against the panes. Trees began to fall,
uprooted from the ground. Our main concern was Jon's paint mare,
Penny, who was in the corral. As the trees began falling over the
fences we could see her darting around, dashing this way and that.
When the storm finally passed over, after lasting about ten minutes,
we went to survey the damage. We had lost thirty to thirty-five trees
in and around the buildings alone, but fortunately none of the trees
had caused much damage—some broken fences—and the mare
had not been hurt. It took several days to clean up the mess, cutting
the trees up for firewood and fence rails and hauling the branches
and tops to a big burn pile.

After the kids learned to ride and had outgrown Buttons we
ended up with a half-Welsh pony that Wesley rode some, but it also
had a mind of its own and some days were worse than others. Wesley
would lose his patience with it and could get into a rage. One day
he came to the house for a gun, saying he was going to shoot it. He
would have been about fourteen then. We had some visitors from
Vanderhoof who talked him out of shooting the pony, and told him
to sell it instead. So it rode to town in the cattle liner with the calves.
On sale day, Wesley rode the pony through the sale ring bareback
with only a rope around its neck and it behaved beautifully. He got
something like seven hundred and fifty dollars for the pony, and was
very happy he had not shot it.

When fall came, Barry generally went to the mountains in
September with friends and the horses. When the kids got old
enough to go he would take them too, starting first with Jon. I worried the whole time that the kids wouldn't be looked after but they
seemed to survive. They always came home full of stories and had a
good time with their dad and his friends.

My boys learned responsibility very young and I could count
on them to do what they were told to do, or in cases where they
had to make decisions they used common sense. One day I came
home and found the three of them—then quite young—changing
the hundred-pound propane tank, as the propane had run out for

the stove. It took all three to wrestle the tank to the stand and remove the empty tank, then hook the new one up. They had a crescent wrench, the pipe tape and a couple of kitchen chairs to stand on, and were just finishing when I came home.

Toby and Doris Cave from Quesnel used to come out often to visit, driving their snow machines from Nazko. We always knew when they were coming, as they would phone. The kids were allowed to walk down the trail to meet them when we felt they were close enough. On meeting Toby and Doris the first thing they would ask for was candy, and then they would climb on the snow machines with them and ride home. Toby said he would ask in the morning which twin was which, and then memorize what clothes they were wearing to be able to know one from the other. Once Wesley was sitting on the back porch telling James, who was in the woodshed a short distance away, how to spilt wood. So for the rest of the visit, Toby called Wesley "Premier Bill Bennett."

My three boys, who I love dearly and who were a great source of help and company, had their days. I am not fond of frogs or snakes,

*The hen looks on with approval as Jon gives his brothers a spanking for chasing her chicks.*

but boys will be boys! One day I called them in for lunch and while we got seated I did not notice the tin on the table with a lid sitting loosely on top. We had just begun eating when the lid fell off the tin and a huge frog's head appeared over the rim. I leapt back in shock, knocking my chair over, while the boys squealed with laughter. It was only a day or two later when another tin appeared on a counter with a shoe sitting on top. I immediately demanded that it be gotten rid of. Then there were the snakes. Garter snakes were very common at the ranch, due to the rock outcroppings, I think, where they had dens. I went to put some toys away while cleaning up once and nearly fainted: there was a tiny snake crawling about in the toy box. What I didn't know was that there were at least half a dozen in there, but I had only seen the one. The boys said they found a snake with a whole lot of babies and they gathered up as many as they could catch. Some ended up in the toy box and some in the toolbox on the back porch, and I could only guess where else. For several days I was afraid to move anything for fear there would be a snake lurking underneath.

Someone gave each of the kids a rabbit. When we got home I put together a rabbit hutch and the boys cared for the rabbits for a short time—until the novelty wore off and they were turned loose. Well, of course we had ended up with two females and a male. They increased by leaps and bounds. After a couple years there were rabbits everywhere, even crossing with the wild rabbits. One time, looking out the window, I counted seventy-six.

While I was feeding the milk cow grain the rabbits would climb into her grain box. She would usually nudge them out of the box with her nose, but this one day she must have been fed up with rabbits as she grabbed a rabbit by the ears using her mouth and gave it a vicious shake, then tossed it to the side. The rabbit hopped away and made no further attempt to get into the grain box. Another time, I set an empty gallon can that I used for grain down in the sloping corral while I went to do something. A rabbit hopped up to the can, smelt it all over, and then nudged it with his nose, rolling the can down the incline. Running after it, he picked it up with his teeth by the rim and packed it back up the hill to repeat the performance. He did this several times before losing interest and moving on. There were rabbits of all sizes, everywhere. The cat would find a nest of baby bunnies and eat till he threw up. While I was milking in the barn one very cold morning, a rabbit came into the barn. She stopped by the cow and gave birth to a baby with a cloud of steam and then hopped off, leaving the tiny creature, which almost instantly froze.

One visitor, noticing the rabbit population, remarked that his wife wanted a rabbit. I told him two would be better, and he finally consented. Leaving him in the house talking to Barry I took a box to the barn and managed to catch eleven fairly small rabbits. Tying the box securely I put it in the back of his truck. I never saw the guy again.

After the rabbit population disappeared, no doubt from disease due to overpopulation, what remained was one big white rabbit. Apparently he was lonely: he followed our dog around the place, running behind him and copying his every move. The dog would lose patience and snap at the rabbit, which would make the rabbit wait for awhile before starting the game again. If the dog was curled up in the sun the rabbit would always be close by, absorbing the rays as well. While I was away for a couple days the rabbit vanished. Whether the dog got it or some predator I don't know, but that ended the rabbits.

Letting the boys have the freedom to grow up like I did was important to us, and of course, accidents would happen. Before Rob was married I cooked for him on occasion, when he had fly-in guests who wanted to be cooked for. Once I was at the lodge cooking when Barry arrived there on his dirt bike with James, whom he thought had broken his leg. How it happened I'm not sure, but James was in a lot of pain and the leg was swelling. He also was covered with dirt, and minus one shoe (the three boys had been digging tunnels somewhere in the horse pasture). We managed to get him on a plane bound for Williams Lake that evening but they would not be able to bring him home in the morning. There was no room in the plane for one of us to go with him, either, so I had to send him alone, and he was only six or seven. I phoned my brother Ken and his wife, Andrea, who lived in Williams Lake, to meet the plane. They did, and took James to the hospital for X-rays, where it was discovered his leg was not broken, only badly bruised. Andrea got James on a flight back to Nimpo Lake the following morning with Floyd from Avnorth Aviation. Floyd left him for the day with his daughter Anna, who kindly bought him a pair of runners so he wasn't shoeless. Late that evening Floyd had a flight in to Tsacha Lake—it was a full load but he said he could squeeze James into the storage area behind the back seat, which he may well have. Barry took the dirt bike to Tsacha and picked up our son, who arrived home still wearing his dirty clothes but sporting new runners and with stories to tell.

As they got older the twins started wrestling each other but those matches started to end up punching matches, as one would try to outdo the other. They were so close in weight and strength that it was usually a tie. But as they got older some of those fights became vicious. I would break them up and try to calm them down; sometimes it worked and other times it didn't. Finally I told them that when they fought in the house I would just get the broom and start whaling on them, I didn't care where or who I hit! So most of their fights from then on were outside, with bloody noses and bruises. This they did till about grade nine. They were both by then boarding in town with Doug and Vicki Weaver, friends of mine, while going to school, and the fighting had continued till one day Doug had to leave work and drive home to stop a fight—which was their last one!

I found out accidents could happen anywhere, with things I least expected. I was out by the hay pen one day feeding some mares we had out in the field. I stuck the pitchfork into the snow and was doing something when the fork fell over. As I reached for it one of the mares stepped on the tines. I wouldn't have thought it was possible but the handle came up and cracked me on the temple, nearly knocking me down. Immediately a huge lump arose, seeming to pull my face skin to the area—then the pain hit. By the next day the lump had gone down some but my eye began to turn black. By the second day the lump was gone but both eyes were black and blue, as was the ridge of my nose. I looked like a raccoon. I had to go to the Alexis place for something and when I got there Peter gasped and said, "Barry hit you?" I told him what happened. He laughed and said, "First time I ever see a white woman with black eyes."

One night, Barry was going to cook supper and had put the cast-iron fry pan on the kitchen stove to heat while he cut up some meat. He had opened the door to the cubbyhole situated just back from the stove on the kitchen floor to get vegetables, when he saw the pan on the stove was smoking hot. He then grabbed the handle of the pan, burning his hand. He leapt back from the stove only to fall into the hole and onto the vegetables. Climbing out, he went out onto the porch and had started down the steps when his feet slipped and he fell down the three steps to the ground. Needless to say he refused to finish cooking supper. No sense of humour, apparently!

But sometimes I was the one who perhaps couldn't see the fun in a particular situation. I not only kept laying hens but a few bantam hens for raising chicks. These I set in boxes in the barn or shop. When the eggs hatched and the hen wanted to leave the nest I checked any leftover eggs under the hen by holding them against my ear, listening for the peep of a chick inside. If I could hear nothing, I gently shook the egg to see if I could hear anything; a rotten egg would have space and the liquid would move, which I could hear or feel. A chick won't move. If I felt no movement I would gently remove the shell and hope to save the weak chick. One particular egg I held against my ear exploded, covering the side of my head with the foulest smelling rotten egg. I ran for the house gagging and at the door asked for a basin full of warm water, as the egg had run down my cheek and neck. The kids and their dad found it very funny and spent some time laughing before getting me water to clean up with.

# CHAPTER 14

# Animals and Their Ways

As the boys got older their interests turned to motorbikes and snow machines. There wasn't any spare money to buy anything new so whatever they had was second-hand, and not necessarily in good running order. They were constantly repairing them. One evening in the winter the boys were out back working on a snow machine and I was inside preparing supper. It was dark outside so the three were out there with a flashlight. I think they had a spark plug out of a snow machine, testing it for spark on a badly flooded motor. Then the back door burst open and there were cries of "Fire!" This was before we had plumbing and the kitchen had its usual slop pail, which contained wash water, coffee grounds . . . anything that didn't go in the hen bucket. I grabbed it, ran out the back door and dumped the contents onto the motor of the snow machine. Well, the fire was extinguished, but then there was the problem of dirty water and coffee grounds in everything, with some carrot peelings clinging here and there.

Jon had been trapping since he was young, as it was something all kids did in the bush to make a little spending money. We probably encouraged him as I had trapped as a child, and when Barry first came to the Home Ranch during winters he had done the same thing. Jon started with squirrels, and then later started trapping martin and mink as well. He had a fairly long trapline, and he would walk it every few days to check his traps. He used the money he made to invest in new humane traps, smaller ones for squirrels and larger ones for the bigger animals. These traps are very powerful and he had to be very careful setting them. But one day he caught both thumbs in a trap and had to run home with the trap on his hands. Only Wesley and James were at home, as we were over at Ed's place doing something. James took vice grips to the trap to try to relieve the pressure while Wesley came looking for us. We hurried home and removed the trap from his thumbs, and fortunately he suffered no ill effects other than having swollen thumbs for a few days. He then had to walk back over his trapline to get his coat and rifle, which he had left behind.

D'Arcy Christensen, who had the general store at Anahim Lake, was also a fur buyer. He had his small plane on skis in the winter

*Barry with D'Arcy Christensen (right), the flying fur buyer.* VANCE HANNA

and flew about the Blackwater country for many years, landing anywhere people lived to buy fur and to deliver groceries and mail. He was known about the area as "The Flying Fur Buyer," and he'd stop at our place and buy Jon and Barry's fur. Everyone always looked forward to his plane coming in winter, not only for the mail but also for news of other people, and the humorous stories he would tell.

At one point Jon was interested in Morse code, so we got him a radio; he learned the code but never did get his licence. He also for awhile had an interest in bow hunting. We managed to buy him a good used bow from a fellow who went caribou hunting with Barry. When he was eleven or twelve he started working at the local lodges in the summer, at Eliguk Lake Lodge and Blackwater Lodge. Between that and school, he never seemed to have time for much else. Later, when he boarded in Vanderhoof for high school, his summers were spent working for people who ran sheep in the clearcuts—it was part of a program that kept the grass grazed off those clearcuts to allow new seedlings a chance to grow. In the fall he worked at the Vanderhoof Auction Mart on weekends. From the time he was eleven, he was not at home much.

On one of Barry's trips to Anahim Lake he brought home for the kids a mongrel puppy. But it didn't matter to the kids. They loved it. It looked a bit like a coyote. After it grew up it started going over to Rob's place. We couldn't break the habit and we had some other dog at the time, so we told Rob to shoot him and not say anything to the kids. Rob did get rid of the dog but since it resembled a coyote he skinned it and shipped the hide with the rest of his fur as that of a coyote, and it sold as one. The kids found out years later; fortunately they were big enough to laugh about it by then. Over the years we had quite a number of dogs. On another trip Barry brought home a Bluetick hound, from Lester Dorsey at Anahim. He was a good dog but not what we needed. He spent all of his time chasing rabbits or whatever scent he picked up. He did keep the bears out of the yard, though. Then Ed accidentally poisoned him. We also had a dog brought as a puppy from Oregon, a heeler–border collie cross we named Bob. He was about two years old and just beginning to be a valuable stock dog when one day he vanished. He was there in the evening and the next morning he was gone; it was the last we ever saw of him. We thought he must have been killed by a wolf and that could well be, except Rob lost a dog about the same time. This was in the winter and there was thick ice on the river. Rob's dog, a female, was found in the spring by William Cassam in a back eddy of the river when the ice went out. She had been shot in the head, and must have been put under the ice. It is possible our dog was shot and put through a hole in the ice as well. He never left home to our knowledge, but stranger things have happened.

But of all the dogs we had, Patch was my favourite. I got him in January 1987. Again we were in between dogs. I had caught a ride to town, as back then we could not afford to put insurance on our truck year-round. The kids wanted a dog, and I found a lady west of Vanderhoof who had puppies to give away. The mother was a border collie and the father was a heeler. The bitch was barely a year old and had had thirteen puppies, which she had weaned much too soon. Patch was the runt of the litter and the last male left. Of course I took him. A friend gave me a ride home and to keep the puppy from crying, afraid it would be irritating, I put him inside my shirt, where he slept, warm and cosy, for the four-hour trip back to the ranch. He barely knew how to eat and had to learn to drink from a dish. He was so tiny he could sit in my hand.

It did not take Patch long to become a fat and very rambunctious pup. Only I could not house train him. I tried the newspaper thing, and he just tore up the papers and raced around the house with them. I tried a box of dirt, which he dug in, with dirt flying in all directions. During the day it was not so bad, as he could be taken outside regularly, but at night he was free to do his thing. And if he was locked up he cried and whined and kept everyone awake. He never did get the habit of chewing on things, so that helped. But he did have a very strong dog odour, which I can't stand, so I bathed him often. He hated that. After his bath I would roll him up in a big towel and set him on the couch to dry with just his head sticking out. He wouldn't move — only his eyes followed me, with a look of pure disgust. One evening he was in front of the stove when Barry was cooking supper, and hot grease spilt on the pup. It caused only a small burn on his back, but it was bad enough that the hair never did grow back. Patch was banned from the house at a young age because he could not be house trained. It was winter, but he survived.

Some years later I went up the hill behind the chicken coop to see if I could see the milk cow in the pasture that ran below the hill. There were a fair amount of willows around the sloughs so I couldn't see her. I called a few times hoping she would come in and save me the walk down the pasture after her. Patch sat beside me for a short time then raced down the hill under the fence and disappeared down the cow trail behind some willows. It wasn't long before he returned with the milk cow hurrying ahead of him, her udder swinging back and forth, head up and stepping lively. I praised the dog and he wiggled in glee. The following night the performance was repeated again. What a wonderful dog! The third night I had company and told them they had to see this. We went up on the hill and I called the cow. Patch sat beside me staring off into space. When I looked at him he'd meet my eye and wag his tail and sit, as if

*My favourite dog, Patch.*

to say, "What do you want?" He never did go get the cow on his own again, and my company never got to see the wonderful dog at work!

Patch was not only a good stock dog; he would also tree squirrels. We tried to keep the population of squirrels down around the buildings because of their destructive nature, but all the pine trees in the yard attracted them. They would chew up saddle pads in the shop and get into the guest cabin, taking the insulation out from between the logs and chewing up the foam mattresses. Not only that, their droppings were everywhere. When one showed up in the yard Patch would tree it and sit under the tree and bark till someone came out and shot it. (This was not appreciated in summer, with the early light, when the squirrels and Patch could be out and about at four a.m.) When the squirrels fell out of the tree Patch generally caught them in midair and gave them a vicious shaking, just to be sure that the bullet had done its job properly. Once, a squirrel was not hit badly, or perhaps he'd only been knocked from his perch, and Patch caught him. The squirrel retaliated and sunk his teeth into the dog's lip. Patch dropped to the ground and began to cry and whine. The squirrel refused to let go and Patch continued to cry. I had to intervene on the dog's behalf.

Patch never took food that was within his reach till his later years, when he started to become senile. He would only take what was handed to him or what was put in his dog dish. During one winter I found a muskrat against the house. It had been frozen out of its home and had nowhere to go. The most humane thing I could do was kill it, rather than leaving it to starve to death. Undecided what to do with the rat after the deed was done, and till I could get it skinned, I dropped it into Patch's food dish on the porch. A few minutes later I looked out the window to see the dog examining the contents of the dish. After a couple minutes of turning the furry creature this way and that he took it in his mouth and tossed it in the air to catch it in his teeth. This performance was repeated several times. He then dropped it back in the dish, turning his head this way and that while studying it with a look of confusion, and then left the porch to pursue other activities.

The boys were always fishing in the summer, and did not necessarily look after their fishing lines. Quite often they were left on the riverbank, and quite often the spinners contained bait—as one did the day Patch decided to eat the tidbit. No one actually saw him eat it, but the foot or so of fishing line hanging from the side of his mouth and the amount of discomfort he was showing made us realize what had happened. Luckily I had a friend visiting who was good with dogs and managed to get Patch's mouth open, to see the hook of the spinner caught securely in the back of his mouth. Rod said there was only one way to get it out, as Patch was now objecting strongly. Getting a good grip on the fishing line left on the spinner Rod gave it a vicious yank, ripping it from the dog's mouth. Patch fled and did not want anything to do with any of us for awhile.

As Patch got older he travelled less and less, preferring to sit on the porch and watch the world go by. I missed not having him to guard the hay pen gates while feeding or when moving stubborn cows. When I called him he would wag his tail and join me at the corrals till I was on my horse or the tractor, then walk slowly back to the porch, as he felt too old to leave the yard. But one day in the fall, just before cattle drive time, two of my guests were going riding and Patch decided to join them. They rode for most of the afternoon and when they returned the dog was trailing a fair distance behind, and no doubt exhausted. I waited out in the yard to greet him. His steps were slow and his head hung down as he passed behind a horse grazing near the buildings. The horse kicked the poor old dog, knocking him flying. He did get onto his feet, and started towards me on three legs. There was another dog visiting at the time, and it saw this as a golden opportunity to run over and mount the exhausted, three-legged Patch. I had to take Patch's side and get him to the safety of the porch, away from horses and excited dogs. Thankfully he had no broken bones and recovered in a few days.

We had a couple of different Holstein milk cows back in the eighties. The first one we got as a calf, at about two weeks old, and I bottle-fed her. One of us named her Buffy and she turned out to be a very good milk cow. She raised many heifer calves, most which turned out to be good milk cows as well. I tried to have one freshen about every three months so we always had a lot of milk; at three months the calves took all the milk and could be turned out with their mothers. Then in summer, when the bulls were on the range, they had to go out to the range with the bulls in order to calf again on time to fit into my schedule. It didn't always work but most of the time it did.

One day I was taking a milk cow out to the range with my saddle horse. I had put her and the calf out the gate and turned them to head upriver, to where there were cattle. She had other ideas, and didn't want to leave home. She went through the buck fence into pastures twice, dragging the fence around till she got through, and I would have to go find a gate with the horse. Once she jumped in the river and got into the field. I was so mad I took her back to the corral and put a halter on her. I then tied her to the ball hitch of the pickup and started up the trail, with the calf following. She didn't lead very well, and even less well when we got out of sight of the buildings. Sometimes she skidded along on all four feet; other times she would throw herself on the ground so I would have to drag her along on her side. It was a mile to the west gate, where I wanted her, and it was a rough mile for her! She lost a fair amount of hair and I am sure her feet were sore. Skidding her through the gate, I removed the halter and left her there. I went back home and repaired the fences she had gone through. Later I went and checked on her. She spent the afternoon lying by the gate but towards evening got up and started upriver with her calf towards the range and the other cattle.

Another Holstein cow we had, which I had called Charlie, was a bit flighty and did not like Barry. Barry rarely milked but this one evening in the winter he went to do it. Charlie was not going to go up to the barn and instead ran down to the lower corral by the river, where we had built a hothouse. Barry sent Patch after her. The dog ran her around behind the hothouse, where the wind had built up a big snowdrift. The cow got stuck in the drift long enough for the dog to chew off the end of her tail. This was a real inconvenience when the flies were out because it was left just the right length to rap me on the side of the head while I was milking, but too short to tie to her leg.

When we first bought Charlie as a heifer, we had a fellow haul her to 157 km on the Kluskus Road and we picked her up there with our pickup and stock rack. It was late in the fall so by the time we got home it was dark. While we unloaded the heifer the kids went to the house to start the fire. When they got to the back door it was open. They could hear noises in the house, and the smell drifting out the door wasn't a bouquet of flowers. They came running back to tell us there was a bear inside! We didn't know what to do, as the rifles were all in the house. Then one of us thought of the pig we had been fattening; it was housed in a shed next to the chicken house. Checking there we discovered the door open and figured out what had happened. Back at the house, we found Emily the pig contentedly lying by the heater and a huge dump by the kitchen stove, which was stinking up the house. She greeted us with a squeal when we walked in, like she lived indoors all the time. She was happy to follow a pail of grain back to her quarters. While in the house she had found a bag of potatoes and eaten a lot of them, and several pounds of margarine that had been on the bottom shelf of the pantry. But other than the deposit on the floor, things were pretty good. While I made supper the kids and their dad went upstairs. They yelled that the pig had been up on my bed! I bounded upstairs with a sick feeling, only to discover them laughing their heads off at playing a joke on Mom.

Moose were a real problem in the winter, getting into the hay pen and destroying the hay. In the days when we put up loose hay, we built high log pens to stack the hay in, which kept the moose out. After we started baling, our small tractor did not have a front-end loader to use to stack the bales on top each other, so they took up a lot of area. The round bales were stacked in long rows end to end, with rows side by side. The moose would get between the bales and walked down the rows till they found a bale they liked, usually the fine meadow hay from the high ground; they didn't bother with the coarse meadow hay or the timothy and clover mix. They ate what they wanted from the bale of their choice, while standing on the rest of it and messing on the scattered hay till nothing else would want to eat it. The next night they would choose another bale. The hard-packed snow around the bales where the moose walked made it hard to pick up the bales.

The hay stacked in a pen by the bridge was the best hay, kept for calving in the spring. One cold winter morning, as it began to get light, I was angry with the number of moose walking around in the bales. Taking the rifle, I started shooting around the moose to scare them away, but not trying to hit any. With one of my shots I heard a different sound when the bullet hit the ground, and then realized I had shot through the aluminium boat leaning against the log fence and covered with snow. I now had a hole in the boat and none of the moose seemed fazed by the shots. Soon after daylight the moose would leap out of the enclosures and cross to the willows, where they would browse for awhile then lay down in the snow to await evening's return. Some moose became really bold and would not leave the pens even in the daytime or when we showed up with the tractor to remove hay. One cow moose with her calf actually tried to run Barry out of a pen. Her neck hair standing straight up, ears flat against her neck, she advanced in a threatening manner. Barry returned to the house for the shotgun and birdshot, shooting her in the rump from a distance. She left immediately with her calf, and from then on left when we arrived. She did continue eating hay for the rest of the winter with no apparent side effects from the birdshot. It took several years but I finally got all the hay pens moose proof, and it was certainly nice not to have the messes in the hay.

Before the first snow in the fall, when the days were getting short, I used to like to walk through the timber and see what the squir-rels did with the pine cones they had gathered through the summer and fall. If the pine cones were stacked up in big piles around their den holes or piled up against fallen logs, with a few big piles here and a few there, we would have very little snow, or what was called an "open winter." When there were just a few small piles of cones under fallen logs and around the trunks of spruce trees where the branches sheltered the ground from the snow we would more than likely have a normal snowfall. If no pine cones could be found, they had all been taken underground and stored for the winter where they were readily available, which meant the snow would be deep. How the squirrels would know ahead of time is beyond me. And the little creatures were seldom wrong.

Animals can also tell a person a lot about the weather. If the temperatures are cold and a cat suddenly becomes very playful, warmer weather is usually on its way within twenty-four hours. Horses become active and restless before a storm. (Of course, now that horses are confined to cramped quarters and cats never go outside, how could they express what is about to happen?) Cows on open range are very apt to come home before the first snow in the fall, and moose will move out of the high country to their wintering grounds at lower elevations before a big snowfall hits.

In September, the pack rats started looking for winter homes. Log barns, sheds and quite often log cabins became favourite places for them. If there were a lot of the smelly creatures, some people thought it indicated a bad winter. I didn't find that so; I believe it just meant it was a good summer for them and they raised big families. I felt there was nothing more disgusting then a pack rat. Being a rat was bad enough, but I guess it was the smell more than anything. Learning to catch rats in the outbuildings was a good way to practise trapping. They love carrots, which could be used as bait. Another bad thing about them: they love to chew on leather. It must be something used in the tanning process that they like so much. They could be hard on the saddles and harnesses hanging in the tack sheds.

Fortunately I can only recall ever finding two rats in our house. One was the one that fell into the water container. The other was discovered above the false ceiling we put in the original cabin to cover the burnt logs after we had a fire. I first heard him running around up there. I could not smell him yet, so I knew he had just gotten into the house. I was able to slip a baited trap up into the area from one corner. I then went to my brother's for several hours. When I returned the rat was in the trap and dead, so I was able to sleep in the house without the fear of the rat running over me.

Being able to foresee what's going to happen in the future isn't an ability that only animals can claim, although people who can make such connections are few and far between. Francis Cassam, the local medicine man who lived downriver at Blue Lake, was well known for his predictions. I guess one would call him a psychic. He had lived in the area a long time and belonged to the Kluskus Indian Band, although he had not been born in the area. For many years he rode about the country on a skinny horse, doctoring the sick among his people, for the fee of one horse. No one knew how old he was because he had no birth certificate; he did have a baptism certificate, although he didn't know how old he had been when he was baptized—he thought about twelve, which would have put his birth date in the mid-1870s. He had suffered the loss of an eye years before and his hearing was bad, and now that he was well past his hundredth birthday he spent his time sitting indoors, or outside on sunny days, while his daughter-in-law Rose waited on him.

Barry stopped by their place to visit soon after the disappearance of a Britten-Norman Islander aircraft owned by Central Mountain Air, which had disappeared on a flight from Campbell River to Smithers in the fall of 1983. There were seven on board, four from Germany and three Canadians. At that time it was one of the largest coordinated searches in Canadian history, covering thirty-two thousand square miles in some eight hundred hours, with no trace of the aircraft. I don't know whether Barry brought the subject up or Francis did, but their conversation was about the plane. Francis told Barry the plane went down near a lake where that man from Lessard Lake had died nearly twenty years earlier in a plane accident. (That accident had been on Fenton Lake, in Tweedsmuir Provincial Park.) He also said it was near the old Indian trail that went from Ulkatcho to Fort St. James, a portion of which was flooded when Alcan put in the Kenney Dam and built Kemano. He went on to say the people on board the plane could talk but couldn't talk, perhaps meaning they spoke a foreign language; this would have been the four from Germany. He also said the plane was blue and white. At the time he told Barry many small things, in detail, about the plane and its occupants (I have since forgotten most of them), and Barry came home a bit spooked. Barry did go flying a few days later with White Mountain Helicopters, in the area Frances talked about, but still no trace of the aircraft was found.

One February four guys came up from Quesnel on their snow machines and spent the night. The following day Barry went with them on his snow machine to spend the day playing in the Ilgachuz Mountains. They left about noon, and I then got the boys on to their school lessons. I am not sure how many hours later it was when two of the machines came back. They didn't stop and come through the gate by the bridge but instead jumped down the steep riverbank onto the ice and came up to the house. They said Barry had been hurt: while he raced along the trail on his snow machine he was hit by a dry snag along the trail, which ran into his thigh and came out his back. They needed a chopper to get him airlifted to a hospital. Of course that was a day that the radiophone chose not to work. I had to relay a message from one CB radio to another till Anahim was reached and the call went out for a chopper. I was concerned that if the message were passed along wrong at any point the chopper would not know where to go. But a short time later we got a message back, relayed through one CB after another, that a chopper would be sent and that an area needed to be cleared for the chopper to set down. A fire would have to be lit at the landing spot, one with lots of smoke that could be seen from the air, so the pilot would know where to set down. The guys took a chainsaw, blankets and a Thermos of tea and took off again for the mountains. It was after dark when they returned, saying that the chopper had gotten in and Barry had been taken to Williams Lake. The following morning two of the guys took Jon back to the mountains to bring Barry's snow machine out. The other two felt they wanted to help me. Seeing as our woodshed was down to the last piece of wood, which was usual in those days, they wanted to get wood. There was a huge dry pine tree in one of the corrals that would provide a lot of wood. I asked one of them to fell it—I hated felling trees, as they never seemed to go where I wanted them. The tree was brought down, only to land on a gate, smashing it to pieces. Well, I could have done that, but I did appreciate that they wanted to help.

While Barry was in the hospital, Woody (Don) Woodward, who was at that time living in Anahim Lake, came and spent a couple weeks with us to help get wood in and help with the feeding. Woody is a very colourful person and very entertaining. I had first become acquainted with him when I was a child of three or four and living at the Home Ranch; Woody had come there with Ronnie Harrington on saddle horse. Neither one of them would have been more than twelve or thirteen. We became friends through the years, and still are today.

Over the next year Barry spent a total of eighty-three days in the hospital with a recurring infection from the wound. A piece of stick about eight inches long had been removed from his thigh when he had reached the hospital.

In the late eighties we had a bathroom put in the back room, and running water. A fellow from Victoria and a friend of his brought all the material for the plumbing as well as what was needed to partition off the room. This they did in exchange for a caribou hunt to the Itcha Mountains, which Barry took them on. A large water tank was put in the twins' room upstairs, to gravity feed water to the bathroom and kitchen. A hot water tank was put behind the kitchen stove and heated with coils of copper wire in the firebox. One of the nicest things I could have had was the bathtub. What a treat that was! We had always had to bathe in the tin tub in the kitchen then pack the water outdoors to be dumped. The best part now was that after a bath I could just pull the plug and the water was gone. There was a shower as well, but not a great amount of water pressure, although it could be used. To fill the water storage tank upstairs you had to start the water pump on the riverbank, which had a fire hose running to the tank. This was fine and dandy in warm weather, but in the winter it was another story. Water could only be pumped when it was zero or warmer, as the water hoses would freeze. First a hole had to be cut in the river ice. Once the hoses were strung out, the water pump had to be packed down from the house to the river, primed and started, and only then could the tank be filled. After that the pump and the hoses were drained and brought back indoors till the next time. The back room was good for storing this stuff. In summer everything could be left out.

# CHAPTER 15

# Cow Stories

We decided to try a Limousin bull and bought one late in the fall. Walt Lampert hauled him home for us along with two Welsh ponies that had been given to the kids. Walt had them in a corral on the north side of the river at his place, so Barry and I rode up there to get them. We haltered the ponies and tailed them together and then let the bull out of the pen. It was a gentle bull but I don't think he had ever seen a horse and rider before. There was about ten inches of snow or we would never have gotten him as far as we did. He took a look at us and started running down the well-beaten trail towards the Y where our road split from Walt's. It was a couple of miles to there and by the time we got that far the bull was fairly hot for a cold day and even our horses were sweating.

We did get him turned onto our road, which then had only the horse tracks on it, but he stuck to the horse trail in the snow for another mile or so till we came along the river. We thought we were okay then: with the river on our right we could keep him going downstream to the ranch. The river was freezing, with ice reaching out from shore, up to four feet in places, and even more where the river was calm. The centre was still open, with a lot of slush and ice chunks floating down on the water. Without any hesitation the bull ran down to the river's edge and jumped in. By the time we reached

*These calves enjoy the warm sunshine in the spring.*

the riverbank he was midstream, bobbing up and down and moving downstream fast. He had jumped in just above the rapids, where the water was deep and fast. As soon as he got near the rapids and his feet touched bottom he went to the opposite shore, breaking the ice to shore and climbing out onto the bank, and disappeared into the thick second-growth jack pines. We went on home, put the ponies into the field and then gathered up about twenty cows and started them upriver on the south side. They were not cooperative, not wanting to leave the ranch fields on a cold November day with snow on the ground, but with a lot of yelling and the dog working on their heels we got them going up along the river. As soon as we neared the area where the bull was, he came to the cows. He had a lot of ice and frost on his hair. We just left them and rode home—they would come back as soon as they made their acquaintances with the new bull. The next morning he seemed none the worse for his swim in the icy waters, or the fight he had with the other bulls when he got back to the ranch.

Before Christmas one year we got a huge dump of snow. It

would have been three and a half to four feet. The cows quit their rustling and came in, pushing through the deep snow. We only had the small tractor and the snow proved too much for it, breaking something in the transmission, so from then on we used the team of horses to feed, dragging the round bales out to the cows. For bringing bales from the far pens we used the front bunks of the sleigh, tying the bales behind and riding on the bunks, as running in the deep snow behind a rambunctious team could tire you out fast. We had to do this all winter, as we didn't get the tractor fixed till early summer.

Watering the cows in the river after cutting holes in the ice worked fine till calving time. Then there was always the danger of new calves falling into the watering holes, which grew in size as the warm weather melted the ice. I often stood a log up in a hole to make it smaller. Usually cows went to water then returned to their calves, but once in awhile a cow would take her new calf with her. Most times, if a calf fell in the watering hole the mamma cow would cause a racket, bawling and carrying on enough that I would check to see what was happening. Still, I couldn't be watching all the time. Over the years I probably had half a dozen fall in and not be able to get out. When they were a few days old they were agile enough to avoid slipping into the water; it was the newborn ones that were a concern. I once had a heifer with her first calf that took the calf down with her and it fell into the water. She lay down by the hole and chewed her cud, waiting for the calf. I noticed her lying there in what I used to call the water gap (fences built out on the ice to reach a deep spot on the river, but not allowing the cattle to escape). Cows didn't lie down there so I hurried over to find the calf with its four feet in the hole. I booted the heifer hard as I could in the head as I passed her, for her stupidity, and pulled the cold wet calf out. Once I got him to stand on his feet I knew he would make it, although he was badly chilled. I think there was only one calf that I reached too late to save. One appeared to be unconscious it was so cold. I packed it to the house and right into the bathtub, filling it with warm water. Linda Karran was visiting and she and I worked on the calf for some time, running warm water on it and keeping its head above water.

It finally warmed enough to start showing signs of life. From there I put it on a blanket on the floor with a propane heater beside it. It took several hours for the calf to warm up. Meanwhile the cow ran up and down the fence bawling for her calf. After I got the generator I built a wooden box with a heat lamp to warm up chilled calves. Not only those chilled from falling in water holes, but also newborn ones that had lain in the snow too long and gotten chilled.

At the very beginning of calving one year I had a houseful of visitors and the hour had gotten rather late before I remembered I had put a cow that had started calving in the barn. She was an older cow and the weather was warm, so I had not felt there was much concern. When I did get around to checking her the calf was backwards, and she had not had it. Because of the hours that had passed the calf was dead when I pulled it from the cow. Calves coming hind feet first (backwards) do not survive long in the birth channel. The next day I put the cow out in the field, where she went off without thinking about the calf—I thought. About a week later I had a set of twins from a heifer. Thinking there might be a chance the cow could be made to take a calf I went and got her. She had begun to dry up. Before I brought the cow into the barn I put one of the new-born twin calves in the stall where her calf had been delivered. The cow went into the stall, saw the calf, mooed to it and began licking it, with the attitude of "Where have you been?" I had to give the calf a bottle for awhile, till the cow came to her milk, but all went well.

All the years we raised Hereford cows on the Home Ranch—and even for the few years at Sleepy Hollow, before we started cross-breeding—I can never remember a set of twins. After we got Simmental bulls, twins were common. In the first set we had one was born dead, so I was greatly disappointed. The second set was to a two-year-old that was as flat-sided as a slab. I had gone out in the afternoon to do a check and there she was with two fairly large calves, both trying to suck. The cow seemed a bit overwhelmed with them. I couldn't believe they were both hers so did a thorough check of the rest, but they were hers.

Over the years a person sees some strange things with cows and calving. One was a calf born with no hair. I was shocked to find a cow under a tree with her new calf shivering in the cool March air without hair, not even any eyelashes. Mamma cow was licking and mooing to her baby, not seeming aware that it was different. I hurried to the house, got the calf sled and loaded the calf into it, and took it to the barn with the cow following behind, and then bedded it in a pile of hay. I quickly made a coat of sorts from an old wool blanket to cover its body. This, the cow didn't seem to mind either. The calf was normal in every other way, getting to its feet and nursing. I kept it in the barn where it was at least not exposed to the cold winds. After about a week there was still no growth of hair. Making some phone calls I found someone who had also had a calf with no hair. They said they kept theirs as well but it never grew hair, and that was a problem: it kept getting sunburnt and constantly had eye infections because it had no eyelashes to protect its eyes. I then decided the calf had to be put down, as it would never have a healthy life.

Another cow gave birth to a calf with a deformed mouth. The

*A cow stands patiently while her twin calves search for the milk.*

mouth ran up both sides of the head to the ears, with a double row of teeth as well. This calf was normal otherwise. It got up and played about and tried to nurse—but it could not. If the calf couldn't nurse it couldn't survive, so again a calf had to be put down.

For a time I had two half-Angus cows that were getting fairly old but they raised such nice calves I had kept them. They stayed together most of the time. One year, they both calved only days apart, and one developed a very bad case of mastitis. She was very sick, to the point she wouldn't even care for her calf anymore. I had been doctoring her but hadn't seen much improvement. The other old cow took over nursing both calves, which surprised me, as she was fussy about that. And after feeding she would return to the sick cow with both calves. After a few days I thought I would see if the sick cow's calf would take a bottle, wondering if it was getting enough milk. When I caught it, there was a fight and the other cow got mad that I would touch her friend's calf. I ended up with milk all over the calf, but it refused to suck the bottle. When I let it go the cow smelt it all over than glared at me. But I ruined a good thing because she wouldn't let the calf suck after that, her attitude being "If you don't like what I was doing, you do it," so I had to find another cow to take it, as the mother was obviously not going to recover soon enough to raise the calf. All I could do for her was pump her full of antibiotics. They finally started working and she began to move around. When she got to where she was eating again I turned her into the field. Her udder was swollen huge from milk and infection, which caused her to have trouble walking. It must have been very painful.

About a week later I was moving a bunch of cattle to the Home Ranch and as I drove them by the cow she wanted to go with them but her udder was hampering her. I rode over to her, meaning to turn her back, but she was determined to go. She tried to outrun me, her udder swinging, then the side of it split open and the pus poured out like it was being dumped from a gallon jar. But it must have been a relief as the cow took off running at full speed and got into the bunch. I figured it was now or never and let her go. That fall I sold her, as she was dry, fat and old. Her buddy died towards the following spring and I never knew why.

People say cows are dumb, and some of them are, but some are not as dumb as people think. One spring the cows were all out in the field and the snow was gone, but I was still feeding. I was down at the barn doing morning chores when I noticed a cow and her calf standing at the gate across the bridge. I walked over to see what was going on, as all the others were a good half a mile away grazing on the stubble. The cow was one that was not gentle or easy to handle. Her udder was full, the calf not having nursed for awhile, and the calf appeared sick with a bad case of scours. I opened the gate, and with her calf at her side the cow walked by me, then went across the bridge and up to the barn. I went to the house and gathered up scour medicine, then went down and got hold of the calf and doctored it, while the cow watched me without any interference. She seemed content to stay by the barn, where I fed her and went on about chores. By evening the calf had nursed a little. The following morning the cow was at the gate across the bridge with her calf, which by then was back on the trail to recovery, it seemed, so the cow was ready to take it away. She did not want me near her or her calf then. I thought she was a bit ungrateful, but she had been smart enough to know that I would take care of her calf when it was sick.

While checking cows one night before bedtime during the calving season, one cow followed me about the bedding ground mooing. There was no doubt that she was in the last stages of labour, but she did not seem to want to settle down and have her calf. I thought I would wait up and give her more time but when she followed me back to the house, watching me with those big eyes, I thought maybe she was trying to tell me something. I went to the barn and she followed me. I put her in and checked the progress of the calf, only to discover the calf was backwards and needed to be pulled out fast. I helped get the calf out and left mamma and baby in a bed of hay, the cow licking and mooing to her wet calf as it flopped about, getting its feet under it.

One cow had this calf that may have been a little short on brains.

It would crawl through the fence and find a place to bed down, then not want to come out. The cow would wander around bawling her head off. I would then go out and look for the calf. I soon learned that the calf always went through the fence so I knew where to look for it. After a couple days of this the cow, when wanting her calf, just came to the front porch and stood there and bawled till I went and got the calf. After about a week the calf stayed on the feed ground with the cow, thankfully.

For some reason this one big Simmental cow would not let her calf suck. She was an older cow and had had a number of calves, so she should have known better. (I could have understood if it had been a first-calf heifer.) Roping her and tying her to the log fence (this was in the days before we had a squeeze chute) I tied her legs together and let the calf suck, but she still kicked and fought, knocking the calf about. I put leather horse hobbles on the cow's hind legs, then let the calf get its fill. When I let the cow loose she stood kicking with one hind leg then the other. I had put them on tight so there wasn't much slack between the legs. I knew she would fight till her legs got sore, then the calf could suck by itself. By afternoon she had gotten down to about thirty yards from the barn and stood with rage in her eyes while the calf slept nearby against the hillside. I walked up to her and did a little dance in her face because I was very confident that she could only move with very short steps, with her legs bound so tightly together. What a shock to discover as she charged that she could travel at a great speed. I barely made the top of the fence without her hitting me, but I took such long strides that I split the seam of my well-worn Levis from the waistband to the fly.

The Cassams ran their few cattle with ours but failed to dehorn theirs. Running on the range it was not much of a problem till one of their cows stuck a horn into one of our calves. The calf did recover but we decided then, with the help of a friend, to dehorn their cattle. About three weeks later Rose rode up on the range to see their cows. She returned to say she had seen all of ours but had not seen any of theirs. I then had to confess we had cut the horns off of theirs, and looking for cows with horns she had not recognized them.

Rob called me fairly early one morning in late August to tell me that all my cows that had been grazing on the Home Ranch were now all lying down on his lawn and he was not impressed. Rob had tried to chase them away but the bull had challenged him to the point he had thought it was best to leave them be. I got my saddle horse and went over for the cows. They were badly spooked, protective of their calves and bawling a lot. We decided then that wolves had been chasing them; otherwise they would not have left the Home Ranch. I took them home and going through them discovered that one calf was gone. I put the mother of the missing calf in a corral and turned the rest of the cattle upriver. I didn't want the cow to go back looking for her calf as the wolves might get her as well. The cow bawled through the night but I awoke in the morning to silence and discovered she was gone, having crawled underneath two different pole gates, knocking them down. I saddled up without breakfast and taking a rifle started for the Home Ranch. I pushed my horse into a trot wherever the trail wasn't so rocky, fearing the worst for the cow. I had just crossed the creek at the east end of Airplane (Cluchata) Lake and started up the sandy grade above the creek when I met the cow coming down the trail at a trot, with her calf running beside her—and two wolves behind. The cow and calf ran by me. The wolves ducked into the timber and faded away. The cow had found her calf somewhere unharmed and was bringing it home. It was the time of the year when wolves teach their pups to hunt, and apparently they had just been running the cattle about, teaching hunting methods. Lucky for the calf they had not been hungry. I was then grateful that the cow had been so determined to go find her calf that she had knocked gates down.

I had a cow calve mid-January one year, when there was no bare ground under any of the trees, so I put her in the barn. She was not the type of cow that liked the barn so there was a lot of crashing and banging going on. I ignored it and went off to feed. When I came back a few hours later, some people on snow machines had passed through the place, leaving every gate open. I also noticed that the barn door was open and hanging on one hinge. There was a lot of swearing about where the cow would be by now. I noticed her tracks going out one gate but had not looked for any others. As I was trying to figure out what direction she had gone I looked over at the barn, and there she was looking out the door. By her tracks I figured she had busted the barn door, found the gates open and done a bit of a tour, only to find no bare ground, and had returned to the barn and had her calf. She was content in the barn as long as the door was open, so I left it that way while she had to be in there. A couple days later she brought the calf out, but for some time still they both went inside at night.

# CHAPTER 16

# On My Own

Barry and I decided in 1991 that our situation at home was not a happy one; we no longer cared enough to even disagree. Barry moved to Quesnel. At the time Jon was in high school in Vanderhoof and the twins were home on correspondence. By around Christmastime Jon quit high school and came home. I wanted him to go back to school but boarding out was not easy, and he wanted to be home. His school friend Steve also quit school and moved in with us for a few months. I was very fortunate to have my boys and good friends to help me so much through those hard times.

As I've mentioned, we had a fairly large woodshed but it was always out of wood. That was the first thing we did that fall: we hauled wood till we couldn't pack another stick into it. As soon as the twins' school work was done we would take the tractor, wagon and chainsaw and go cut dry trees. The twins were twelve by then, and drove the tractor and ran chainsaws like adults. We took the box off the wagon and hauled the wood in about twenty-foot lengths on the wagon bunks, stacking it in front of the woodshed, then we would cut it into stove lengths and stack it under cover. Weekends that Jon was able to get home before he quit school, he came and helped as well. Never once was the woodshed empty again!

In February of 1992 the snow machine races were on in Anahim.

Grace and Gordon McNolty from Fort Fraser left their place in the care of one of their daughters and came to look after mine and feed the cows so I could go for a few days, as I had not been away from the ranch since October. The twins were in Quesnel visiting their dad and Steve had gone back home, so there was just Jon and I at the ranch. I finally got talked into going and away we went. We were gone for four days and I really did enjoy myself.

On the way home, late in the day, we ran into some ladies moving horses at the end of Eliguk Lake where the creek remains open year-round, but has a solid rock bottom. One of the young horses they were leading refused to go into the open water. They asked us to shut off our snow machines and wait till they got the colt across. We sat on our machines for a long time and the sun was dropping

*The twins cutting firewood in October 1991.*

into the trees while they begged the horse to wet its feet. I finally lost my patience and got a sturdy willow, walked around behind the colt amid their protests and whacked that colt on the rear hind. He leapt nearly the full width of the open water. I could tell no one was impressed except Jon. I told them it was called gentle persuasion. We then we got on our machines, ran them through the open water and headed home. Jon beat me to the house. Gordon asked him if I had had a good time. He replied that I had been totally wasted for four days. I thought that was called fun!

A few months later Gordon and Grace came back to the ranch with their diesel generator as they had gotten power in to their place and no longer needed the generator. They also bought material to build a generator shed and enough wiring to wire the house. Everything else was forgotten while we built the shed and wired. What a difference power could make, with the brightness of light bulbs. I also inherited their propane fridge when they got their new electric one a short time later! After Ed passed away Joe Whittitt had moved back to Quesnel, but now he wanted to come back to Sleepy Hollow and live in Ed's cabin. We had bought Ed's original two quarters of land from my brothers after Dad died, but gave Ed the same as he had always had, estate for life, so he had his home and his animals. After his death the cabin sat vacant for several years, except for a short time when a retired conservation officer had occupied it. I was more than happy to have Joe move back there and he was always available when I needed help. It was with Joe's help that I finally got all the hay pens built high enough to keep the moose out of the hay in the winter. Joe's specialty was digging postholes. He would often say his nickname was "Posthole Joe." The kids spent a lot of time with Joe and would tease him and play tricks on him constantly, which he didn't seem to mind.

One time, I needed to get some rails to fix a fence. Ernie John had stopped by on one of his horse trips and laid over a day. He wasn't keen on going into the timber as he said there were a lot of hornets about then, nesting in the ground. We had a lot of hornets on the ranch that summer, but I could not remember ever being bit by one, so I couldn't see a problem. We took the tractor, wagon and chainsaw and went up behind the house to cut rails. We'd no sooner started felling small trees when I stepped into a hornet's nest in the ground and was bitten several times on one leg, which immediately became quite swollen. I still insisted they had never bothered me before — that this was the first time. Only a day or two later I was out in the field mowing hay. There were quite a few horseflies about and what I thought was one landed on my lip. I caught the fly between my lips intending to end its life, but to my surprise, then shock, it was a hornet — and it bit me. My mouth swelled up till I had trouble talking. Well, that was twice. A few weeks later I had a sick calf in the pasture and went to doctor it. The calf went into the heavy willows along the river. It was a hot day and I was in cut-offs and a tank top. As I followed the calf along a cow trail I had to walk bent over to get under the heavy willows that hung over the trail. I got into a nest of hornets and was bitten again, a number of times, on the backside. From then on I watched for them and knew it did not pay to ever say something doesn't happen.

It was a cold day in May and I had been riding range up the river to see how the grass was growing, as it was nearly time for the cattle to be turned out. As I rode down a cow trail by the river on the way home, Buck, my big buckskin gelding, wanted a drink so I let him go out onto a sandbar, where he waded out into the river a short distance before he lowered his head to drink. What spooked him I don't know but suddenly he spun in a circle and I lost my seat, falling into the icy water while he plunged into deeper water, and then ended up crossing to the other side. I was about two miles from home and soaking wet. The wind was cold that day and blowing strong. Buck had always ground hitched so I knew that he would be standing in the willows on the other side with his reins on the ground, waiting for me. The fastest way home was with the horse, even though it meant I had to wade across the river with the water nearly to my armpits. But I was wet anyway so I waded across and climbed through the willow bushes to find the horse waiting for me. Grabbing the reins I swung into the saddle and put Buck into a lope.

We raced along the river following old cow trails till we hit the open meadows and the cold wind. I had to stop and open a gate—my teeth were chattering from the cold—and when I was back in the saddle I took my reins and hit the horse on first one side then the other, seeing as it was his fault I was all wet, and we raced across the hay meadows to the bridge and then into the corral. I pulled the saddle and bridle off him, dropping it to the ground. Running up to the house I found it cold, with the fires out—the boys had gone someplace. Stripping off my wet clothes I climbed into the tub for a warm bath but only got a trickle of water, not even enough to wash the sand from between my toes, as the tank was dry. There was some swearing as I then had to dress, start the fire and go pump water, when all I wanted was to warm up.

In the winter after Jon had quit school he came back from Vanderhoof driving his Volkswagen with bald tires. He drove right into the ranch, even with the poorly ploughed road, and managed to make it. Of course that car was much like the motorbikes and snow machines, always sputtering, missing and backfiring. One evening it was parked two feet from the back porch, while Jon was working on the motor. Marlin Chantyman, an Indian lad from Kluskus, was with us at the time and was helping Jon. I was again preparing supper. By this time I had the diesel generator, thanks to the generosity of the McNoltys, so we had lights, and we'd had running water for a few years. As I worked at the counter in the kitchen Marlin appeared in the doorway to the back room, leaning against the door jam, and quietly told me something. I didn't catch what he said so I asked him to repeat it. Still quietly, he repeated, "Car's on fire." I looked up, and then saw the reflection of flames on the back window. I grabbed a pail, filling it with water from the kitchen tap as fast as I could, then ran out the back door to the flaming motor. Throwing the water onto the flames, I put the fire out. In spite of the fire, Jon managed to get the car running and later on took it onto the river, which was frozen. There was very little snow on the ice—it was a nice smooth roadway with lots of curves. While passing under the bridge he broke through several layers of ice, causing me great anxiety to the point that I thought I might have a heart attack. I'm not sure how he managed to get it out of there but he assured me he would be all right.

When the Volkswagen finally died a slow death and refused to run anymore the twins would drag it to the edge of the rock outcropping just west of the house with the tractor. One would get into it and put a helmet and a seat belt on, and the other twin would push the vehicle over the edge with the hay prong on the three-point hitch of the tractor. The Volkswagen would bounce down the short incline, and once in awhile roll over. This, they told me, was so they could experience what it was like to go through a wreck. The poor old bug was finally taken to the dump where it could rest in peace; it still remains there today, minus a lot of parts.

It seemed things were always catching on fire behind the house. Once, James had taken my dirt bike out to do something and when he came back he parked it in the woodshed and nothing more was thought about it. Joe had come over and we were having tea when Joe noticed smoke drifting across the yard. We went out to discover the bike on fire in the woodshed, and some of the woodpiles were beginning to burn. James ran and got a lariat and managed to get

*Vehicles always seemed to be catching on fire behind the house—we saved the woodshed but my dirt bike wasn't so lucky.*

a loop over the handlebars of the bike—we were able to drag it out, away from the wood. Several pails of water dampened the wood enough to let us throw the smouldering pieces away from the rest. It was lucky we saved the woodshed but the bike was left with only a metal frame, it had burnt so fast and so hot. The only thing we could think of was that some wires must have shorted out.

The twins got a brainwave one day and strung a rope across

the river from a tree on the hill to a post on the south bank of the river. They had attached to the rope a couple of pulleys. They would take turns climbing up the tree, taking hold of the hooks on the pulleys and kicking free of the tree. The pulleys raced them down the rope, over the hill, across the fence and over the river to slam into the post on the other side. Jon was very upset that I would let his brothers do that: the water in the river was quite high and neither one could swim. He was afraid they might drown. There were days that I did not have enough energy left to protest the shenanigans of the boys. I could only pray that they would survive their activities.

At the age they were by then, the boys were old enough to use big rifles. One time, when there had been a black bear hanging around, they wanted to hunt it and kept bugging me to let them go after the bear. I thought they probably wouldn't find it anyway so I finally told them to go ahead. There was another lad staying with us at the time, so the four of them set off, armed with rifles and all the ammo they could find. I decided to wash my hair and had just gotten my head all lathered up with shampoo when I heard gunfire close by. I ran out onto the porch and heard the boys yelling and shooting just west of the house. With all the yelling I thought the bear had attacked them so I ran for the truck with shampoo dripping down my neck and running in my eyes. I took off in the direction the shooting was coming from. They had found the bear right on the road and scared it up a tree. Then the four of them had emptied their rifles, not only killing the bear but nearly cutting the tree down as well. They were very excited and laughing when I drove up with shampoo dripping from my hair, my eyes watering, and a look of panic on my face. They choired, "Oh, Mom! Stop worrying!"

One year, when the twins were about ten, they decided to build their own cabin behind the house, next to the woodshed. First, they would fell the trees with the chainsaw and haul them back to the building site with the tractor. All the logs were then peeled. It took them several years but they did complete the log cabin, which was about eighteen by twenty and had a porch out front and a couple of windows, one in the side and one in the back. They built close to the house, as they felt secure there I guess, but when they were teen-agers and came home with their friends, staying up half the night with their loud music, I wished they had built a lot farther from the house.

When the twins reached grade eight I was unable to teach them anymore. I had had very little education myself and it had been a struggle to get them that far. Jon had gone out to public school starting with grade eight and Wesley was the next to go, partway through grade seven, boarding with a family outside of Vanderhoof. They came back home for the summer when school was out. In September both the twins went out to school and boarded together with a family in a rural area, catching the school bus to Vanderhoof. Then I was alone at the ranch, except for Joe up the road. I missed my boys so badly and looked forward to the times they came home. I had different people who came and helped me out over the years, especially through calving and haying—I had to have someone but

*Half built in this picture, this is the cabin that the twins constructed behind the main house.*

could not afford full-time help—and the kids came home as often as they could on holidays and for some weekends. I used to so look forward to the weekends when they came home with their friends. By then Jon had gone logging, but he was able to get home the occasional weekend as well.

I had a real nice Simmental bull back then, which I put out at the Home Ranch for the summer with cows. It was along in August that he disappeared. I looked for him for some time and one day found him in a patch of willows along a boggy swamp, where he had clearly been for awhile. His front ankle and leg were swollen to twice the original size and he was not putting any weight on them. I didn't want to tackle him myself and none of the kids were home at the time, so when I got home I called a neighbour, Jim Chadwell, who met me there the next day on his dirt bike. I had ridden saddle horse up there with ropes and a good dose of antibiotics. Jim got the bull out of the brush a bit, then scratched slowly along the bull's back until he got up to the shoulder. Picking up the swollen front foot he put it between his knees like a farrier would. Taking out his Leatherman knife, he slowly dug into the foot, removing a nail that was imbedded in the hoof and flesh. The bull didn't move the whole time, other than to gently shake his head whenever the horde of flies got into his eyes, nor did he move when we gave him a number of shots with the syringe. Four days later, when one of the boys was home, we went back and found that the bull had relocated to the banks of Pan Creek and the shade of a few trees. He was not nearly as docile but we were still able to catch him and tie him to a tree without much resistance, and give him another round of antibiotics. He never did completely recover. The ankle remained large and he had a bad limp but he did make it home to the ranch in October, just several days behind the main herd. And I got him to market—it was a very slow trip out to the loading chute, but I did get him there.

One August when Wesley was home we would hear the odd shot from a small rifle, more than likely a .22. At first we thought it was someone on the trail passing through, but several times the sound came from across the field and up in the timber, where there was no trail. We would take the bike and cross over to the edge of the timber and yell, asking who was there, but received no response. This had gone on for some time when a fellow came down on a quad from Eliguk Lake to visit. He said there were cattle grazing about at the drift fence west of the place and there had been someone walking among the cattle with a fishing pole. Rod watched him from the trail for some time, then called to him. The guy quickly slipped into the thick bushes, out of sight. Between this and the shooting about the place, we suspected that someone was camping in the area and did not want to see anyone, and was hunting grouse with a rifle. It would have been several weeks later that Wes and I came in late from the hayfields and I noticed a slip of paper on the radiophone with a strange phone number written on it. It was not my writing, and Wes confirmed it was not his writing, nor was it a phone number that either one of us knew. It was then I knew that whoever was about had been in the house when we were in the hayfield and had used the phone. I kept the number and checked the next phone bill. If he had reached his number it had been a collect call because no

*Linda, Rob, Melvin, Diana and Helen at Sleepy Hollow.*

charge showed up. We never heard anything else about the place after that day, so he must have left.

In the 1990s, the Mackenzie Trail Lodge and the Blackwater Lodge did a booming business, and a lot of that was fly-outs. Guests were flown to outlying lakes with a guide to fish for the day. At the peak of the season these fly-outs would start in the early hours while I was still sleeping, and at least one of them seemed to fly up the valley. The Beaver aircraft would come right over the house very low, the rumbling motor causing the windows to rattle. It would of course wake me up. I am not a morning person, so many mornings I got out of bed grumpy. After Bill died and the lodges changed hands, it was the end of the heavy air traffic. And eventually, both places closed. (In the wildfires of the summer of 2010 the Blackwater Lodge completely burned, leaving very little evidence that there had ever been a lodge and cabins on the site.)

One Labour Day weekend a bunch of people came out and we were enjoying a fun evening—we even moved the table back and danced, the first time in the house—when an early storm blew in. It was snowing, but that didn't bother us, as we knew it wouldn't amount to much. Near dark a float-equipped plane flew up the valley, quite low, its lights flashing, and there were some comments about the lateness of the hour and flying in the middle of a snowstorm. I said that those pilots flew all the time in bad weather and they knew where they were. A short time later the plane returned, again flying very low. We all rushed outside to watch, thinking it was attempting to land in the field even though it was on floats, but it continued down the valley and disappeared into the blowing, swirling snow. Nothing more was thought about it and the evening continued. The following morning I received a phone call asking if I had seen an aircraft the night before, as it had not made it back to home base. I reported that the plane had been headed east at dark. It was located a short time later north of the ranch on Adrian Lake. The pilot had gotten confused in the storm and crashed on the edge of the lake. The pilot and one passenger had been killed.

One passenger had survived the crash but was badly injured; he had gotten out of the plane and spent a very cold night under some trees.

The 1990s was when the cattle drives became what my father would have called the "annual picnic." As many as a dozen friends would come out with their horses from Vanderhoof several days ahead of the drive date to help bring the cattle home, or if the cattle were all off the range they would come out to just ride. These were great times, spent with good friends, a lot of laughs and good food. I always shipped cattle on the Thanksgiving long weekend, and generally the weather was good. We would drive on the Thursday, taking all day to move the cattle the fourteen miles to the corrals at 157 km on the Kluskus Road. People driving pickup trucks, including mine, would follow behind the cattle. Every cow whose calf was going to market was driven to 157 km. Earlier drives had been harder, with the cows not wanting to leave home in the fall, but by this time they were used to the annual drive. They would actually begin to trot as we neared the corrals, as it meant feed and water and a chance to lie down.

On one of these drives I was riding a four-year-old mare that was doing very well. We were in the timber after a stray when she jumped a large log that lay on the ground among the standing pine and spruce trees and landed on an old, fairly rotten raincoat that must have been lost years before, probably on an earlier drive. It was bunched up on the ground half covered with leaves and pine needles. As the saying goes, all hell broke loose when she landed on the jacket with both front feet. I was caught off guard as the mare turned inside out, leaving me on the mossy ground, then raced off down through all the cattle, scattering cows and riders in every direction. People were yelling at the cows and the horse, and asking what happened. I wasn't harmed but I was always a little red-faced when I lost my seat. For a long time after, the mare was quite skittish when she couldn't see well in front of her, and terrified of anything plastic.

A big camp would be set up at the corrals and chute and Clifford Irving always barbecued steak, making a great dinner. There were many laughs through the evenings, and if we were lucky it would be fairly warm—but most times frost covered the ground and the water pails would have an inch or so of ice by morning. As the evening progressed we'd make the campfire bigger and put coats on. It was hunting season, so hunters would be driving up and down the forestry road and some would stop to visit and share a drink. This applied to the loggers working in the area as well. For a couple of years friends came out from Prince George with their musical instruments and played music for us at our end-of-the-trail barbecue. The first year they didn't get my directions right and were lost part of the day and got into the Yukon Jack a bit early, so they had a head start on us before they arrived. They were later sitting side by side on a log, playing and singing, when the lady fell over backwards off the log and lay on the ground. Her partner hardly glanced at her and kept playing. When he finished his number he remarked that the Yukon Jack must have gotten to her, and went right into his next song. The following morning we sorted cows, loaded the cattle liner and broke camp without any movement from their tent. I picked up the bottle of Yukon Jack off the ground, which was still about a quarter full, and set it on the log fence by their tent. The next cattle drive, the following year, it was still sitting there. The amber liquid had bleached out from the sun.

As pre-arranged, the cattle liner would always arrive early Friday morning. The calves would then be separated from their mothers and loaded into the liner for their ride to market. The cows would be turned loose to wander about bawling for their calves for several days, and then they would return home. Sometimes the trucker would arrive in the middle of the night and park by the camp and go to bed in his sleeper till daylight while we all lay in our sleeping bags and listened to the diesel motor vibrating its sounds out through the quiet night. It was pretty well the end of one's sleep when that happened. Once I had two replacement bulls come out on the truck. You cannot imagine how much noise two animals can make in a trailer, on a cool, quiet night, over the throbbing of a diesel motor. One of my more outspoken friends got up in the middle of the night and woke up one driver, and told him rather rudely to move the blank, blank truck down the road.

I had been alone a couple years when I met Ron Bryant from Soda Creek, south of Quesnel. We had a lot in common as he ranched there. We took turns going from one ranch to the other to visit and do things together. In 1995 Ron and the boys improved the road into the ranch a great deal with Ron's small crawler and his 931 loader. Matter of fact it was good enough by November 14 that Ron drove his logging truck in to the ranch. History had been made: it was the first logging truck on the Blackwater. The boys came home for the long weekend as well, with their friend Chris, and Rob and Linda came over and joined us for supper. The following day Ron and the boys fell trees and loaded the truck with a load of logs. Bright and early the next morning they all left for town. I always had an empty, lonely feeling when the boys left, but I knew they had to go to school. There was not much for teenage boys to do on an isolated ranch other than work, and they did that every time they came home.

Ron bought the Home Ranch two years later and that fall he had a bridge put in at the Lamperts' place in order to move equipment into the ranch. Going through the Lamperts' was the shortest route to the Home Ranch from the main road. But a few months after the bridge was put in, before he even got the chance to use it, Ron died in a tragic accident.

# CHAPTER 17

# Riding in the Itcha Mountains

One fall, friends and I decided to do the mountain trip, not so much to hunt but to get out and ride and camp, and see the Itcha Mountains. I had lived in the Blackwater area all my life but had never really spent much time in the Itchas; the guiding I did was mostly in the Ilgachuz Mountains. Barry had usually gone up to the Itchas every year with friends, and quite often took the boys along. Chester John from Stoney Creek had worked for me that summer haying, and wanted to go as well as he had never been there. Five other friends came out from Vanderhoof with their horses. One of them had spent quite a bit of time in the Itcha Mountains so at least we had one person who knew where we were going.

We left late the first day with my team, Andy and Maude, pulling the wagon with all our gear. We planned on only going as far as the Home Ranch and camping for the night. Two others, John and Billy from Vanderhoof, would catch up to us there with their horses. Once at the Home Ranch I needed to run the bunch of horses in and catch one for Chester to ride. My saddle horse was tied behind the wagon and Chester rode on the wagon with me. When we reached the Home Ranch we made camp by the old cabin near Pan Creek. I then ran the loose bunch of horses into the tumbled-down corrals and caught a buckskin mare. I wouldn't have worried about shoes

*Riding in my favourite spot in the Itchas.* SHEENA MARTINEZ

*Maude and Andy hooked to the wagon.*

for a week of riding if it had been around home, but the mountains are very rocky, so I had brought shoeing equipment with me. While the others organized camp, I shod the mare. The front feet were no problem but she did not want me handling her hind feet. After a considerable length of time messing with her, I tied up one hind leg. This she objected to, and she started backing up, trying to get her foot free. I let her go and as she gathered speed I could see that bad things were about to happen—to Clifford and Linda Irving's dome tent set up on the creek bank, for one. Fortunately none of their belongings had been put in the tent yet. The mare hit the tent with her rear end, taking it with her as she flipped upside down into the creek. She thrashed about in the water getting her three legs under her, and the tent popped up and started to float downstream. One of the guys leapt into the creek and caught the tent, while I jumped into the cold water and untied the mare's leg so she could scramble up the bank. I, of course, found it all hilarious and laughed my head off. I am not sure that the rest found it so funny. From then on the

*Refusing to be shod, the buckskin mare tumbled into Pan Creek—bringing a tent with her. Here, I am untying her leg so that she can climb out.*

mare decided it was probably best to tolerate the shoeing and things went much better.

The only other excitement was when one of the horses was tied to a spruce branch and kept pulling on the branch till it broke off the tree. The horse raced around with the large branch dragging on a short halter shank, spooking the other hobbled horses, which ran every direction and nearly flattened the camp. But once the branch was removed, calm was restored, and a beautiful warm evening followed. Unfortunately it was warm enough for mosquitoes and blackflies to be biting—as we wore t-shirts—till the sun dropped behind the mountains and the cool night air reminded us it was late September.

The next day was another extra warm one as we travelled up that rocky trail and over the top, camping just on the Anahim Lake side at what is known as Burnt Cook Camp. The camp got its name a few years before, when Barry went up there with Wesley, John Dunn and several others and met Dean and Winnie Phillips there, and a blonde lady whose name may have been Melanie. On one of the mornings, because John was going to stay in camp, Winnie put a caribou roast in the Dutch oven and set it near the fire to slowly cook, telling John to watch it, and to add water if it began to dry out. Then everyone began to saddle up for a day of riding in the high country. Melanie then decided she too would stay in camp. Later on in the day, Melanie told John she was going to have a bath in the creek and asked John if he could see without his glasses; he said he could not. She then said he could take off his glasses and wash her back . . . well, then no one was minding the dinner and it burnt!

A white toilet seat had been brought along on our ride and this was set up on a log on a ridge out of sight from the camp, for everyone's use. Chester laughed and laughed, that a white man would actually pack a toilet seat into the mountains. We had set up a really nice camp and were very comfortable. It was on this trip that I was given the name "Blackwater Hattie," but I can't remember why. Each night we tied the horses in camp. During one night we had a problem with a bull moose that kept coming into camp, spooking the horses with his grunting and presence. The guys finally had to get up, and only then he left.

On reaching timberline above Burnt Cook Camp we could look west onto the Ilgachuz Mountains, and see all the country towards Anahim Lake. To look out over so much country while being on the ground always gives me a feeling of wonder, to see so much beauty in detail. Riding over another hill we were able to look north out over the Blackwater River basin and east towards Nazko. Another day, on another peak, we looked towards Anahim Lake and caught the reflection of the sun on a tin roof in the little settlement.

We rode most days in the high country, seeing small bunches of caribou here and there. About the third day we ran into a larger bunch, which had an older bull with an exceptionally nice rack. Ken, also from Vanderhoof, could not turn it down, so he shot it. The guys dressed it out and left the meat lying on some juniper boughs to cool off overnight. We returned the next day with Andy and Maude to pack the meat back to camp using pack saddles I had brought in the wagon. As we approached the site where the caribou had been killed the horses did a lot of snorting and were very

*A herd of caribou from across a lake in the Itchas.* BETH GARIEPY

nervous, smelling the scent of a grizzly that had circled the kill. The bear must have been right there in the scrub junipers somewhere, as the meat had not yet been touched—he must have arrived about the same time we did.

On another day we had ridden up a side canyon off of Smoke Valley and stopped for lunch. It was another very warm day. We hobbled our horses and lay in the rocks, enjoying the warmth, the company and the beauty of nature all around us. I climbed way up into the rocks to where I could see for miles and miles in all directions. I felt at peace with the world and close to God. I didn't want to go back down, but everyone else wanted to ride some more.

Down through Smoke Valley runs a well-trod trail, coming into the valley from the southeast end, following Shag Creek to the end of the valley, then turning up through the scrub pine to the east, continuing on to Itcha Flats. Back in 1966, Anahim Lake cattlemen had moved five hundred head of cattle onto the Itcha Flats (now referred to as the Plains of Abraham) in the Itcha Mountains. Tommy Holte, D'Arcy Christensen and George Gilson were supposed to have taken their cattle in the first year. Bob Cohen, John Brecknock and Monty Mooney were others on the drive, although Monty returned back to Anahim the second day. Al Elsie was the cook. Upon reaching Itcha Lake, they built a small cabin to accommodate a cowboy and a log pasture to hold his horses. Why the cattle were only taken there a short time—I believe it was four years—I don't know. I have heard it was because the flies were really bad, making the cattle drift too much, and another was that the BC Fish and Game Branch stopped cattle from grazing at that elevation because of wildlife habitat.

While riding above timberline the last day it was cool and windy; my lips were getting chapped and I had forgotten my ChapStick. I asked John if he had any. He said no, but handed me a container of Vicks, saying that was all he had. It wasn't really what I had in mind but decided it was better than nothing and I stuck my finger in the jar, and then rubbed some Vicks on my lips. I passed the jar back to John as we rode along, asking him why he carried Vicks. He said he had these hemorrhoids . . . Needless to say I never licked my lips!

We returned to the mountains again the following September but the weather was miserable, with a lot of rain and snow as well. Whereas there had been seven of us the first year, there were ten of us the next. I asked everyone to keep their personal effects light as the team could only pull so much.

I had lost my workhorse Andy in the summer, from what I believe was blood poisoning caused from something in his foot. I'd then bought from the neighbours a dapple-grey mare called Sadie. She had been used for logging but I wasn't sure she had had much time on the wagon. The first day we went beyond the Home Ranch to Tire Camp at the foot of the mountain. The last couple miles I asked Ron to ride ahead of the team to encourage Sadie to keep pulling, as she was very tired. It had been uphill all the way and I knew the wagon was badly overloaded. The second day was a short day, just up and over the highest pass on the trail. We didn't camp at Burnt Cook Camp but went down a mile or so farther to what is called Lynn Camp. It was named after Lynn Harrington, when she and Richard accompanied us with team and wagon to Anahim for

*Here's Sadie and Maude and me going to the Itcha Mountains.*

the rodeo in July of 1960. My dad liked to name things after ladies as they were always thrilled, and he would beam with pleasure. We had more horses with us that year, and Lynn Camp had more horse feed. On the steepest grade downhill the mares were holding back the best that they could and the wagon was still pushing them. Maude stumbled on a rock and I thought she was going to lose her footing and fall but fortunately she caught herself. If she had fallen it would have been an awful wreck, as one horse alone would not have held the overloaded wagon on that very steep rocky grade.

When the wagon was totally unloaded I could see why the mares were having a hard time. There were camp chairs, a table, propane lights and propane tanks, and a small heater for the tent (which came in very handy on cold, rainy days, I have to admit, while we sat around playing cards). And of course the food was unbelievable. We even had all kinds of appetizers, and plenty of refreshments. There was a lot of cribbage played as the rain beat down on the tents and the horses turned their rumps to the cold driving rain. The only things out and about were the ravens, squawking as they flew overhead.

Two fellows from Victoria wanted caribou and on one nice day we did get out to hunt. As we glassed the mountains from a ridge at timberline looking for movement I commented that there was something white on an open hillside above timberline several miles away. I said it was an old bull caribou lying in the sun. (Younger caribou would be darker and not show up at that distance.) Nobody would believe me, saying it was nothing but a white rock! We rode most of the day and late in the afternoon on the way home we did run into a herd of caribou with some trophy heads. The herd ran down a draw with the guys in hot pursuit. I followed behind and gathered up the abandoned saddle horses tied to scrub trees. When the herd vanished some of the guys circled back up a different draw to get their horses and found them gone. Then the yelling and swearing began, their voices echoing off the rocky slopes of the mountain. Finally everyone got back in the saddle without a shot being fired. As we crossed the ridge on our way back to camp I glassed that slope again and that white rock had gotten up and walked away.

Back in 1970 when Dad had sold the Home Ranch, he had bought a small John Deere 1010 crawler and walked it all the way from Anahim Lake to Tsetzi Lake. While passing through Lynn Camp he had pushed up a mound of dirt just below the campsite for whatever reason. Now, twenty-five years later and covered with grass and weeds, this pile of dirt resembled a grave. For awhile I had some of my guests convinced it *was* a grave. We left the mountain after a week. It had not been the same trip as the year before, but it had still been a relaxing one. The weather doesn't always cooperate.

Nipper, a friend from Quesnel, came to the ranch with his dad in the fall for several years to hunt moose. Nipper had sometimes come to do hunting trips to the mountains, but this year they were just going to hunt from the ranch. I got them horses and they were getting ready to leave for a day of hunting. I had given James's horse, Too-good, to Nipper to ride, as he was a very relatable horse. Nipper always had a cigarette in his hand and he had one that day as he got on the horse. He did not swing his leg far enough and it went down under the gun scabbard against Too-good's flank. As Nipper tried to wiggle his leg free the motion must have tickled the horse, which caused him to take off. Nipper had hold of the reins but only at the very end. So there he was with both arms in the air, one trying to get some leverage on the reins and the other holding his cigarette, with the horse gathering speed. Of course it was a wreck looking for a place to happen. And it didn't take long. At a very rocky spot just out from the tack shed, Too-good changed course suddenly and Nipper lost his somewhat unstable seat, landing in the rock pile. I ran over to find him lying on his back, beating his heels into the ground to kill the pain, but still holding his cigarette. Between bouts of hysteric laughter I told him not to move, as his back might be broken. After some time he was able to get up but it was the end of that hunting trip.

Another fall a couple of guys came out and planned on spending awhile in the Itcha Mountains with their horses. As they were leaving my place, Bill had a problem with his horse and it went over backwards, landing on him. He was very fortunate not to have any broken bones but he was badly bruised and in a lot of pain. They returned to the house, where Bill lay on the couch. John tied the pack horse to a tree and went off hunting downriver. I was busy doing something when I noticed the pack horse had gotten tangled in the rope and was choking, with long wheezing gasps coming from him. I ran through the house and grabbed the butcher knife, explaining to Bill, who was still lying on the couch, what was happening as I ran out the back door. The horse at this point was fighting for breath and pawing the air. While I was trying to get the rope cut and not get hit by the flying hooves, Bill came stumbling out of the house to help me, groaning in pain. As he reached me he suddenly said, "I think I am going to faint." I told him to get back out of the way. He fell to the ground just as I managed to get the rope cut. The horse backed up, gasping for air. I turned to Bill, who was on his back in the dirt, uttering faint moans of pain, feebly trying to fend off the dog who was leaping all over him. And me without a camera!

# CHAPTER 18

# The Changing Seasons

I've always loved the rain, unless it was haying time. There is something comforting about going to sleep with the gentle fall of it. The peaceful sounds of the rain as it falls through the leaves and tree branches to hit the ground. The hushed beat of it on the roof. Almost like a lullaby. When it stops the air smells so clean and fresh and everything seems washed, like the earth has been bathed. The grass appears greener and the flowers brighter. The birds sing more after a rain. Even the thunderstorms I don't mind; the rumbling of thunder off in the distance, then lightning streaking across the dark sky. The wind rushing through tree branches is a pleasant sound at night, while I lie in bed waiting for sleep to come; it is nature's music.

Sometimes the rain continued till everything in Sleepy Hollow was soaked. Water ran in little rivets down the sloping ground, carrying pine needles, dirt and small pebbles, till it all formed a tiny dam and held a little water back; then the water would break loose and continue on again. I tried to stay indoors when it was really wet, to do housework and get caught up on stuff I had let go. But sometimes I just felt lazy and would lie back with a good book. On some rainy days I could be excused for just taking a day off.

In our area, it seemed that one day it was summer, then

*Our driveway was very discouraging for those who came to visit.*

*The pastures east of the building in spring flood.*

overnight fall arrived—the hot days were only a memory. The geese would return to the fields on their way back south, circling and calling as they left their V formation and slowly settled down onto the stubble fields. Thousands and thousands of sandhill cranes passed over on their migration south. Those large bunches never landed, flying very high, but the din of their cries could be heard. The green leaves quickly became yellow, then orange, a few slowly drifting to the ground. Then one day a strong wind stripped them from their branches, leaving the trees like bony skeletons. The days got so much shorter, and the crisp, cool mornings warned me that the warm days would soon be gone as well. Once the sun rose and warmed the earth, the frost would melt away and the days would be warm again—till an overcast day, with no warmth, and having to face the fact that winter was coming. That was the season I liked the least. The lack of daylight kept a person confined to the house. The long evening hours of darkness had to be passed, doing something. I'd have to watch the temperature closely, then. If it was dropping the wood heater had to be crammed full of wood for the night, to keep the house warm. On really cold nights the house creaked and groaned as the cold penetrated the logs. The trees outside cracked and popped as well, and if you were outside at the right time you could hear the booms coming from the different lakes, as the ice fractured from the cold. During a cold spell all the trees would be frozen, and then when a thaw came the frost would come out of the trees and there was a lovely smell from the spruce and poplar. I never noticed it so much with the pine trees, but the other two emitted very pleasant smells as they thawed.

When the river started to freeze, water holes had to be opened every day to allow the cattle to drink. I'd start at the shore, and as the ice got thicker the holes were moved farther out. Once I was sure the ice would hold cattle I'd use the chainsaw to cut a water hole out where there was a bit of a current or ripple, as it slowed down the freezing of the holes. I weaned the replacement heifers in November, putting them on feed. When the first snow came to stay, I would bring in the first calf heifers to feed as well, and move the other cows and bulls outside my property fence, onto the Indian reserve upriver from the house. There they would stay till the snow got too deep or crusted, or it turned really cold. They would come in when they wanted to be fed; usually it was around New Year's before I had to feed them. Once I went and got them January 17, as they did not appear at all interested in coming home. The reserve grew mostly thick slough grass, and the Indians never used it so I took advantage of it. This slough grass stayed green even after freezing, and provided excellent rustling for both horses and cows. When the snow came the cows would bunch up and work in a circle, digging the grass out of the snow. They would bed down in the heavy spruce where there was no or very little snow. In the morning they would come off the bed ground in single file to a sunny spot and stand in the sun, getting some warmth. Then they would go rustling. Joe or I would go up about noon and open up water holes on the river for them to drink from after they got full from rustling. As darkness came they would all line out again, one behind the other, to the timber.

The horses that I kept at home (the main bunch stayed year-round at the Home Ranch) I would move from one field to another. When the snow came I put them at the very east end of the place, in an area that was not used in summer. They rustled there till the cows came in to hay. Then I would move the horses up onto the reserve land for the rest of the winter. The horses knew when I showed up with the snow machine and a bucket of oats, giving some to each horse, that it was moving time. They would run in single file behind the snow machine, through a gate and into the next field.

In order to hold animals in the corrals and get water to them in the winter I had to build what I called a "water gap." Once the river ice had frozen solid enough in the fall to hold me safely, I cut holes in the ice and dropped posts into them. After they froze in I would build a fence using the posts, extending it out far enough to be in the main current of the river. Then I'd use the chainsaw to cut a water hole at the end of the gap and remove a panel of the corral fence, and there would be water for the winter. When the ice weakened

*A mare and her foal at the ranch.*

in the spring the fence rails would be removed and stacked on the riverbank for the next season. The posts I'd let go with the ice when it moved, as they were hard to get out.

February would more than likely be a windy month, and the wind would continue into March. The wind would come from the southwest down the valley, blowing the snow. If the snow was a bit crusted it was sometimes worse, as the strong wind would pick up the fine snow crystals and blow them. It would be a solid front of snow moving over the crust, rushing madly to wherever the wind ended. (I once saw a sandstorm in Arizona that made me think of that blowing snow.) I hated to go to the field when it was like that. The tractor trail would be drifted over and hard to follow, and when you got off the trail it was hard to get back on. Often it was better to just make a new trail. The cows were hesitant to come out of the shelter of the trees or up from the river, where they were sheltered by the riverbanks. Normally I fed on the fields but when the wind was like that it would just carry the hay across the crust, rolling it into miniature bales and carrying it away till it hung up on the bushes or whatever obstacle got in the way. So on those days I fed in the sloughs, which offered shelter from the wind. Or if it was really cold I would take the hay to the timber.

Sometime in February the days became warmer, the snow started to melt and the winds were warm. On these days the squirrels chattered endlessly and the chickadees chirped. The snow fleas hatched on the snow. The ravens seemed to be more active, flying about and calling and diving after each other. Mornings, the snow would have a crust. Then the squirrels would travel on top and run through the timber for farther distances, visiting other dens and chasing each other up and down the trees. The coyotes would pair up and travel about on the crust and become very vocal with their yapping. But the cold of winter was still never far away, and would often return.

The spring was always the nicest season, I thought. The days became longer and warmer, and the snow all melted. The new calves arrived, and more than likely a colt or two. The birds returned to sing and the water birds splashed on the ponds. The sandhill cranes were my favourite: when they returned I knew all danger of cold weather was past. The flies buzzed against the logs of the buildings warmed by the sun. Butterflies suddenly appeared, floating about on the gentle winds.

As soon as it was possible I would burn all the old grass. This made for better grazing, cut down on the mosquito population and helped limit the fire hazard. Once leaves came out it was too late to burn, as the bush was then too dry. I loved the smell of grass smoke. As a child I would ride with my father for long days while he burnt rangeland. Once the grass was good enough the cattle went to summer range, and there would be ten weeks before haying—time I would use to do some project that needed to be done. This was also the worst time for mosquitoes, and they could be bad! Evenings and overcast days were the worst. Once summer came and things dried out they would die down, but then I could look forward to the blackflies, and in July the horseflies came to torment the livestock. I would start to hay about the first of August. By then the hay was usually headed out and the weather was apt to be nice. I liked to mow hay. It was my favourite job in the summer, watching it fall behind the sickle bar and enjoying the smell of fresh-cut hay. As a child on the Home Ranch I would follow my dad for hours behind the horse-drawn mower, watching the hay fall.

It was always nice to wake on a winter morning and find the temperatures had risen during the night, offering a balmy morning. The chickadees would be singing outside. Then I'd want to go out and enjoy the daybreak. This one particular morning I was in my pyjamas with my coffee and decided to go outdoors. Slipping into my lined coveralls and felt packs I wandered outside into the warm air and the silence that surrounded the place. I then decided to take the snow machine and go for coffee at Rob's. An early morning run would be nice. You can imagine my embarrassment upon arriving at Rob's to discover when I kicked off my boots and coveralls that I was still in my pyjamas and bare feet, although if they hadn't had company, it wouldn't have mattered.

One fall I was fattening a cow to butcher, and because I was home alone Rob agreed to come and help me. It was November, but the weather that day was nice. We had a log tied about ten feet high between two trees close to the corrals to use for butchering, with a block and chain for pulling carcasses up. Rob arrived about noon wearing a long coat that nearly reached his ankles. I got a bucket of grain and the cow followed me out of the corral and to the trees, where I dumped the grain on the ground so she could be shot right where we wanted her. As she started to eat the grain Rob stepped around in front of her with his 30-30 for a good head shot. His coat flapped about his legs, and seeing that, the gentle cow threw up her head and bolted. She was loose in a five-acre pasture, which she ran all over like a wild deer before we got her cornered behind the barn and Rob managed a good shot. I still don't know what actually spooked her, but she transformed from a lazy, gentle cow into a wild animal. I then had to use the tractor to drag her carcass to the hanging area. We skinned and gutted her, then left the carcass hanging till the next day, to let the meat cool out before we quartered it. But during the night the temperature dropped to about thirty below. So now there was seven hundred pounds of rock-hard meat hanging there. The only way to cut it up was to use the chainsaw. After draining the chain oil out, the cow was cut up into quarters. It was the toughest meat you could imagine. I don't know if it was the quick freezing or her thirty minutes of running around the pasture.

James and Wesley both quit school in November 1995, the fall they turned sixteen. They went logging for the winter. Wesley was working in Vanderhoof and James in the Tatlayoko area. In the spring, when breakup came, James went to work for Sven Satre on his family's ranch in the Tatlayoko valley. In June, James and Sven were out looking for cattle. The area the cattle were in had a lot of underbrush and thick bush, which was hard to get through on horses. James went into it on foot with Sven's only rifle for protection, as there was a large population of bears in the area. Sven stuck to the more open country with a saddle horse. They were to meet at a rendezvous spot later in the afternoon for the ride back to the ranch. James arrived at the meeting place but Sven did not show up. James then started to look for Sven, becoming very concerned when he could not locate him. After several hours of looking he went for help.

Now young loggers, my sons James, Jon and Wesley return home at spring break-up.

With four other young men, Edward, Matt, Troy and Henry, James returned to the area and began to search again. At dark Sven's wife Denise became alarmed and went out to look for the overdue men, leaving her two young sons with a neighbour. She met up with the five searchers, who still had not located her husband, then went to the nearest phone to call for more help.

The young men spread out in the darkness, searching the underbrush with flashlights and calling loudly. Their calls were not answered, and the area remained dark and quiet. About midnight Sven's saddle horse was found, with the halter shank tied tightly to the horn of the saddle, which was on the ground with a broken cinch. More men arrived to help, backtracking and searching in vain. The search party then waited for the first little bit of light in the eastern sky before continuing — armed with more rifles, as by this point there was little doubt that the worst had happened.

They were just a few minutes off the main road when a black bear was spotted. The bear showed no fear till the party got close, and then he moved off. It had been guarding the partly eaten body of Sven. Several of the men waited there with their rifles and the bear returned within a few minutes, snarling, bristling and chomping its jaws. It was shot.

It was determined from the telltale tracks in the sandy soil of the trail that the bear had followed the horse and rider for at least half a mile, while Sven rode along cutting alder branches hanging over the trail with a small hatchet he carried on his saddle. The tracks then indicated that the bear and horse began running hard, with the bear claws digging into the ground and the horse's hooves gouging out dirt as it fled down the trail for a short distance, before veering off the trail. This was the spot where Sven's hat was found. The grass and brush was flattened down for some distance and the hatchet was also located there. It appeared that the search party had passed very near to the body and the bear several times during the dark hours, and the bear had moved farther from the trail each time.

Wesley and I drove to Tatlayoko to be with James and offer our support to the family. I had intended to stay with James in a mobile on the ranch where he lived with a couple of other young men but Denise insisted I stay in her home with her and her sons. I had the opportunity to get to know this very strong, caring and beautiful lady. She told me late one night while we talked that she loved her husband with all her heart, but if someone had to be killed it was better it had been Sven rather then James, because if it had been her son who was killed she never could have lived with it; a mother should never have to lose a child that way, and it *could have easily been my son!*

Denise felt it was important for people to know that the black bear that killed Sven was not undernourished. The necropsy showed it to be a healthy and normal animal. There was a lot of forage in the area, and an abundance of deer. This bear was not protecting a kill, or cubs. Rather, the bear had lost its fear of people and saw this man and horse as prey.

Denise returned to Australia with her children a year later, as she no longer felt safe raising her sons in Tatlayoko, with the increasing numbers of bears and cougars and the government's policy of maintaining predator populations to a maximum. Another reason for her leaving was that gun control was being introduced, limiting the availability of firearms, and she felt that people needed to be able to protect their families. Sven had wanted to buy another rifle but needed to take the FAC training in Williams Lake and had not found the time to do so, or he would have been packing one.

Wesley and I returned to Vanderhoof after Sven's service. James stayed on at the ranch for haying and to continue to help Denise and the boys through that terrible summer. He thought a great deal of Sven, and wanted to be there for his family.

For several summers Gordon McNolty brought one of his quarter horse studs out to the ranch. I had lots of pasture and lots of mares. Not that I needed any more horses—the number had reached about thirty-five—but it was a beautiful stud, so of course I took advantage. I bred several mares each time the stud was brought out. It didn't seem right when spring came not to have several mares in foal. While I was growing up on the ranch we always had a stud, and sometimes two, as my dad raised a lot of horses.

It was early one summer in the mid-nineties that a mining company moved down a logging road north of the ranch and began drilling. It shattered the silence of the wilderness, having the drill whining 24/7. One of the holes they drilled was less than a mile from the ranch. The drilling happened for a number of summers. To this day nothing has been done to develop a mine, but as far as I know there are still claims there and some work is done each summer.

In July of 1996, Linda Irving, Gail Kristensen and I drove down to Kamloops to see Armand and Beth Cordonier in Barnhartvale. Every summer, for many many years, Armand went up on the mountain range behind Shuswap Lake, on Scotch Creek. It had been his range back when he had ranched and now belonged to someone else, but Armand still did the summer riding there. We had been invited to go up with him to move the cattle from the valley bottoms to the high country. The heat was what got me, there. We would start riding at about four in the morning and by ten it was too hot for the horses. After lunch I would go with Armand on the quads, with the dogs on the back of the bikes, and we would take logging roads to high side hill areas where cattle would sometimes be found in the clearcuts. It was steep, logged-over country. Some of those roads scared me on a quad, and the thought of being in a loaded logging truck was even scarier. Armand said he gave me the bike with the best brakes, while the ones on the bike he rode were not good. Well, the bike I had did not have much for brakes at all, so his must not have had any! When we found cows that high up, the dogs would jump off the quad and herd the cows down off the mountainside while we followed slowly behind.

When Armand felt we had all the cattle, plans were made to move them up to the top of one of the mountains starting at first light the following morning. When the cows were finally on the alpine meadows, we sat in the grass and had a bite to eat, resting our horses, before starting back down.

One of the guys there had a stock dog, a border collie that he had spent a lot of money training. Near the alpine meadows we were on was an outcropping of rock with a canyon below that dropped down for about three hundred feet, not straight down, but it was fairly steep. Before having lunch the fellow rode his saddle horse over to look out over the canyon, and as he sat there his dog came at a full run and never slowed down, and sailed out over the cliff and disappeared. The man was feeling bad about the loss of his dog when it appeared on the rim, packing one leg and bleeding from the mouth, but alive. It hopped on three legs all the way down the mountain.

It was August of that year when I awoke in the morning to the mountains white with snow—it was time to start haying! But the early snowfall didn't last; several days later it had all disappeared. While it had been snowing in the mountains it had been raining at home, and we had a thunderstorm as well, with a lot of lightning. The cattle at the Home Ranch must have been crossing Pan Creek for shelter in the spruce on the west side of the creek when lightning struck the Charolais bull in midstream. Someone came by and told me the bull was dead in the creek, and I needed to get him out of the water before he contaminated people's drinking water downstream. Modern civilization was reaching the backcountry. I chose nature's way and left the bull there. Besides, how was I going to move a dead animal that weighed in the neighbourhood of 2,500 pounds? I wasn't about to drive the tractor seven miles on that rocky trail to do it. The next rainy day I took my dirt bike and went up to check cows, and then ran over to the creek. The bull was gone and on the opposite shore the willows were broken and there was a trail flattened through the grass into the thick spruce. On a muddy back channel on the creek, huge bear tracks were displayed in the mud. I quickly left; nature had taken care of the problem.

Wes came home for a few days in the summer and while he was there we had a huge windstorm, about noon one day. Wes and I were both in the house when it hit. It only lasted a few minutes—although it seemed a lot longer as the house shook, the windows rattled and trees fell. When it first hit Wes ran out the back door saying my truck was parked right in the path of the biggest tree in the yard. By the time he finished the sentence he was back inside saying the tree had fallen on the truck. When things were calm again we went out to survey the damage. The tree that landed across the hood of my truck was at least twenty inches through, a big pine for that area and the biggest one in the yard. The damage was extensive. Another tree had glanced off the hood of the tractor but fortunately only put a small dent in the top of the radiator and ripped off the grille. No leaks from the radiator. A tree had fallen parallel with Wes's truck. In back of the shop I had three snow machines lined up under a big spruce tree; a pine had fallen alongside of them but hadn't touched them. None of the buildings were hit but a lot of fences were and would have to be fixed. We got into Wes's truck and drove around to Joe's and the Carter place, to see what had happened, but other than fences things looked okay. The young couple in the old Carter place had company and were playing cards; they hadn't realized the wind was blowing, even though two huge poplar trees in the yard had fallen.

I called for a tow truck to take my truck to town. When the driver arrived the next day and I gave him coffee and lunch, he asked me not to tell his boss what kind of road he had driven on to get my truck. The only reason he had come that far off the beaten path was because he knew my boys and had always wanted to come to the ranch.

The rest of the summer was spent haying and whenever I was not haying, Joe and I were fixing fences. I certainly did not need the extra work, but what could I do? Wes had to go back to work but came out whenever he could to help bale hay.

Wesley was on his way home again in October with an old Honda car and said he would drive right in. I felt the road was not good enough for a car but he insisted, so I stayed home. But I thought he'd never make it, so I took my dirt bike out to see how he was doing. It was a good thing I met him on a straight stretch as he was just flying, with very little regard for the car. I think he said it took him something like twenty-eight minutes to get from 167 on the Kluskus to the ranch. At that time it was a record, and it may still be. For awhile, the boys, their friends and I had been trying for the best time. Generally the winter was the best for times, as the driveway, once ploughed, was in better shape than it was in the summer. My best time from town to the ranch was two hours and thirty-nine minutes, I think. Good conditions all the way and no logging trucks.

The Honda was like the Volkswagen—it never left the ranch either, as the drive in had left it with all kinds of ailments. It was driven around the ranch for awhile. At some point first and second gears vanished; starting in third was tricky. Wesley and I were going up the road in it for something once when Patch decided he wanted to come. He did not like riding in vehicles but was always excited when the boys were home, and would want to be included in everything. When we climbed in, he did too. Wesley had the motor just screaming to get going, and then we had to stop with a jerk at the gate. When I opened the door Patch shot out with his tail between his legs and ran back to the house. Enough of that!

At that time Wesley was logging in Vanderhoof and staying at a logging camp at 118 km on the Kluskus, so he came home fairly often, which was nice. James didn't make it home for Christmas of 1997—it was the first Christmas he'd missed, and it didn't seem right not to have all three of the boys home. The neighbours all got together at Rob and Linda's to welcome in the new year and thankfully the weather warmed some, as it had been down to minus forty-six between Christmas and New Year's.

Because the banks of the river in the valley were just sandy soil they were constantly washing away, and I think increase in the beaver population on the river, with them putting feed houses and living quarters in the riverbanks, encouraged it a great deal. That was what probably happened to the bridge abutment on the south side of the river: the soil washed away and the bridge began to sink. But I knew it had to be fixed before the next high water runoff or I would lose the bridge. With help from Rob and Joe, I had gotten enough logs to the bridge site to rebuild the support on the riverbank, but the whole bridge needed to be raised up in order to build it. Bill Cash from Prince George, who moved houses, came out with everything we needed. The ice was good and solid under the bridge so everything was set up there. Clifford and Ken came out from Vanderhoof to help and Rob of course was there. I can't remember everyone who was there but I know that I was very fortunate to have such good friends pitching in. We raised the bridge, rebuilt the abutment and lowered the bridge down on its new support. I never had another problem with the bridge.

Jon and Wesley came home the end of March as breakup was on and they thought I needed a holiday. I had a chance to go to Medford, Oregon, with Wayne Reavis to spend awhile with him and his wife, Jackie. They lived in the little town of Jacksonville, just a few miles out of Medford, in a beautiful old house. This little town had one of the first placer gold mines in the area; gold was discovered in 1851 or 1852. It also had the first Chinatown in Oregon. There was a lot of history there, and many neat old houses remained from its early days. Wayne and Jackie's yard was large, with a lot of shrubs, trees and flower beds. Because I was used to keeping busy I spent a lot of time in the yard, cleaning out the flower beds and trimming the shrubs and trees. One neighbour was visiting over the fence with Jackie and said she had had a conversation earlier in the day with Jackie's new gardener. We had a giggle over that. I also walked a lot and while on one of my long walks I encountered a couple of old gentlemen out for a stroll. We stopped and talked for some time and the conversation got around to the weather, which had been beautiful, but that afternoon a thin cloud layer covered the sky, although the sun could still be seen through it. Around the sun a faint ring of light could be seen as well. I remarked that a ring around the sun generally meant a storm was on the way. The old boys looked at each other, and then asked where I came from. I told them Canada. They said that a ring around the sun might mean rain in Canada, but it certainly didn't in Oregon! They looked at the sun for a long time, like people seeing something for the first time. I think they thought I was nuts. When I awoke in the morning it was raining. I took my walk down the same road, hoping to find those old gentlemen, but they must have chosen to stay dry.

Jon called one morning, a few days before I was to start home, to tell me there had been a bad storm with horrific winds and snow. The cattle had started running with the storm and had crossed the river in spite of the bad ice. Most had made it across but they were sure six cows had drowned when the ice gave way. They were still trying to sort out which ones and locate the young calves, and Wesley had gone into town to get milk replacer. I said that the red milk cow would calve soon and that would help. "Well, Mom," he said, "I have more bad news: she is one of the cows in the river." When I got home a week later, they had two calves on milk replacer, one had been put on another cow, one had gone to a neighbour's and the fifth had became an avid stealer and fared quite well.

# CHAPTER 19

# A Trip Down Under

Dave Chapman, who I had known for many years, had property in Port Bundaberg in Queensland, Australia, and had spent a number of winters there. In January of 1998 he bought me a plane ticket to go there. With the young couple living on the ranch in the old Carter house, and Joe to help, I had no excuse not to go. Joe moved into my house so the water system would not freeze up. I left the ranch on January 8 and drove to Prince George; leaving my truck there, I caught the bus to Abbotsford where my friend Susan picked me up. I stayed with her at her home in Deroche till I got my visa and passport. I probably would not have gone if it hadn't been for her, as she drove me about to get my paperwork done and then took me to the airport and went with me as far as she could. I was a bit of a bush bunny and was sure I would end up on the wrong plane or lost in the masses of people. But on January 16, I was on my first overseas flight.

The flight left about six p.m. and our first stop was Honolulu, at about midnight, where we arrived late due to the departure time being delayed and the strong headwinds we encountered over the Pacific. I sat between a couple from New Zealand and a couple from Tasmania. They were a lot of fun and interesting to talk to, so the time passed very quickly. Sean from New Zealand was a rugby player and a very big boy. The seats were too small for him so as soon as the seat belt sign went off he got up and sat on the floor just in front of us, as there was a divider right there, and space. The couple from Tasmania had two small children who promptly fell asleep, and they were put on the floor in front of us as well. The stewardess complained about it but neither parent paid any attention. The next stage of the trip was a flight from Honolulu to Sydney. I did sleep some but the seats were very uncomfortable. Watching the sunrise out the window was pretty spectacular. We were cruising at 35,000 feet and it was forty-two below.

Vancouver airport was so small compared to Sydney's. On landing, I was taken to a bus that delivered me over to the domestic airport and on to another flight that took me to Brisbane. By the time I landed there it was 11:15 a.m. It had been about seventeen hours since I left Vancouver, and I had four hours there before going on to Bundaberg. I felt so hot and so tired. I thought some fresh air would make me feel better so I went out a side door at the terminal. The heat hit me, and it was like a sauna. I could not go back in the door, as it was an emergency entrance only, so had to find my way around the building to the main doors. Fortunately there were benches placed along the building—probably for idiots like me, as I had to sit twice before I reached the main entrance, for fear of passing out from the heat. Once inside I went to a place that served drinks and was advertising milkshakes. I ordered a vanilla shake only to discover it was vanilla-flavoured milk. That was a real letdown.

The flight to Bundaberg took a little over an hour in a small aircraft. The trip was extremely rough, flying half the time with the nose down and through a lot of thick cloud. Pressure built up in my ears so much I had a painful earache. Landing at the small strip in Bundaberg made me realize for the first time I was in a foreign land. There were so many plants and trees that I had never even seen pictures of. The palm trees were the only ones I recognized. And then there were the birds, which I learned never cease to make noise, whether it is singing, squawking, crowing or calling; it goes on night and day.

Dave's place was about twelve miles away at Port Bundaberg, set up on a man-made hill and built of brick with lots of windows. The floor was concrete with a finish on it, and was very easy to keep clean. I learned to love that floor because you could see anything on it: bugs, ants, spiders, cockroaches—and apparently snakes, although none got in while I was there. I was told there was a carpet snake in the garage when I arrived, so I stayed away from that place!

Living in the tropics was certainly different from living on the Chilcotin Plateau. Keeping the ants and the cockroaches under control was a constant battle. You had to keep tabletops and countertops wiped clean and all containers sealed. And the mud wasps over there have a sting that is like an electric shock. One bit me, and it caused my whole leg to go numb. I also had the pleasure one day of meeting the huntsman spider that lived in the attic and supposedly ate poisonous spiders. He came crawling down the wall, a huge hairy-looking thing. Made me sit up and take notice! While I cowered in the corner, Dave took the broom and chased him back into the attic.

Little geckoes ran all over and quite often inside, if they found a crack. Reptiles are not my things, even that small. And there were snails everywhere but I was not aware of them till one came out of its shell by my foot. It had a fairly long body with antennas on its head. It moved away, slowly, packing its home with it. Little crabs are common as well. When you hear rustling in the leaves you freeze, expecting a snake, but it might be a little crab.

In the mornings I would walk with the Filipino lady from across the street, generally going down to the port. The paved road was bordered by high grass, and while we were walking one day a frill-neck lizard appeared at the edge of the grass, with his neck expanded and hissing. I nearly climbed up on that tiny lady's shoulders, it scared me so much. They were so ugly!

But of all the creepy crawly creatures in Queensland, I think the snakes were the worst. I was very concerned about the snakes, so for the first few days I would not go outside without boots and coveralls. I soon learned it was much too hot for that. Everyone kept the grass short around their houses as it discourages snakes if you eliminate their hiding places. The first thing I was told over there was do not step where you can't see and don't put your hands where you can't see. Australia has about 140 land snakes and about 32 sea snakes. Roughly 100 of these snakes are venomous, but only 12 are likely to kill you. The taipan is one of the deadliest, probably in the whole world. The king brown snake is the one that was very common in the area I was in, and it could kill you. We came home one day to find a king brown about four feet long on the patio. It got away before it could be killed. A neighbour lady stopped by one day and she and Dave were looking for red back spiders when she discovered a small king brown under the garbage can. She jumped up and down on it till she killed it. People told me stories of finding a king brown snake under their carpet, curled up on their coffee table and in their dryer. A lot of homes were built off the ground, and that stopped the snakes from coming inside. We went one day to a garden restaurant for lunch. There were beautiful gardens, walkways and ponds with ducks and turtles. I thought it would be a place where I could relax, till I discovered a snake curled around a planter not eight feet from our table, although I was told it was a tree snake and not poisonous.

One day I discovered that a green tree frog lived in the shower drain; apparently that was very common in homes there. It looked almost like it was made of plastic, as it was a very shiny green. When the water got too hot or soapy it was apt to leap onto your leg, using the suction cups on its feet to hold on. Dave had named him Kermit or something like that. When I showered, which was often in the heat, I would put a bowl over the frog, if he was in the shower stall; no frog was going to hang on my leg! Dave took him to the pond three times and he always came back.

Dave kept fish in his pond out back. The cane toads that are everywhere in Queensland were thick by the pond. At night, especially after a rain, their croaking would drown out the loudest of noises. Lots of birds spent time at the pond too, like doves, swallows, Willie Wagtails and many I didn't know the names of. In the fields there were wild hares, pheasants and sometimes kangaroos.

Dave also had a big white duck he had named Spud. He loved

to admire himself in the hubcaps of the car (or fight with himself, I am not sure). He would hiss and bob about in front of a hubcap. Dave put a mirror down by the pond so he divided his time between there and the car. Dave thought he'd been shorted in the brain department, and it could well be.

The most pleasant time of the day was early in the morning, sitting out on the patio with as little clothing on as possible. It was a little cooler in the mornings, as a breeze came in off the ocean and there were no bugs. The evenings there were nice too, but the bugs would be out. After dark it was beautiful: the stars were so bright, and there seemed to be so many more than in the northern hemisphere. You couldn't see the dipper there, but you'd see the Southern Cross.

Most of the time, the best clothing was a loose white cotton shirt and shorts or loose cotton dresses, worn with sandals, a hat and sunglasses. The T-shirts and cut-offs I had brought with me were too hot. My body was constantly covered with a film of sweat. You could burn there in about twenty minutes, and you could also dehydrate very fast. Once your body was overheated it was hard to cool down, so I had a lot of cold showers. While I was in Australia there were places the temperatures reached forty-five degrees and cattle were dying from the heat.

And sometimes the wind howled there like you see in old western movies: when the big storm comes in, and everyone huddles around a small campfire clutching their tin coffee cups and sitting back on their spurs. If I let my mind wander while the wind howled I could have dreamt up tumbleweed blowing by.

Often in the evenings we drove to Bugara, a short distance away, and walked in the breakers. The spray felt good and cooled us down. There was no swimming there as sharks fed close to shore in the evenings. Another nearby place we used to go to was Elliotts Heads, to walk on the beach. If the locals didn't go in the water, we wouldn't either.

I was in Australia two weeks before it rained. Then the humidity was so bad that my glasses kept steaming up. January 26 was Australia Day, and the following morning the kids went back to school after summer vacation.

But that kind of a climate has its plusses, too. For the first time in my life I grew beautiful fingernails; when I got home I was asked if they were artificial. And I needed to get my hair cut every couple of weeks over there. There were many flowering trees and shrubs; I was told they were not at their best because of the drought, but still, they were beautiful. I really can't remember seeing a flower garden where there were just flowers, not shrubs and trees. Bundaberg was cane country and there were miles and miles of cane fields, but crops were poor, again due to the lack of rain, and some were being ploughed under.

One type of vine there grows very rapidly. As it grows, it wraps itself around the nearest tree, going around and around all the way to the top. More vines grow from it and over many years the vine kills the tree, which rots and over time disappears, leaving a very interesting looking tangle of twisted wood extending high in the air, with enough growth for the vine to now support itself.

I visited a banana grove one day to see how they grew. The trees were eight to twelve feet high with a cluster of bananas at the top. Along the trunk of each tree near the bottom was a new shoot, called a sucker. The ones in this grove varied but most of the suckers were about three feet high. When the bananas were ready to harvest the tree would be cut down to about two feet off the ground, and then all the goodness in the trunk would go to the sucker, which would grow up to produce the next cluster of bananas. The best banana I have ever eaten was fresh off the tree. Mangoes were in season, so we ate lots of them. At first I didn't like them but in time I did develop a taste for them.

As far as food went, you could get the same things in Australia as here, but they were different. Like a hamburger: over there it was a bun with a meat patty, a slice of pineapple and a slice of beet. It took some getting used too. And the coffee was so strong it would curl your hair, so I only drank what we made at the house. The fish and chips were excellent, though, and I enjoyed the best corn I've ever eaten—so sweet! The chicken was very good too. But I could not get a salad to save my soul. When I would ask for one they wanted me to tell them what to put in it, and even then I usually got mostly beet and pineapple anyway, with a wilted piece of lettuce. We quite often went to a nearby pub for lunch; they served very good roast beef and fried chicken, but the temperatures were so hot I found it hard to eat a big hot meal.

I only knew two people in Australia and found one, Denise Satre, who had returned to Australia after Sven's death and lived about three hours away in Tanawha. In a country so big it was hard to believe I was lucky enough to find her so close. We went to Tanawha to see her. She had told her boys that James's mother was coming to visit. And Zak wanted to know why I didn't bring James with me. He remembered James from Tatlayoko, when James worked on their ranch. The youngest son cried because I had not brought James with me. A few weeks later Denise came to Port Bundaberg with the boys for a weekend. The boys went through the house looking for James and the youngest cried again, when James was not there.

I had never really been able to swim, but Denise taught me how to float and swim and even snorkel when she visited. The water there was so nice, and the tropical fish were beautiful. It was hard to believe there were so many colours, sizes and shapes, and I only saw a few.

At the port right beside Dave's place, sugar was loaded into huge ships from all over the world. They loaded twenty-four hours a day, and there were always ships at anchor out in the bay, waiting to be loaded. The warehouse was so large it covered acres, and I was told that they moved the raw sugar with large Caterpillars, onto conveyer belts that carried it out to the ships' holds.

One time Dave took me to where they held cattle sales a short distance from his place. Quite primitive! The cattle were in pens with an alleyway running alongside of the pens, where the buyers gathered and moved from pen to pen, as the auctioneer stood on a walkway above the pens and auctioned the cattle off. Each pen held one owner's cattle. The animals were not sorted or weighed before sale, and their sex was determined by the colour of paint spray on their back. You could buy one animal, or all of the same sex; then they'd move on. The cattle were weighed after the sale was over. At the scales, the number of each lot, the weight, the price and the buyer would be announced over the PA system. Of the cattle sold there, most were a breed called a Droughtmaster, but there were straight Brahmas and Brahma Hereford crosses as well. The animals were all very thin and very cheap, but then, this was only a small sale yard selling local cattle. I did see more beefy looking cattle in other areas, like Hereford and Angus. Never did see a black cow, not that they didn't have them. There were also a few Holstein cattle around the area, but they are called Friesians over there.

While out for a drive one day down a country road lined with gum trees and tall yellowish grass waving in the wind, we came across a small arena where several people were working with some horses. We stopped, and just like in British Columbia everyone away from the towns and cities was friendly. I was talking to one fellow who asked where I was from. When I told him BC, he said he had spent eight years there training horses. I asked him where and he said, "Oh, a little town you probably never heard of, called Deroche." We had a laugh when I told him that I had just spent a week in Deroche and until I got there I'd never heard of it either.

The country roads there were paved only wide enough for one vehicle. When another was met the outside tire of both vehicles would drive out into the gravel or grass. And everyone drove on the left-hand side, which confused the hell out of me, and intersections were usually circles—any vehicle already in the circle would have the right of way. Pickups there were called "utes." The ones I saw didn't have regular pickup boxes like we have but what is called a tray box, a flat deck with steel sides about twelve inches high with a grate over the back window. The majority were Toyotas. It was rare to see a Ford or a Dodge.

At the beginning of February we went on a walkabout, which is when you go out on a trip travelling some distance away from home. We travelled past miles and miles of cane fields, all the way to the little town of Childers. The streets were very wide there, with cars parked on each side and down the middle of the street as well. The soil was very red all along the roadway and in any bare patches of fields or schoolyards. This seemed to be more like cattle country, with a lot of horses (brumbies), ponies and donkeys, and even a one-humped camel. Farther on past Biggenden we saw a lot of cornfields but the ground was much rockier, with piles of rocks in the fields. At Ban Ban Springs we stopped to shower in the public showers. This was where the tribes of Aborigines gathered for many years; it is now considered sacred ground. Around Kingaroy, the peanut capital of Australia, there were peanut fields as far as you could see. I had always thought peanuts grew on trees, but they grow underground, much like potatoes. There were many fields of sunflowers as well.

The Bunya Mountains, which rise out of the flat country, would not by any means be considered mountains here, but I guess in Australia, which is pretty flat, they are mountains. It was beautiful country. There were huge bunya pines with acorns the size of basketballs, and apparently edible. The Aborigines used to climb the huge trees, cutting toeholds as they climbed, to reach the acorns and knock them from the trees. (Once they fall on their own they are no

*On holiday in Queensland, Australia, feeding the birds.*

longer good to eat.) On some of the really old trees, these cuts are still visible.

We rented a house in what I think was called the Bunya Mountain Rainforest Estates, behind locked gates. It was a beautiful house, with a veranda around three sides, kitchen, living room and bathroom, with one bedroom on the ground floor and two bedrooms upstairs. It had hardwood floors throughout. The grounds were well cared for, with a lot of trees and shrubs. There were about thirty homes there already and more were being built. A lot of colourful birds were about, including wild turkeys, and wallabies everywhere—hundreds of them. When they were not lying under the houses, which were all built off the ground, they were eating, many with babies in their pouches. And there was a lot of fighting with hind feet when their space was trespassed on.

Leaving the Bunya Mountains, we were back to the gentle rolling hills and the gum trees. Other than the bunya pine, I think the gum tree is the only kind of tree I saw. They even withstand wildfires, which leave them black and charred, but they return to green the next season. We then drove through the Darling Downs, beautiful farm country with very rich-looking soil and crops of corn, cotton, sunflowers and sorghum. The lack of rain showed, as some of the crops were poor and wilted-looking. We passed through many small towns where nothing ever changes—not even the population, I was told, because when a girl gets pregnant a boy leaves town.

Then we reached the Gold Coast . . . surfers' paradise. White sandy beaches, with turquoise water as clear as clear can be. High-rise hotels and apartments along the beaches, stretching as far the eye can see. There were large crowds of people, and there was heavy traffic. We stayed in a backpacker hostel. A lot of Asian people worked in the shops and sat outdoors along the streets. I visited with a man from Cambodia who had come to Australia sixteen years earlier with his brother, after the civil war in Cambodia in which three and a half million people were killed, including his parents, ten brothers and three sisters.

The Gold Coast was one of the most beautiful places I had ever been, but the crowds of people were too much and I was glad when we left.

On the return trip we spent a day in Sydney, a city with about three million people at the time, with endless harbours and rolling hills. We rode around on the ferries to different areas. I would have been totally lost but Dave knew his way around. It was somewhat cooler in Sydney and I slept with a blanket for the first time in six weeks and put on a pair of jeans.

I am grateful to Dave for giving me the opportunity to see what I did of Australia. If I had been a young person I probably would have wanted to stay and see more of that country, but I missed my boys and the ranch, so it was time to go home.

*Enjoying the beach in Queensland, a far cry from BC.*

# CHAPTER 20

# The Good with the Bad

I arrived back home March 5. I had been gone eight weeks; it was the longest I had ever been away from the ranch. It was good to be home and everything seemed to be in good shape. Within a couple days of my return to the ranch I went to check on the horses that were rustling around the Home Ranch. Dick Taylor from Washington state, who was looking after Rob and Linda's place while they were in Thailand, came with me. We located the horses and discovered Baldie was missing from the bunch. Baldie had always been a special horse and a truly good one, one of the best workhorses anyone could ask for. He no doubt had his mother's genes, as she too had been an excellent horse. His breeding was mostly Clyde but he had some mixed blood as well. By this time Baldie had been retired for probably ten years and left to run out with the loose horses, as horses should be allowed to do. We had snow machines and back-tracked on the horses' rustling, following the trails in between the rustled areas and ending up at Sill Meadow, a hay meadow we used when we lived on the Home Ranch. On the west side of the hay land was a very large swamp and out towards the middle was a spring that overflowed in the winter. With the overflow and freezing it built up a small ice hill in the middle of the swamp.

I noticed the ravens as soon as we drove out on the swamp—that was where Baldie had chosen to die, up on the ice hill. It seemed to me an odd place for a horse to go. All three mountain ranges could be clearly seen, as well as the Naglico Hills to the north, but I hardly think an old range horse was looking for a view when he decided to die. But you can never know what goes through an animal's mind at a time like that. He had to have been about thirty years old, and probably enjoyed a good horse life. We had always treated him well and he had had the life horses were meant to have, living with the seasons in natural surroundings and dying the same way. I could not help but shed some tears, with Dick awkwardly patting my shoulder. It was like losing an old friend. He had pulled the wagon many miles over the rock-and-mud terrain, and had probably travelled every wagon trail in the area at least once, sometimes with teammates who had shirked their job, so he had pulled their share as well.

In the spring I usually worked with some young horse and rode it while checking cows in the field. The Lampert kids had started quite a few in the past number of years but they were grown and gone off like my boys, so there was no one around to do that now. I had brought in a four-year-old paint gelding that belonged to Jon to work with. After several days of ground work in the corral and riding him in the corral he seemed to be quiet and sensible, so I took him out in the small pasture. I rode him there several times but I was busy with other things so I did not have all that much time. He had tried to get his head and run once, but settled down and seemed to forget about it. Several days later I had some sick calves in the field and the bike refused to start so I saddled up the paint, tied the stuff I needed for the calves to the saddle and climbed on, riding up the field to where the cattle were. He went really well, and stood quietly while I caught and doctored calves. On the way home he kept trying to run and if he could have gotten his head I believe he would have bucked, but he did have a very soft mouth so I was able to hold him. Then I did some thinking. Here I was not exactly a young woman anymore, out in gumboots riding a green horse, all alone and no one knowing where I was. Had I gotten hurt, how long would it have been before someone came looking for me? I turned the young gelding out the next day and got in my well-broke one to ride.

Joe was very good at helping fix fences, digging postholes and doing chores while I was away, but he didn't really want to run machinery so I had to look for someone to help hay when haying season came. I was able to find a fellow who came out. He also liked to ride so when we couldn't hay he spent his time riding about. But he had a habit of smoking a little too much pot sometimes, and it interfered with his work. We were in the field one day, and I was raking the windrows of hay together while he baled. We would pass one another a short distance apart every once in awhile. I noticed at one point that he seemed to be flopping about in the tractor seat. Stopping my tractor I watched him going down the windrow, his body swaying from one side to the other to the point I thought he might fall off the tractor. The irrigation ditch was coming up and the baler was nearly ready to dump. I wondered if he had it together enough to know what was happening. He did turn the tractor at the end of the windrow before driving into the ditch, and then dumped the bale and continued on. I just shook my head and avoided watching him after that because my stress level rose badly.

Coby Mero from Quesnel, a young fellow my sons' age, came out for a few weeks and rode some horses for me, including the paint. When most of the hay was in, Coby and I decided to ride down to Lower Euchiniko Lake. I took my buckskin gelding and Coby took the paint and another four-year-old mare, riding one and packing the other. Because they were young he took turns switching between them. Leaving late the first day we only went to the Chadwells'. The next day we rode down the old wagon road towards Kluskus. We passed Antoine Baptiste's place, where no one had lived for years. The main house had burnt down but there were still remains of the foundation. Small sheds stood scattered about the building site, but they were in a sad state and the home of pack rats. Down the creek from the old building site a cabin had been built within the last fifteen years, but it looked to have been unused for some time.

From there on we began to pass old trucks on the side of the trail. Some had been stripped of tires, others had hoods up or doors left open and still others had been burnt. Several had been rolled down small inclines along the trail. We also passed snow machines that had quit along the trail and been left behind, some with seats torn open, skis and headlights missing. We even saw a chainsaw that must have fallen out of a truck or off a snow machine. None of this litter had been there the last time I went this way. It did not improve the look of the wilderness countryside, and it continued for as long as we travelled along that trail. We reached Kluskus Village a couple of hours after passing through Antoine's. The Catholic church, which had probably been built in the 1920s, still had not seemed to age a

*Coby Mero, a young friend from Quesnel, on our trip to Lower Euchiniko Lake.*

great deal over the years. On the hillside to the west of the church was where most of the new log houses were built when the people returned to Kluskus, before most moved to Quesnel. The school built there had been used for only a few years; now the students went to school in Nazko or Quesnel. There was also a large recreation centre made of logs. A gravity-feed water system had been put in to supply the homes with water. Pickup trucks were parked here and there, although most looked like they did not run. Somewhere I could hear the throb of a large diesel generator, which I was later told ran 24/7. The place seemed abandoned—with the generator running someone had to be around, but we saw no one. For many years I had remembered Kluskus as a spot of wilderness beauty, but now with the rebuilding of the village with its modern homes and the broken-down trucks scattered about between the houses it had lost that pristine look. The generator chugged away and a mongrel dog up the hill barked at us as we slowly rode by. Other than the dog, there was no sign of life.

Passing out of sight of the buildings we followed the trail, now wider and badly rutted from 4 x 4s, through the heavy spruce and poplar timber up from the lake for about four miles, then crossed the wide, shallow creek at the end of Kluskus Lake, on a rather badly constructed pole bridge. The Alexander Mackenzie Trail turned left at the top of the hill after the bridge, and this would take us down to the Blackwater River. I had never before crossed at that crossing, which was referred to as Chantyman Crossing. The trail down to the river was very steep, and our horses slid part of the way down. Upon reaching the river, in the thick spruce that covered the south shore, we found the crossing was very wide and the water very dark, so it was hard to tell how deep it was. The shore had a lot of boulders and rocks. I wasn't interested in going into the river as I am afraid of water, but the young are much braver and Coby finally got the mare in the river. She argued a lot till she lost her footing on some rocks and fell in the water, and decided to cross. About halfway across, the water was nearly to the saddle skirts, but my buckskin was a lot taller so I followed. The pack horse was not that tall so the bottom of the pack got wet but at least the sleeping bags were on top.

The trail on the north side had not been used in some time. After climbing up the steep bank onto the shore we encountered a lot of windfall. Winding around through the thick spruce and poplar for some time we found a well-used trail and turned east. Some time later we came out at an old abandoned reserve known as Jerry Boyd's. This was where the Blackwater River drained into Lower Euchiniko Lake. There is another river crossing there at the mouth of the river, but it is very deep and has undertows. I remember crossing there once years before as a little girl, with my mom, Mickey Dorsey, my brother and four of Mickey's boys, on a return pack trip from Batnuni. We had used a raft to cross and swam the horses. The raft was now long gone, washed downstream or just rotted away, although there was a wooden boat turned upside down under the trees on the south side of the river.

The last time I had passed this way there had been fences and buildings standing at the old home site overlooking the lake, but the only thing that remained was the old log barn and it had settled into the ground over the years, the open doorway leaning at a odd angle, and most of the shakes had blown off the roof, leaving the wooden stringers bleached white from the sun. In a couple of places one could see evidence of the log fences that once ran behind the barn. We found where the cabin had been, which had burnt. There were pieces of rusted tin sticking out of the ground, from items that had been in the cabin, and small piles of dirt within the perimeter of the cabin, which were now covered with grass, indicated that it had had a sod roof. I could find no remains of the garden, although I could remember talk of the huge rhubarb that grew there.

As the sun neared the treeline we thought we'd better hurry up as it was still a good hour's ride to Dave and Maureen Harrington's, or Euchiniko Lakes Ranch as it was better known. Bunch and Oscar Trudeau had homesteaded there back in the early 1960s, I would guess. Bunch had lived there alone for many years after Oscar left, and when she moved to town her son Ted had lived there, operating it as fly-in fishing camp, and ran a guiding business too. The Harringtons had bought it a few years earlier and had built more guest cabins and a new lodge, and operated on a bigger scale.

We managed to get in before dark and put our horses in the pasture. I hobbled my buckskin, as I knew he would head home if there were any possible way. Being hobbled would put a damper on his looking for a way out. We laid over the following day and did very little. The second day Dave and Maureen lent us their quads so we drove downriver with Steve (Dave's brother, who arrived soon after us) to Pan Crossing on the Blackwater River and crossed there, the water being low enough to do so. We then went up to Pan Meadow. No one lived there anymore and the place showed signs of neglect. The fences were falling down and the buildings were sagging and home to a lot of pack rats. The last time I had been there was in 1970, when I drove my cows to Nazko.

Early the following morning we left for home, planning to do it in one day—a long one, as it was about forty miles back. My buckskin danced sideways for the first five miles, wanting his head to go home, before he settled into his fast walk. We retraced our steps near Chantyman Crossing, then continued upriver on a very good trail that petered out when we reached Church Crossing (another crossing that years ago came out behind the church at Kluskus, but now came out farther down the lake from the village). We didn't cross but continued upriver on the north side on a trail I had never been on before, but I was always interested in new trails. The horses were happy as we were still headed west and that meant home. This trail was not very well kept but we had no trouble following it. (This trail is now called the Messue Horse Trail.) It stayed close to the Blackwater River most of the way, through stands of poplar, spruce and willow, and alongside hill country that was sometimes quite steep and covered with trees, and other times partly open grassland. In places the river widened out to form miniature lakes, and in other spots it narrowed up to fast-moving water. Other times it was still and dark, while the water moved around large boulders scattered across the channel. We passed Upper Euchiniko Lake, riding above it, as the shore was steep along the north side. At the west end of the lake the Blackwater River drained into it and a short distance up the river we reached Messue Crossing, where we let the horses feed and rest for an hour and a half on an island in the middle of the river, by the crossing. There were cattle ranging in the area so the feed was short along the river, but for some reason they never went onto the island so the feed among the willow bushes there was plentiful. When we left the island we climbed steadily for several miles on a better-used trail called the Messue Wagon Trail until we met up with the trail to Kluskus, just east of Antoine Baptiste's place. We got home well before dark with tired horses, but the young ones had learnt a lot on the trip.

A few weeks later I took the young horses into the Itcha Mountains for several days, camping with friends. The ride to the mountains was a pleasant one: the weather was good and there were no flies. It was nice to ride along and listen to the horses' hooves thudding on the ground, and then occasionally their shoes would strike rocks and emit a ringing sound. There was also the creak of saddle leather and the scraping of branches on the tarps of the packs. We camped in Smoke Valley and rode to Itcha Lake one day. We also spent a day riding up above timberline. The third morning we woke to the tents sagging under wet snow that had started falling during the night. We tied the horses to trees at night, letting them loose to feed in the morning. That morning their backs were white with melting snow. When we put them out on hobbles to eat they took off down the trail for home, and we had to run to get ahead of them. And when it came time to pack up they didn't want to do that either, and the paint gelding tried to buck the pack off. We rode out of Smoke Valley down to Rat Cabin, one of my dad's old hunting cabins, then took another trail that led us to Shag Creek Hunting Camp. (This was the base camp for the hunting area that once belonged to my dad.) It was a good thing the packs were tied on well, as it was an awful trail, crossing a lot of swampy ground where the horses had to lunge in the mud, jumping windfall and squeezing between trees. It might have helped if we were on the trail the whole time but with the several inches of snow we kept losing it.

We were soaking wet by the time we reached the hunting camp, from the snow falling into the saddles. Two of the guides were in camp with no hunters so they made us welcome. It was nice to get into the warm cabins and dry out. My boots were soaking wet so I put them by the stove to dry and ended up getting them too hot. When the leather dried they were rather misshapen. I did get them on in the morning but by the second hour they were killing my feet. I couldn't stand it any longer and pulled both off and threw them in the bush, and continued the remainder of the ride in my sock feet. We stopped for a few minutes at the lodge at Tsetzi Lake to talk to Rob. A lady guest kept repeating quite loudly that I had no boots on, while I continued to ignore her.

Joe had bought a couple pigs the year before and the sow had produced thirteen young ones earlier in the summer. It was now late October, and he thought that the males should be neutered. I had never had such an experience, but I had done calves and once a stud, which had the choice of that or being shot, and he'd lived. Elaine Scott was house-sitting for Rob and Linda, who had gone away on holidays, and she had a couple friends visiting from Bednesti Lake, so I invited them over to help. They were always game for something new. We gathered at the pigpen in the afternoon, which was sunny and warm, with a case of beer to quench our thirst. Joe had the sow barricaded in the hog house and the little ones were left running around the pen in front. He was to catch the piglets and pass them to Clarence, who was to hold them upside down by the hind legs, with the help of the other two, while I did the dirty deed.

The first piglet Joe got hold of set up such loud squeals it set the sow off screaming in the hog house and banging on the walls. The rest of the little ones started a choir of their own. The hens that were scattered about scratching in the dirt lit off running low to the ground for shelter, wherever they could find it. Even the dog slunk away like a thief, trying not to be noticed with his tail between his legs. There was no way that the pigs could be held still, so it wasn't the cleanest job. We decided after the first one they should have been done when they were a lot smaller, but it was too late now.

There were six or seven males and by the time they were done one had escaped somehow and run squealing for the bush, never to be seen again. After we were finished, Joe informed me that the incisions should have been vertical rather than horizontal. I thought it was lucky the job got done at all; it was like trying to keep up to a ping-pong ball.

Everyone stayed for dinner and I prepared the little delicacies for hors d'oeuvres but they were not that popular with my guests — although Elaine did try one, looking like someone who had a gun to her head, then bolted out the door.

Then there was the job of getting rid of the swine. A few weeks later, Joe and I built a large crate, loaded it in the back of my truck and again caught all the pigs, dropping them through a hole in the top of the crate. Off to town I went to deliver them to buyers who had answered the ad we'd put in the paper. Joe later butchered the sow, and there never was another pig at Sleepy Hollow.

One of the hardest things I went through that fall, though, didn't have anything to do with the ranch, but with my mom. In her later years, Mom had moved into the Dunrovin Lodge in Quesnel, a facility for the elderly. She was getting terribly crippled, to the point that she walked with a cane, then a walker, and later was confined to a wheelchair. It seemed like I didn't spend much time with her, which I had a hard time doing, living so far away, but when I was in town I would try to take her for drives about the countryside. After she was in a wheelchair the drives stopped, as she was too afraid to let me lift her into a vehicle, for fear I would drop her. I remember the last drive I took her out on: we drove out to Nazko fully intending to drive about all afternoon. The first place we stopped was at the Harringtons' (who were still living on the Nazko Ranch) to say hello. Just Ronnie was home — Betty was away — but Ronnie asked us in for coffee. My mom said no as she felt she would not get up the steps to the ranch house with her walker. Ronnie picked her up out of the truck in his arms and packed her inside, setting her in a chair by the table. He made us coffee and Mom was so happy to have coffee with fresh cow's cream. Through the big picture window we could see down into the corral, where there were a number of cows with young calves. There was also a cow having a calf, which mom watched the whole time, saying it had been years since she had seen a calf born. From the birth, to the new calf getting cleaned by the mamma cow, to the calf getting to its feet and having its first feeding, Mom watched with an expression of contentment. By the time she was ready to leave she just wanted to go back to the lodge, having spent a happy afternoon. That was our last drive. After that, when I visited I would take her out in her wheelchair if the weather was nice and we would go down along the Fraser River on the river walk. She enjoyed Chinese food, so I often got takeout and we would eat together at Dunrovin in the little coffee room at the end of the hall.

On November 13, 1998, the hospital in Quesnel called, saying my mother had been brought in with what they thought was a heart attack. I called Rob and we started for Quesnel in the middle of a snowstorm, arriving late in the evening. Mom had not regained consciousness since being brought in. The next day my brother Ken and his wife came up from Williams Lake and my three boys drove down from Vanderhoof. Mom passed away early in the morning of November 15 without ever waking up. She was eleven days from her seventy-ninth birthday. We decided to have her cremated and hold a memorial the following May; with the weather and road conditions, it was not the time for people to be on the road. Most of Mom's remaining family and friends were elderly and did not want to be out on the highways that time of the year, and family would be coming up from the coast and Washington state.

My boys all came home for Christmas that year and as a gift bought me a satellite receiver and dish. Christmas Eve was spent setting it all up. It was the first TV to be viewed in the Blackwater. The first program the boys watched was the Christmas segment of *South Park*—I could not believe that they aired such garbage on TV. I thought I was broad-minded, but apparently my mind (at least that day) was a bit narrow. The year ended with a good New Year's party at Rob's, with a lot of people from Anahim snowmobiling over. My boys and some of their friends were there. We went out on the snow machines New Year's Day and the weather and conditions were good.

I had to drive to Quesnel in early February of 1999 to take care of some of Mom's things and on my way back the roads were icy. By then I was quite used to driving that road with icy conditions, but something went wrong at 118.5 km and the truck spun a few donuts and went backwards into the ditch, with the front of the truck out on the loaded lane. Now I knew how the story went, about the guy who was calling an empty km on his truck-to-truck radio and lost control of his pickup and was saying "empty . . . loaded . . . empty" as he spun down the road, trying to decide which way he would be headed when he stopped. Well, I didn't have time for that, clutching the steering wheel with white knuckles and wondering how it all was going to end! But I was fortunate, as all I ended up with was a dent on the side of the truck box. The first empty logging truck that arrived pulled me red-faced from the ditch and I continued on. A few days later a group of people out snowmobiling stopped by and one of the guys worked at a body shop. He got under my truck with a block of wood and a sledgehammer and popped the dent out.

When Joe was away, Rob and Linda would come over and help me feed, which I really appreciated. Patch used to be my right-hand man but he was getting older: instead of waiting by the gate hoping a cow would try to get into the hay pen so he could chase it out, he would either not pay attention or stay home altogether. I considered getting another dog but that puppy stage they all go through convinced me I didn't really need another dog.

It seemed William and Rose Cassam were gone a lot that winter, so Rob and I took turns going down to feed their cows every second day. He put up loose hay so it was just a matter of forking loose hay off the stack then scattering it about on the snow so the cattle could all feed at the same time. The cows would usually be down on the river feeding on the bare riverbanks, or in the willows feeding on the willow branches, but they would come when they heard the snow machine's motor. They were hardy cattle. The weak died and the strong survived. We had always fed the cattle when the Cassams were gone but this winter it seemed they were gone more than they were home. They were the only Indian people left living in the Blackwater country. There were a few at Kluskus, but most had moved to Anahim, Nazko or Quesnel for what they thought was a better life. They gave up their small herds of cattle years earlier, and then quit trapping, and they seldom used horses anymore—trucks replaced them. The elders, I believe, would still have preferred the old life, but the younger ones refused to live away from everything the reserves near town offered, and the elders were too old now to live in the bush alone.

In early March, while feeding cows with a German lady who was a nurse, I found a cow in labour on the feed ground. She did not want to be taken to the corrals; apparently her nest had been chosen,

*William and Rose Cassam's nieces, Roseanne (left) and Tillie, with their horse Hocksey in front of the barn.* VANCE HANNA

and she made that quite clear by taking some rather angry runs at us. I returned to the barn, got a rope and a few things I thought I might need, and roped the cow. I dallied the rope onto the bale lifter on the back of the tractor and then handed the end of the rope to the German lady, telling her to take up the slack. She got behind the back tire and the running board of the tractor and was pulling in the slack as I chased the cow up closer. Then the cow went ahead of the tire as well and crowded up to the little gal, who by now had her head under the steering wheel, back against the gearshift, while the cow stood very close in front of her, head over her blonde one. I asked her if she was all right, and a small "yes" came from under the cow's neck. I proceeded to pull two dead premature calves from the cow, and she never moved. Then I reached over and grabbed the short piece of twine on the breakaway hondo, releasing the cow, which backed up and walked away. The lady straightened up, no worse for wear. I told her, "That was called delivering in the field."

# CHAPTER 21

# The Fire

I always did my branding in mid-May, as turnout time was May 15. That is, if the grass was good enough on the range. Branding time was always fun as a group of people would come out with their horses to help and to ride, although by this time it seemed fewer and fewer people bought horses. That year, Don Hogarth drove out with Clifford and Linda Irving as I had asked if he would castrate a two-year-old colt for me, one that I had brought down a few days earlier from the Home Ranch, where he had been since he was born. I caught his mother in the broken-down corrals and led her home, with the colt following as he was still nursing. He was as tall as the mare and it looked a little ridiculous, seeing him nurse. I put him in the round corral and turned the mare loose to go back to the Home Ranch, which she did without a backward glance at her overgrown baby. Unless they are in foal again, range mares will let their colts continue to nurse unless they are taken away.

As soon as Don had taken care of the colt we ran him down into the pasture, where there were a few other horses, to get him away from the dirt in the corrals. He immediately jumped into the river—which was bank-to-bank full with spring runoff water—swam across, climbed up the muddy bank through a tangle of willow bushes and galloped across the field to disappear into the timber on the south

*Newly branded calves at Sleepy Hollow.*

side. He jumped the fence somewhere along the trail and went back to the Home Ranch. He did all this right after being castrated, but survived without any harm coming to him. I noticed the next time I was at the Home Ranch that although he followed his mother he no longer nursed. The couple days away from him was all she needed to decide enough was enough.

When we were done turning out the cattle, I went to Quesnel to arrange my mother's memorial service. We decided to have it at the Legion, and the Ladies' Auxiliary would do the tea. My mother had been raised going to the Greek Orthodox Church, but since moving to Quesnel she had not gone to any particular church, instead choosing to attend different ones over the years. I talked to a young pastor from one of the churches that had been recommended to me. I also mentioned that I would like an organist to play some of my mother's favourite hymns, and he recommended the lady from his church. I asked him to keep the service fairly short, as the crowd I knew would be attending would be inclined to get restless if it went on too long. He agreed to that. I gave both him and the organist a modest fee, in cash.

The twenty-second of May, the day of our mom's memorial, was clear and the sun shone brightly—a good omen, I thought. A large crowd came, including relatives from the Lower Mainland and Washington state and friends from all over BC.

The organist arrived having forgotten her music sheets but carried on anyway. I have no ear for music but even I could pick up her mistakes. Everyone was talking in muted tones, at least, so hopefully not too many noticed. She played and played, because the pastor was half an hour late arriving. And on his arrival, he was dressed like the militant, and his service went on and on and on. If I had had a rifle, I would have been tempted to shoot him off the podium. Toby Cave gave the eulogy and several others spoke as well. The Legion's ladies served a very nice tea and the crowd lingered for hours, visiting and renewing acquaintances. So I guess all in all it turned out okay. I hoped it was something my mom would have liked; I know she would have enjoyed seeing the crowd of old friends.

I had a plaque made in the memory of both Mom and Dad, and had a tree planted in their memory. The tree was planted in one of the parks by the walkway in Quesnel. The plaque was set into the ground at the base of the tree. The town, which honoured pioneers of the area, arranged it; there are many such trees and plaques throughout Quesnel's parks and by the walkways.

Someone suggested to me that building a cairn at the Home Ranch in the memory of my parents would be nice too, so I had a headstone made. At the end of July, Bill and Barb Mero brought out everything that was needed to build the cairn, and about fifteen friends from Vanderhoof and Fort St. James came to help—some came with quads and some by saddle horse. Rob and Linda were there to help as well.

I was to use my team and wagon to haul all the stuff Bill needed to do the rock work, plus sleeping bags, tents and food. I seldom used the team anymore. Maude was her usual self, always the dependable animal, while Sadie was flighty. I harnessed Maude and went to throw the harness on Sadie, when she decided to display the behaviour of a young, unbroken colt. She would not stand, jumping back and forth as much as her halter shank allowed. Losing patience I put a pair of leather hobbles on her, which still didn't help enough to let me harness her. Turning her loose in the five-acre pasture with the hobbles on, I got on my bike and chased her. At first she ran along the fenceline, happy to run, but soon she was dripping sweat and no longer wanted to run. Then she was glad to stand while being harnessed. While I was doing this Bill and Barb had loaded the wagon. I hooked the team up and started for the Home Ranch.

As soon as the team moved the wagon, I thought we were a bit overloaded. We had two steep climbs, the first out of Sleepy Hollow and the second out of Tsetzi Lake. On the level ground the team handled the load fine but the first hill we hit they were digging to get to the top. I rested them for a minute and we continued on. The second hill was steeper and longer then the first one. Halfway up they were digging in but couldn't go farther—they held it as long as they could, then down the hill we started, backwards. I turned the

*It was quite the event putting up the cairn for Mom and Dad at the Home Ranch.*

scrambling team and jackknifed the wagon, till the tailgate came up against some trees, stopping it. The team were very glad to stand, sides heaving and shoulders quivering, blowing hard. The sweat dripped onto the ground. I informed Bill and Barb, who were on saddle horses and had stayed with the wagon, that we had too heavy a load. Too much sand and gravel for the rockwork that was to be done, I discovered as part of the load was taken off. After we took about a third out the team was able to get the wagon up to the top of the hill without too much trouble, and I felt that they could handle the hills ahead. Rob, Linda and Elaine hauled the rest of the load to the Home Ranch with their quads and trailers.

A spot had been chosen for the cairn on the north side of the field, up on a jack pine ridge, where the pines were sparsely scattered, allowing a view of both the Ilgachuz and the Itcha Mountains, as well as the field, and the homestead, although only the barn roof could be seen as the meadow brush and willows had grown a great deal. Back in May of 1964, while we still lived on the ranch, Len Cave had been killed in his aircraft out on the ranch strip, while coming in for a landing. That fall his ashes had been buried in the very spot that had been chosen for the cairn. Len's brother had planted a blue spruce at the time, which had done well till we sold the ranch in 1970, then died within a few months. We stopped at the cairn site first and Bill did the concrete pad, so it would set for the construction the next day. We then went down to the building site, pitched camp and hobbled the horses, turning them loose to feed.

The following morning everyone assembled at the cairn site to gather rocks and do whatever needed to be done, although the lion's share fell on Bill's shoulders, as he knew what he was doing. Our mother's ashes were placed in the centre of the rocks and concrete of the cairn. The headstone, which has a team and wagon and mountain scene etched on it, says, "In memory of beloved pioneers, you will always be remembered." This was placed on the face of the cairn. Four posts were put into the ground and a roof was constructed over the top and a fence around, to keep cattle and horses from rubbing on the cairn. Bill had even brought shakes to cover the roof with. A guest book in a covered box has always been there and many, many people visit the site, travelling on horseback, quads, snow machines, on foot and by team and wagon.

I have always felt that I deserted my mother, leaving her ashes there on the abandoned ranch, even with Len's remains there. But my mother never would say what she wanted done when the time

*The completed cairn and headstone at the Home Ranch.*

came. At the time it seemed like the right thing to do, and maybe it was. I have visited there many times in the past thirteen years, and I always leave with sadness and regrets.

Soon enough it was September, and all the haying was done, although there were some bales left to haul. Joe was fixing the last of the hay pens, replacing some posts that had rotted. It had been a cold, overcast few days with strong winds, and I noticed some of the roofing paper had come loose on one of the roofs. I went out to the shop and found the plastic pail of tar I had stored there, which I took to the house and set on the top of the warming oven of the stove to warm up. It was taking forever to warm up it seemed so I crammed the firebox with pitchy wood and wandered off to do other things. Before I knew it I was in the north field hauling bales with the tractor, the tar long forgotten. I had been there a couple hours when Joe pulled up alongside me on my three-wheeler, shouting something. I shut the tractor off and he told me the house was on fire. I leapt from the tractor and Joe got off the bike. I jumped on the bike, telling him to get on behind, but he said he'd walk the half a mile back to the buildings. Driving as fast as I could, my heart in my throat, I reached the first gate to find Joe had come through it and stopped long enough to close and securely tie it with an array of knots. I finally got it untied with shaking hands. Praying all the time, I threw the gate open and left it that way as I raced on to the house. As I came through the yard I noticed that the windows were all black and black smoke curled out of every small crack in the place. But at least the building was still standing. I went up to the door and tried to see through the blackened windowpanes but it was impossible; touching the door I found the wood hot.

Water, I needed water! Sprinting down to the river I started the pump and luckily it didn't argue but started right up. Running back up the hill I was wheezing like a wind-broken horse and shaking all over. I found the ladder, propped it against the roof and with the hose spaying water all over I climbed up on the roof. Getting near the crown of the roof I ripped up shakes with my bare hands, then threw dirt out of the way, and finally, ripping up the plastic, I located a punching that wasn't nailed down and got it pushed to the side enough to get the water hose through. As I sprayed the water around I heard the windows breaking, as the cold water hit them. The smell of smoke was strong and burnt my nose and eyes, but I couldn't see any flames. About then Joe showed up. I told him to take my bike and go get Rob. I continued to run water around inside the room. It suddenly dawned on me I had two one-hundred-pound propane tanks that could explode if they got too hot. One was on the porch against the wall, with a line through the wall to the propane cook-stove, and the other was by the side of the building, hooked up to the refrigerator. Leaving the hose running inside the house I climbed down the ladder and luckily the crescent wrench was hanging on a nail by the one propane tank. I quickly shut off the tank, unhooked it and threw it off the porch. I ran over and did the same thing with the other. Then I rushed back up the ladder to the water hose.

After some time the smoke seemed to have died down, although the smell was strong. I realized my teeth were chattering and I was freezing—the wind was blowing hard, and I was soaking wet, sitting up on top of the roof. Throwing the water hose off the roof, I climbed down and then picked the hose up again and went to the door and opened it. I then started to cry—I do not know if it was the mess that met my eyes, or relief that there were no flames. Everything was black, and curls of smoke rose from the sofa, recliner chair and the open closet where the coats had burnt off the hangers—the remains had fallen to the floor and lay there smoking. My Australian long rider coat was the only thing still hanging on a hanger; the cotton liner had burnt out of it and the leather collar had curled a bit but otherwise it looked fine. I reached for it only to realize it was hot. I had left the potholders on the countertop, but they were now just burnt material resembling ashes—it took me a minute to realize what it was. I knew without a doubt that the pail of tar I had left on the warming oven had finally warmed up, and because I had built the fire up in the cook-stove the bottom of the plastic tar pail had melted. The black tar, running all over the cookstove and onto the floor, had burst into flames. Some of the logs behind the stove were badly charred, as was some of the floor surface around the stove, but the rest of the floors and walls had not burnt—they were only black with soot. The stringer logs on the ceiling above the stove were charred, and the exposed punching was as well. Everything was black with soot. No fire had reached the back room or upstairs, I discovered later, only the room I was standing in: the kitchen and living room.

I tried to figure out what some of the things were on the table, as they had melted, along with the Arborite tabletop. I picked the salt shaker up off the table and the salt ran out. The rubber stopper in the bottom had burnt away, but the shaker was not broken. My stereo on top of the TV stand had melted down to about four or five inches high from its original twelve or fourteen. The receiver for the TV looked normal, as did the TV, although neither ever worked again. On a shelf under the coffee table were my photo albums; the covers were blackened but the pages were fine—the water had not even reached them. The kitchen range and propane stove that sat side by side were beyond use, as was the refrigerator, while the Valley Comfort heater was unharmed. Why the whole place had not ended up in flames was beyond me, as there had obviously been flames, but they had gone out. As I stood there in that blackened interior, my nose and throat burning from the smoke, silent tears running down my face, listening to the dripping water, I realized the courage and the strength that I'd had all my life were badly shaken. I felt more discouraged than I could ever remember being in my entire life. I waited for my inner strength to tell me it was all okay, and I could fix all this, but it never came, only despair.

I walked outside and down to the pump and shut the water off. Then I went to the small shed next to the house where I stored extra coats and stuff. I stripped off my wet jeans and pulled on a pair of wool pants that I found hanging on a nail. I was trying to decide what coat to put on when I heard Rob yelling my name. I stepped out the door and told him I was okay. He was standing in the door-way of the house, staring at the mess inside. Linda arrived about ten minutes later, then Joe another five or ten minutes after that. By this time it was getting late in the day. We made sure that there were no hot spots in the house then closed the door. I went to Rob and Linda's for the night. There was no way I could have stayed in that house. My eyes were red and swollen and my lungs hurt as it was. My eyes could have been a mess from crying as well.

Rob and Joe had made plans a few weeks before to go to Alberta, so it was decided that they would go anyway while Linda and I started a cleanup. I got the tractor and wagon and parked it by the door. Just about everything went into the wagon, to be hauled to the dump. The blackened pots were stacked on the porch as were the dishes that had not broken. My collection of about 350 videos had melted together, but the videocassettes were fine. On the back wall, one picture frame was badly charred but none of the others. My beautiful houseplants were like overcooked spinach, hanging down the sides of rather misshapen flowerpots. The canned goods in the pantry in the back room had blackened labels but were salvaged; everything else went to the dump. Upstairs, the bedding was saved and later taken to the dry cleaners but the mattresses were thrown out. The wooden dressers were saved too, as they could be washed and painted. Most of my clothes could be cleaned; it was only my suede jacket that couldn't.

The following day the boys and some friends came out and helped remove the heaviest items from the house. My clothes, blankets, linen, pillows and towels were taken to town, and my friends washed and cleaned them. What couldn't be washed was taken to local dry cleaners, and there was no charge for the cleaning of the stuff.

My boys took time off work to come out, bringing anything that was needed and to help. So many people came to help. Talk about good friends, and even people I had never met before came with donations and help. It was decided what was to be done, then someone would hurry off for the three-and-a-half-hour drive to town (one way) to get whatever we needed. I am not mentioning names, as I know I would miss someone, but I will never forget those people and the incredible help they provided. One of the first things to arrive was a very nice kitchen range; it was used but had been well cared for, and we badly needed to cook and to heat water for cleaning.

After the log walls were washed they were painted—every room received two coats of donated paint. And each hour the place got brighter. Windows appeared and were installed. A false ceiling was put in, and a new water system from the holding tank upstairs to the kitchen range. Someone else rewired for lights, so at night we had lights again. Jon suggested a big window be put in the front wall where the cookstove had been, to eliminate the worst of the charred logs, so one was found. It really brightened the place up, letting in a lot of light. On the busiest day there must have been half a dozen ladies painting. People getting in the way were dabbed with paint. Guys were wiring and sawing material. Someone would unplug an extension cord for their own use, and someone else would yell and ask what happened to their power. People brought food. And in the evenings we had guitar music and laughter.

The only big pieces I could save from downstairs were the coffee table, the rocking chair and the heater, which after a cleaning seemed okay. My kitchen chairs and recliner I later took to Quesnel and had recovered. The big round table needed refinishing and new Arborite. A friend hauled it to town and stored it in a building that later caught fire, and nearly all burnt to the ground but the area where the table was stored survived the flames. I did eventually get it to Prince George a few months later to have it redone. Jon said to return my receiver for the satellite dish to Star Choice and tell them it didn't work, and they would send me another. I said, "But Jon, it has been overheated." He said that if it couldn't stand a little heat it wasn't much good. (I did send it back, and did receive another.) I can't remember where I came by the second TV; it may have been my mother's. Well, I once had the nickname of Blackwater Hattie, but after this it became Tar Baby. One thing I received was a plastic pail that contained a calendar, small staple gun, scotch tape, pens, pencil, sharpener, eraser, note pad, paper clips, writing pad, measuring tape and rubber bands, a pair of scissors and nail clippers. All those little things one wouldn't think of but are used around the house almost daily, and all mine were gone! Every week the place improved and soon the strong smell of smoke was nearly gone.

Upon opening a closet I would get a whiff of strong smoke, but it was getting better. I bought a new bed and one was donated so I had beds upstairs again. I was given a big sofa and chair and got another propane stove and fridge. With the big window on the front it was brighter in the house and I did enjoy the sunshine on winter afternoons as it streamed in the window and halfway across the room.

William Cassam came back in November and drove his cattle to Walt Lampert's place and Walt hauled them into town and they were sold at the Vanderhoof Auction Mart. The Cassams had been the last Indian family living in the area, and now they too had given up their bush home for life in town. I would miss them, as they had been good neighbours and good friends. Their horses were left behind to run on the river bottom, west of Tsacha Lake. There was a small bunch of horses in the river valley year-round, mostly William's, but there may have been a few from Blackwater Lodge too, as in the eighties they had a few horses that ran out there year-round as well. It started with a paint stud colt, no doubt an offspring from the little paint mare that used to be my dad's, which I sold after his death to William for his niece Roseanne. There were an assortment of mares, saddle and draught cross, that produced the colts, and many of them were paints. As the young studs grew up they were run off from the main bunch by the herd stud. I believe most stayed in the valley but the odd one travelled upriver, coming to my place to knock down fences, fight the geldings and breed mares to produce more colts I didn't want or need. The studs became a problem. William had made an attempt of sorts to keep them downriver, but once he was gone they went where they wanted. The ones that made their way to the ranch were shot as soon as they were discovered, but usually a mare or two would have been bred by then. Most of them arrived in spring and breeding season. I did not like to shoot them so if someone else was around and willing I let them do it. After they were shot they would have to dragged as far away from home as I could get them and off the beaten track, as naturally it was a feast for bears and the last thing I wanted was bears around.

One March I went down to the river valley, and it had been a deep-snow winter with a lot of crust. There were several colts with the bunch that were in very poor condition, and I was not sure they would live long enough to see green grass. Three of us took snow machines and a skimmer down one day and thought we might get close enough to rope one of the colts—in its weakened condition we could wrestle it down, tie its legs together and haul it home in the skimmer. But that thought was forgotten when we came face to face with the herd stud. At that time it was a big bay, not a bad-looking horse but extremely threatening and aggressive. He kept between the horses and the snow machines as much as possible, head down, ears flat, as he moved back and forth. I lost interest in getting a colt pretty fast. The only way I would have attempted catching a colt would be if we had first shot the stud.

The guide whose area the river valley was in camped there that fall with his horses to hunt moose. I know there were more studs shot than moose, as they would come into camp and fight with his hobbled and staked pack string of horses.

When I was going out the main gate of the ranch one day, standing at the gate were two studs. One was a young sorrel, about three years old, and the other was a big paint stud that I had seen a number of years before. I was surprised that he was still alive, because he would have been eight or nine years old. Where he spent his time was a mystery to me, but he definitely belonged to the Cassam horse bunch. Around his neck was a ring of white hair. Somebody somewhere had roped this stud and he must have had the rope on for a long time, or at least long enough to wear a sore around his neck. Later when he had healed the hair had come in white. It was a too perfect a circle to have been natural. I started them down the trail towards Tsacha and never saw them again.

One day there no doubt will be a government grant handed out to someone who will study the wild horses of the Blackwater and will trace their ancestry back to the Spanish horses of long ago. No one would ever want to admit that these horses could and did start as feral horses, much as the wild horses of the Chilcotin did.

CHAPTER 22

# Snow Machine Trips

It was late in the fall when Joe came over one morning very upset, as something had gotten into his henhouse and killed most of his hens. I went over with him to see what I could do to help, along with a guy who was working for me at the time and another couple. There were dead hens lying all over the floor of the coop and lots of feathers scattered about. The remaining hens crouched in the corner, not moving, traumatized by what had gone on in there. While we were all crowded into the small log coop, close to the door and staring at the devastation, a martin that was hiding in the punching of the ceiling decided to make its escape and came down the wall and ran between our legs and out the door. There was yelling and screaming from us women as we fell over each other rushing to get out of its way. The martin then sought refuge in the old cabin, which was now used for storage. We followed him into the dark, dusty building, squeezing through the door, which by then barely opened a foot because of the old building settling down. Joe had stored some boxes in the cabin and over time a bunch of stuff had collected there. Armed with clubs we began moving things to find the furry creature. Joe ran up to his cabin and returned with a rifle. This bothered me, as Joe's eyesight was not always the best, plus there was an old case of dynamite stored in a big wooden box in there—if it was hit the whole place might explode. Spotting the martin, Joe fired a shot, which caused more yelling. Luckily he had hit the animal (not one of us), which then decided to escape through a broken windowpane, and make its getaway. The martin never returned: it either died of its injuries or decided the place was not where it wanted to be.

While on a quick trip to town — I was supposed to meet the boys for lunch — James called me on my truck-to-truck radio to ask me to come to the hospital: Wesley had had his hand chewed up by a dog. Upon arriving I found it was not as bad as I had feared, but bad enough. The ring finger on his right hand was bitten off at the first joint. They told me that the two of them had been in James's truck and had stopped at the store in Stoney Creek. While Wesley ran into the store James stayed in the truck with the motor running. An old dog from one of the houses close by came and lay down unseen in front of the front tire, and when the truck started off the old dog didn't move fast enough and was run over, resulting in serious injuries. Not wanting to leave the badly injured dog in the parking lot, the boys put him in the back of the truck and drove over to the home of a fellow they knew who had a rifle. James did not want the dog shot in the back of his brand new truck, and Wesley was lifting the dog out when he was bitten.

While we waited in Emergency for the doctor to come, there was a phone call to the desk. The nurse came and told James that he had better speak to the guy on the phone. James came back, with a small grin on his face, saying it was their friend with the rifle (who may have had a drink or two) saying he had looked in the dog's mouth for the finger and had not found it, so did James want him to open the dog up and look in the stomach? About that time the doctor arrived and said that the finger could not be reattached anyway because of the damage to what was left of it. After that, when people couldn't tell the boys apart, some would look at their hands. Not long after, James was using a cutting torch under a machine in the shop of the outfit he worked for and put his hand down on a red-hot piece of metal, burning the palm of his hand badly. When something happened to one of the twins it always happened to the other as well.

On one of my trips to town Elaine met me with her snow machine on the back of her truck and we started home, her truck behind mine. There were a lot of trucks on the road and the radio was extremely busy. We waited at km 18 on the Kluskus, at the junction of Kenney Dam Road, till an empty truck went by and then followed him. This way I could listen to the radio but could rely on the trucker ahead of me to get into the pullouts when loaded trucks were coming. The busiest time was mid-morning, and it seemed we were spending more time in pullouts than driving. It was around km 105 that I heard "107 loaded for three." The empty truck went into a pullout and we squeezed in behind. One truck went by and right behind it was the second. Then the empty truck pulled onto the road and went. I thought I must have heard wrong about the number of trucks coming so I went too. Right at the first corner was the third loaded truck. How the empty one and the loaded one managed to pass each other was beyond me. I turned my pickup against the hard snowbank as far as it would go and stopped. I tell you, those off-highway trucks driving on icy roads with their over-width bunks and huge loads are intimidating. I never looked back to see how Elaine made out but at least she hadn't come to the corner yet. I kept going behind the empty and at the next pullout the truck pulled in and I followed behind and stopped. The driver came running back to me and asked if I had a cigarette. I asked him what he was thinking, as the truck had called for three. He said he didn't hear it, as he was too tired to keep the calls sorted out. By then Elaine had pulled into the pullout. We wished the driver luck before we got into our vehicles and got on the road; his block came up a few kilometres later and he turned down a side road. For the next thirty-five kilometres I had my ear glued to the radio and never missed a call. But once we passed km 142 there were no trucks hauling so I could relax a little.

Usually I left town in the late afternoon, when most of the trucks had done their two rounds, but I still had to be paying attention all the time. Some people wouldn't even drive the road because they didn't have a radio. I felt the radio was only false security as not everyone called, or you could miss calls. Your best defence was watching the road, always prepared to pull over. As soon as you passed the first truck they knew you were on the road and knew whether you had a radio.

Going into town with the loaded trucks was much easier, as I only met the empties. And if you wanted past, the drivers of the loaded trucks would tell you when it was safe to pass. Most of them drove at a modest speed but there was the odd one who clipped right along. I once followed a truck for at least ten kilometres before he started down a gentle hill on a straight stretch, and that's when he called and said I could pass him. By that time I was doing 110 and he was fast pulling away. I told him I would pass him if I could catch up to him. On another trip I had picked up Jeb, Linda's son, at his dad's place and was taking him home to his mother. He was about ten years old at the time. As I called the odd empty kilometre on my truck-to-truck radio, Jeb asked if he could call once. I told him when to call and he did, in his young voice. A trucker came right back on his radio and said, "I hope you're not driving."

While the kids were small I seldom went to town. Meeting those logging trucks scared the daylights out of me. After I was alone on the ranch I had no choice and started driving the road, often with the wheel in one hand and the radio mike in the other. It was not uncommon, after meeting the first truck, to hear the driver say on the radio, "Ms. Rempel is on the road again." I think I went to town at least twice a month. When the trucks were at their peak it was not unheard of to meet seventy-five loaded trucks. How many got onto the main road from side roads after I passed was anyone's guess.

Elaine came out a lot the last few years I was on the ranch, and we would go out with our snow machines to visit the local people, but often just to play in the snow. March was the nicest month to be out as the days were longer and warmer, yet the conditions were still good. But the cows usually started calving about mid-March so we had to go before then, or else when there wasn't much happening in the maternity pen. On one of Elaine's visits to the ranch we decided to take an overnight trip to Euchiniko Lake, so we fed for an extra day and then took our snow machines down the north side of the river to Tsacha Lake, where the Blackwater Lodge was. The lake is about ten or twelve miles long, with many places where there is usually bad ice; there are quite a lot of islands and bays. The sooner I could get off the lake the better I liked it. Once we were on the lake I opened my machine up and took off following the shoreline till we passed the first island, and then headed out to the centre of the lake. About three or four miles down the middle of the lake I glanced back to see where Elaine was. On that big of an expanse of white, even the smallest dark object could be seen—but I saw nothing. I stopped my machine and shut off the motor. There was only silence. I started my machine and went back up the lake. Near the end, very close to shore, sat Elaine. The motor on her machine had blown up before she had gotten a hundred yards. While waiting for me to come back she had removed the drive belt and hooked up the tow rope. There was nothing left to do but tow her back to the ranch. We were both at that time driving Summit 583s so towing her wasn't a problem.

The trail back upriver is a fun trail to ride, but not necessarily fun to tow a dead machine over. There are a lot of hills and sidling places as it winds its way along the river through the big spruce and scattered pine. It also has steep south slopes, which lack snow and are covered with boulders. As I was towing Elaine up a rather steep hill my oil light popped on. When we reached the top I stopped to cool my machine off, and turned around to Elaine to tell her my machine was overheating. She sat on hers, steering with one hand and a beer in the other, and told me her machine wasn't hot at all.

When we came in close to the river, above the rapids about two miles as the river winds from the house, I turned onto it. It was a lot easier towing the machine on the river ice. Elaine was on a fairly long tow rope, which made it interesting when I got my speed up on the winding river. As we came to the last place along the river where I could get off the ice and onto the field I was going a good speed, and I took a sharp turn up the rather steep bank and through a bunch of willows. This gave Elaine a real jerk—she came around and nearly rolled her machine, but it came up the bank. As mine tipped over in the field, hers tipped over in the pile of bush. There we were with both machines on their sides, but we had made it home. Laughing, we righted the machines and ran across the field, over the bridge, up through the corrals and around to the loading ramp. It was a little harder to get a dead machine in the back of her pickup but we managed, and as it was still early in the day she headed for town.

A year later when Elaine was out, we went to the Lamperts' then came down Tsilbekuz and Cluchuta (Airplane) Lakes. On Cluchuta Lake we hit overflow. And it was deep. There is always a feeling of panic when I am so far from shore and the snow begins to roll ahead of me, and I knew there was a lot of water underneath. We had been running side-by-side down the lake till we hit the overflow, and about then my machine began coughing and spluttering and slowing down. Elaine veered to one side and kept going till she was out of the mess but my machine quit. By the time I got it going again and managed to bog my way through the slush to dry snow I was soaking wet. And by the time I got home I was freezing cold, although it was probably plus two or three. I would have hated it to be really cold—we would have had to get to shore and build a roaring fire to dry out.

After feeding the next day, Elaine, Daryl Miller (who worked for me at the time) and I went off to visit the Chadwells. We went down the north side and hit Tsacha Lake, which was fairly clear of snow, and travelled down the lake till we got off at Mackenzie Trail Lodge and went up to the Chadwells' place. We spent several hours there, and when we went to leave my machine refused to start. We discovered it had major problems and it was not going to make it home under its own steam. Elaine said it was payback, and out came the tow line. We decided we would stick to the trail on the south side of the lake on the way home. Things were going okay till we came to the Mackenzie Trail Lodge's airstrip about half a mile above the lake. The trail down the strip was blown full of snow. We had up till then been going fairly slowly, with no problems. When Elaine saw the trail was blown full she took off at full throttle going as fast as she could. The snow and ice crystals were blowing in my face to the point I couldn't see. I didn't have a helmet, had never worn one, but if I had had a helmet and a face shield things would have been better. I tried yelling to tell her to slow down but of course she couldn't hear me. I thought if I put on the brakes she might look around to see what was happening and I would get her attention. But that only pulled her off the trail and into the powder so she increased her speed to get back on the trail. As we flew along I knew if she didn't slow up when we reached the timber I was going to have to bail off, as it was like riding the devil's train. Fortunately when she reached the timber she did stop to find out how I was doing, and I quite loudly told her. Daryl was nowhere in sight. She was going so fast he couldn't even keep up. From there on it was a bit better except on corners where there was a log that had been cut off and it stuck out on the trail a bit. I frantically steered this way and that to avoid hitting them. When you're running on your own power they are not a threat, but with someone jerking you along, powerless to stop, it was not much fun. I was glad to get home in one piece.

Once Barb and Sheila, a couple of ladies from Quesnel, came out on their snow machines and were looking after Rob's place while he and Linda were on a short holiday. Elaine was out also. After feeding was done the four of us would go play in the snow and then we would have dinner at either Tsetzi Lake or Sleepy Hollow. One particular night we dined at Tsetzi Lake. Rob had told the girls that they could help themselves to the wine in his wine room, and we may have overdone it just a wee bit! Elaine and I did manage to get back over the hill to Sleepy Hollow but it took us longer than usual. It seemed the trail had a lot more hills and curves that night. We were to radio when we got home, but by the time we contacted Tsetzi Lake they were already suited up and ready to look for us. We did have some laughs over it.

The four of us did a trip to Anahim Lake as well, and spent the night there. Later on we went to Euchiniko with a few more friends. The trip down was good. We travelled Squirrel Lake and through the Kluskus village, which seemed deserted, then left the Kluskus Trail about six miles past the village and went down to the Blackwater River, getting onto the ice by the Chateau—a private lodge on the river, next to Deadman Crossing, where the river drains into Lower Euchiniko Lake. There was only a caretaker at Euchiniko, Harrington being away, but he let us into a very large cabin where we could spend the night.

On our return trip I decided we would follow the river up to Upper Euchiniko Lake, then cross it and get on the trail near Missue Crossing. I didn't like following the river as there was a lot of open water. The river opens up to form a lot of small lakes and the ice is not always good, but I knew that the north shore was safer than the south shore, which had more springs feeding into the river near the shore, making the ice thin. In some places we had to get up onto land to get by open water, but there was already a trail broken, which was easy to follow. When we reached the largest lake that the river formed, the old tracks ran down the south side. Without realizing it I followed them. I began to hit air holes and as I passed them the water came splashing out. That was when I realized my error and that the ice was very thin. I was instantly scared spitless, and knowing speed was all I had I gave it full throttle as I flew across the ice. I never looked back for the others—it was everyone for themselves, and the devil for all. When I reached shore a few minutes later, where the trail went up on land again, I stopped. Marianne was the first one to pull up, and said, "What an adrenaline rush!"

We continued on, hitting the river one more time before we got onto Upper Euchiniko Lake. Although the ice is usually good on that lake I was still nervous about crossing it. We started down the middle of the lake, everyone spread out, and we went as fast as the rough ice would allow. Marianne had a plastic barrel tied on the back of her machine with bedding in it. This came off about halfway down the lake, bouncing and spinning across the ice as those behind her tried to avoid coming in contact with it. Some brave person stopped and picked it up. I was glad when we reached shore and took the trail from there home, avoiding Tsacha Lake. I knew I could not handle running another lake with bad ice that day. But still, it all had been fun.

# CHAPTER 23

# My Last Years at the Ranch

In the spring of 2001 Wesley came out with Katie for the weekend. I didn't know it at the time, but she was to be my future daughter-in-law. In April James brought Tammie home—another future daughter-in-law. In November Jon introduced me to Dawn, who was to be my third daughter-in-law.

In March, when Wesley and Katie drove out with John Mowry for the weekend, we had talked about burning the old cabin down at the place where Joe lived. The old case of dynamite was still in the big wooden box, where it had been for years, and I had been told that it gets very dangerous when it is old. The kids wanted something to do so at dark the three of them went down to burn the cabin; Joe was away at the time. Katie stayed up on the hill while Wesley and John went up to the building on my snow machine and three-wheeler. They sloshed diesel around, lit it up and ran to the machines. One rolled the snow machine and the other hit the fence with the three-wheeler, they were in such a hurry to leave. They expected an awful explosion, but the building quietly burnt with little fanfare. It was rather a shame to burn it—there was a lot of history there, with the cabin having been built in the thirties when the Frontier Cattle Co. used the place for haying and wintering cattle—but not only the dynamite was unsafe, but the building itself. A year later I burnt the

old barn as the roof had caved in on it; again, it was unsafe. People
from the city seem not to realize the danger in those buildings, and
all I needed was someone to be hurt in one of them.

We also tore the old woodshed down at the main place and rebuilt it, as it had begun to have a dangerous lean to it and the roof
was leaking badly. I put a tin roof on the rebuilt one, which I liked
to be under when it was raining, listening to the rain beat its rhythm
on the tin. I had built a small tool shed next to the woodshed a
few years before, and it was handy to have it closer to the house.
In May the boys brought a hoe out and did a lot of ditching on the
road. Bigger rocks were dug out of the roadway. We borrowed an old
dump truck and hauled in some gravel, although gravel is hard to
find. Gravelling the worst places certainly made it better. The boys
had come by some old culverts and put some of them in as well. All
the work made such a difference to the road.

Then I finally made the hard decision and listed the ranch for
sale with a realtor. All three boys had set up house with their lady
friends and had less time to come home. And ever since I had the
fire in the house, it seemed that the meaning of my life had changed.
I had lost interest in all the activities around the ranch. It was more
like drudgery now, rather than something to look forward to with
enthusiasm.

Soon after I listed the place for sale a fellow out hunting stopped
by and I invited him in for coffee. He asked me why I was selling
the place and what I would do. As we talked about it I mentioned
there were three things I had always wanted and never had: Hydro,
a landline phone and an automatic washing machine. He only then
realized that I didn't have those things, living where I was. I probably
could have had an automatic washing machine, but they use a lot of
water and in the winter it would have been a problem. I would never
have the other two. The diesel generator served the purpose for
power but the generator was not always dependable. The odd time
it refused to start and in cold weather it was worse. When it reached
about thirty below or colder I would get up during the night and
start it and let it run for awhile so that it would start in the morning

without a hassle. If the generator wouldn't start the tractor wouldn't start, as I needed to plug the block heater in. The other alternative was putting a tarp over the tractor and using the propane torch. That was more trouble, and dangerous. And the radiophone would work beautifully one day and may not work the next day, till it was good and ready to come back on again. It might be as long as two weeks before it worked properly. Plus with the radiophone the whole country listened to one side of every conversation. My average phone bill was two hundred and fifty dollars a month, so it wasn't cheap. Some people out there were starting to get other phones, like satellite ones, but they were very costly, and beyond what I could afford.

On the July long weekend of the last few years I was on the ranch I had "camp and ride," as I called it. The first year I had seventeen people who came out with their horses and pitched their tents in the yard. We spent two days riding around and the evening sitting around the campfire after eating a big meal. We never rode that far or hard but went to the waterfalls downriver on the Blackwater and some would try fishing. We always rode to the Home Ranch the second day. We would sit in the grass and eat our lunch and I would tell childhood stories and answer questions about the old buildings or what life had been like living there many years before, while our horses hobbled about grazing. My cows that summered there always came to stand around and watch us.

The second year I had the camp and ride we discovered a cow lying in a slough close to the buildings at the Home Ranch, apparently struck by lightning. She had been there a number of days. The birds had been at work but no larger animals. Of course there was talk like the time the bull was in the river, about how the carcass should not be left in the water, as it would cause contamination to the waterways. After the guests left Rob, Joe and I took our quads up to the ranch to drag the old girl out of the water. When we reached the field, instead of going straight down to the barn we cut to the right and took the summer road along the edge of the field that took us in the back way to where the cow was. The first mudhole had grizzly tracks in it, big ones and small ones that meant a sow grizzly with at least one cub. We backtracked and went down the field to the buildings so we were not driving blind up to where the dead cow was. We then approached from the old house, where we could see into the slough without being right in it. The carcass was gone. The most likely spot for it was in the thick willows on the high side of the slough, but we couldn't see anything. We leaned against the cabin that was on high ground above the slough, and waited. It didn't take long for the sow to smell us and tell us, with a lot of loud roaring from the willows, that she knew we were there. I think she was warning us that she would appreciate us moving on, which we were glad to do.

Only a few days later, I was going into town with my pickup. I had crossed a culvert on the Kluskus Road at km 161 and gone around a corner when a grizzly came down off the low bank to my left and ran across the road in front of the pickup. I had to brake suddenly to avoid hitting her. She had an unusual build for a bear, with very long legs, which made her seem larger than she probably was. She had the usual brown body but her neck and shoulders were silver tipped. She went up a cut bank on the right hand side of the road. I turned my attention back to the road just in time to avoid hitting three tiny cubs that darted out of the ditch in pursuit of their mother. I thought later I should have run over all three, but I swerved and missed them. Then I was looking in the rear-view mirror and glancing back over my shoulder as I drove, trying to see where the big grizzly had gone. The road along that section had very little maintenance and was rather rutted and rough, so I was not driving very fast. I was still trying to locate the bear, thinking she must have taken her cubs and headed into the heavy timber, when I realized she was running alongside the pickup. That gave me a shock, being that close, and I sped up in spite of the rough road conditions and left her behind. My last look in the rear-view mirror showed she was broadside in the middle of the road, jumping up and down with her hair standing up, swinging her head back and forth, and I am sure she was roaring, as her mouth was open. If I had had three flat tires I still would not have slowed down. I realized afterwards that if I had been on a quad it would have been the end of the line!

It was two years later, in June, when she showed up at the ranch with her three cubs, which were by then almost as big as she was. I knew as soon as I saw her, with her long legs and silver neck, that it was the same bear. I first knew there was a bear around when the cows came home bawling and were against the drift fence a mile upriver and refused to leave. Rob came over and we went up to the cattle to look around and that was when we saw the sow and her cubs just beyond the bunched up herd. She never killed anything but kept them stirred up and bawling and wanting to come home. She was around for three or four days then left, all the time keeping the cattle against the fence and upset. I was nervous when I knew she was about. Rob and I looked for her up and down the valley. While we were up on the side hill northwest of the buildings above the cows, where you could see most of the valley, the bear and the cubs were out in front of the house grazing on the clover. When we returned home she was gone and the cattle upriver began bawling. A friend came out and hunted the bear with Rob for a couple of days but she was always a step ahead of them. Then she left.

Over the next year there were stories of a pickup on a side road in the area being chased by two big bears and another pickup out on the Kluskus Road being chased, between 167 km and 159 km. I can only guess how many incidents there were that I never heard about. At the time there was a fair amount of logging activity in the area, as well as drilling at the mine site just over the hill from the ranch. Then in the fall I was talking to a fellow who was in the area hunting, I believe, who had been on a very narrow haul road coming down a steep hill in his pickup when this bear stepped out on the road in front of him and stood up. He said it had a very threatening manner so he opened his door and shot it. Describing the colour of the grizzly and the long legs I was pretty sure it was the same bear, and I could only say I wouldn't miss her. She was a dangerous bear and would have one day killed someone. After that there were no more stories of trucks being chased in the area.

I rode to the Home Ranch one day with some friends and while crossing the small creek at the end of Airplane (Cluchata) Lake we noticed a trout flopping around in the grass on the creek bank. Thinking it was a shame to leave it there to die I dismounted and caught the fish. I knelt down on the bank of the creek holding the fish in the water as it kept wanting to turn belly up, and as I knelt there it came to mind why the fish was on the bank in the first place and how it had got there. My saddle mare was nervous and pulling on the reins, and I thought she just wanted to get moving, but then it came to me that the fish was on the creek bank because no doubt a bear had thrown it there and we had interrupted its fishing. I dropped the fish to fend for itself, live or die, and jumped on my horse, which was in a lope before I was in the saddle. The horses had more brains then we did that day!

It was in midsummer and I had friends from Mission visiting for a few days. The guys had gone biking and Sharon, Joe and I had been building a fence upriver and came in about noon for lunch. After eating we were out back of the house when I heard the chickens squawking. I went around to where I could see the henhouse but there didn't seem to be anything around. Then slowly backing out of the henhouse was a bear. I'm not sure what had interested him, but something had lured him into the coop. Well, if he would go into a henhouse, he might come in my house! I went inside and got a rifle, and resting against a tree I got a good shoulder shot. I knew I had hit him but he started over the hill, so I hit him again. I then ran through the corral and up onto the higher part of the hill, so I could look down and see where the bear had gone. He had not gone far and was lying in the trees against the fence, not moving. I came back and told Sharon, that's what happens to bears that go into henhouses. Being a city girl I am not sure she approved, but when the guys came back they said they should have stayed home—it was more excitement than they had had.

In November 2002, Elaine came out to watch Rob and Linda's place while they took a holiday. She came over to my place most days and on one of them we decided to take our quads over to 153

*Bear trouble—I shot this black bear while it was raiding the chicken coop.*

kilometres on the Kluskus Road to visit the family that had moved in there the year before. We had about eleven inches of new snow but it was fluffy and didn't hinder the bikes at all. At Tommy Valley, about two kilometres from the Kluskus Forest Road, two sets of fresh bear tracks came onto the road. They were from two big grizzlies, and I tested the tracks with my hand and found that the snow had not even begun to set. These tracks were really fresh! I am afraid of bears, especially grizzlies, and I had not brought a rifle. Elaine, riding behind me, wanted to know what the problem was. I told her it was fresh bear tracks. She told me to get on the bike and ride. We continued for a short distance and the tracks turned off the road into the spruce; no doubt the bears had heard the bikes. As I drove by I felt those beady little eyes watching us. I had increased the speed a great deal and about ten kilometres down the road Elaine pulled up alongside me and yelled something. I stopped and she asked if the tracks had been grizzly. When I said yes, she grinned and said, "Ignorance is bliss." On our return trip we saw no sign of the bears, which suited me fine.

Along in the spring, the cows were calving and we still had patches of snow about. Rob had come over and was visiting with the guy helping me out through calving. I was dozing in my recliner when the dog on the porch began to bark. The barking continued and I began to get annoyed, as it was disturbing my nap, when Rob got up and opened the door to speak to the dog. Standing next to the porch was a cougar, and it was no doubt hoping the dog would come down off the porch. When Rob opened the door it ran. Both guys took rifles and went after the cat but it had disappeared. There was not enough snow to actually track the animal and what snow we did have was hard, not leaving any clear tracks. With all the cow tracks it was next to impossible to figure out which way it went. That was the only time the cougar was seen.

I had had the ranch listed for a year and only one couple had come out to look at it and they had no intention of buying—it was a game of theirs, visiting ranches to pass the time. I switched realtors with hopes that things would improve. The real-estate market was hot at the time so the realtors were busy and were not really interested in some land back in the boondocks, a three-and-a-half-hour drive from town. So there was nothing happening, and it was very discouraging.

The last few years on the ranch I had begun to want a gentler horse, as I was getting older and rode mostly on my own, with no one really knowing where I was. My reliable buckskin horse had begun to favour one shoulder, especially riding up and down hills, and the mare I had gotten was pretty hyper. The other horses I had were barely broken so I was on the lookout for an older gelding that had seen a lot of wrecks, and nothing would excite him. I ended up with a retired rodeo horse in his teens that some kids had had for a short time. When I first got him I rode him several times and he seemed just what he was supposed to be: a reliable, well-broke horse. That was just before haying time, and once I got into haying I wasn't riding. About six weeks after the horse arrived I decided to move the replacement heifers out to the range from the pasture they were in. I caught the gelding, tied him to the hitching rack by the tack shed and got my saddle. Even before I threw the saddle on I began to suspect that the horse had things on his mind. He seemed too interested in every move I made. His head was up and his ears back. I finished saddling him up, put the bridle on and would have mounted right there but I wasn't comfortable with it, so I led him down to the pasture around the hill from the house before getting on. Once I was on I nudged him with my heels and the horse humped his back before moving off very stiff-legged. I knew I was in trouble, but what was I to say to the guy I had gotten him from: "I want my money back, the horse was going to buck"? I had to see it through, and it didn't take long. The gelding started off but kept humping up and then very suddenly bogged his head between his legs and away we went. We were headed east when he made his first jump and we were going west when I came out of the saddle, a good way off the ground. By the time the ground and I met I was on my head and my neck has never been the same since. The horse started eating grass right beside me, as I lay there deciding if I was still in one piece, so I knew he had done this many times before. I finally got to my feet with my spine and neck aching and grabbing the reins of the bridle, started walking back to the house. The horse hurried right alongside of me and I swear he was grinning. I gave the reins a vicious jerk and said, "Make one more wrong move you SOB and I swear I will kill you!" I think he understood English because he dropped back behind me and stayed there all the way to the tack shed, where I pulled the saddle off and let him go. The first chance I got he went down the road to where all undesirable horses go.

While living with the waiting game of what would happen with the sale of the ranch I did have some good news. James and Tammie had come out at breakup for the weekend and told me that I was going to be a grandmother! I was so excited at the thought of a baby in the family again. The baby was due in October.

Katie and Wesley were married August 10, 2002 at the Skye Ranch at Mapes, a rural area east of Vanderhoof. The day was beautiful and there was a good turnout of family and friends. My sons looked so handsome in their suits. I had bought a long dress with slits up both sides and while getting out of the truck I managed to tear one of the slits much higher. (One should never dress a redneck

*My three handsome sons—Jon, Wesley and James at Wesley's wedding.*

*Wesley and Katie, married on August 10, 2002.*

woman up then let her out in public.) Wesley was driving highway trucks at the time and took his bride on the road for the honeymoon.

My first granddaughter, Teagan Rena Jane, arrived in the wee hours of the morning of October 7. I was in town staying with Katie and Wesley, and Katie and I were there at the hospital when Teagan was born. I'm not sure who arrived at the hospital with a logging truck, and of course I had a pickup, and I think Tammie's mother MaryAnn drove a pickup. John Mowry later remarked that you could tell the families were rednecks when one person arrived in a logging truck and the rest in pickups and SUVs.

Daryl Miller had come to stay and work for me earlier in the year. He liked the isolation and the quietness, and always seemed to find things to do. Whenever there was some spare time we cut bug trees around the buildings, as the mountain pine beetle had come to my beautiful valley in full force and the whole valley had begun to turn red. Probably eighty percent of the trees that grew in the area were lodgepole pine, so it was a pretty good indication of what the future held. We had a good supply of firewood stacked up and the woodsheds full at both my place and Joe's. Daryl also borrowed an Alaskan mill and the big trees we cut into lumber, which was always in need around the place.

I had a lot of timber on the ranch, mostly lodgepole pine, and some really nice trees. There were some ravines with very large spruce as well. In the eighties we had talked about logging it but I was always against it. After Barry was gone I was approached by one of the mills in Vanderhoof and offered a good price for the timber. I declined because at that time I felt the market would always remain strong, but I had not anticipated the mountain pine beetle. By 2004 there was not a mature pine on the place that had not turned red. If I could have foreseen the future it would have been logged—it would have been better to log the trees than to see them die and fall to the ground to rot. It was very sad for me to see.

Wes, Katie, James, Tammie and little Teagan came out for Christmas that year. We postponed Christmas dinner till Boxing Day, waiting for Jon and Dawn, and Dawn's children, Jared and Amanda, to get there. It was to be the last Christmas the kids would spend at the ranch, and the only Christmas I had a grandchild there.

Just as calving was starting in March the weather turned cold. The nights were anywhere from twenty-six to thirty-five below. I was very glad to have Daryl with me then. We rolled out bales of hay in the corral by the barn and would put the cows that were anywhere near calving in there at night, along with the few that had already calved—the new calves did okay bedded in the hay. With the cows in hay and near the barn, any one that started to calve could be put inside at night. I think those old girls thought they had won a lottery, getting all they could eat in the day and then again at night, and being bedded in it as well. On the coldest night, two heifers having their first calves started to calve about bedtime. We put both in the barn, checking them often. When the first calf arrived it was placed in the calf sleigh and taken into the calf box in the house.

At midnight we pulled a huge calf from the second heifer. We let her smell the steaming calf in the calf sleigh for a couple of minutes as she lay in the barn refusing to get up. Daryl took the calf to the house while I stayed with the heifer for a time, trying to get her to stand. Finally I covered her with hay and hoped for the best. Twice during the night I visited the cows and the heifer was still down but she had switched sides, which was a good sign. In the morning the heifer was up. We took both calves to their mothers. I was afraid they would not claim their babies, these being their first calves and only having had a couple of minutes with them, but bless their hearts both heifers took their calves with a moo and a lick and let them have their first drink.

Elaine came out during calving for a few days with her sister. While they were there Rob called over to say one of his cows was having trouble calving. The three of us ran over on our snow machines to see what could be done. Rob had the cow in his corral. After roping her we tied her to a tree and went to work to see what the problem was. The calf was upside down, and it was a large one. I wasn't strong enough to get the calf turned over, even with both arms, and Rob was only able to work with one arm due to the lack of room. Finally the cow lay down in the slush and manure in the corral, and I lay down in my coveralls in the slop behind her, trying to get a rope around the calf's head. I had my head buried in between the cow's thighs, my coveralls off my right shoulder, when I must have taken the pressure off the bladder because the cow let go. As I lay there the hot liquid gushed down around my neck and into my coveralls. For a few moments it was nice and warm—I was beginning to get cold lying on the wet ground—and I was so close to accomplishing what I wanted that I didn't dare let go. We had all been quiet up to this point but right then everyone burst out laughing. Mary Jane had her camera and took photos but later lost the film, which was kind of a shame. I finally got a rope around the calf's head and Rob was strong enough to pull the calf's head up and it turned over. We were then able to get it out. The calf was dead but the cow survived. We then went to the house where

I gratefully showered and shampooed my hair, and Linda gave me clean clothes.

Every time there was a break in the calving I ran into town to see the kids. It was a good thing Daryl didn't mind staying home. Teagan had grown so much and could leap wildly in her Jolly Jumper and squeal really loud. I would stand in front of her and jump with her. She thought that was great fun; her mom thought I was nuts. Wes and Katie had bought a house with acreage east of Vanderhoof so I would go see them as well, then grab some groceries and run back to the ranch.

I had bought in Vanderhoof a longhorn heifer calf when it was weaned off the cow. I wanted to grow a big set of horns for a wall display. At the age of two she was in calf, and of course this was bound to happen. When she started to calf and the hours passed, I knew she couldn't have the calf. She just didn't have enough room, for even the small calf she had in her. By then she already had a nice set of horns and I didn't want to ruin the skull by shooting her in the head, so I phoned Rob, who told me to shoot her in the neck. Then, bless his heart, he came over and did it for me. After she was shot we opened her up and removed a little red calf, which was up in a matter of minutes, bouncing around as if all was well in the world. We dressed the heifer out for hamburger. The following morning another heifer had her calf on the riverbank in a pile of willows; she only had five or six acres to choose from but it had to be there. The calf fell in the river and by the time I got there the calf had drowned, so she got the orphan calf and they took to one another right away.

*My two beautiful granddaughters, Teagan and Reagan.*

Elaine came out in the beginning of May to feed cows for me as Daryl was away for awhile. Wes and Katie were going to be parents and I was going to be a grandmother again, and I wanted to be there. Elaine would feed and watch the cows while I went into town. Wes phoned late one evening saying that I had better come in. We had had a busy day and I was tired so I got up early and went to town, but by that time my second granddaughter, Reagen Jacoba, was already seven hours old. I spent a day in town with the grandbabies before going back to the ranch. There was something about those grandchildren that made everything worthwhile.

# CHAPTER 24

# Leaving Sleepy Hollow

I had finished up the spring work and got the cows out to range, and later the bulls. Elaine and Leone (a friend of ours from Prince George) and I planned a trip into the Bella Coola Valley with Wanda and Roger Williams from Anahim Lake, who take trail rides in the area and into the mountains. So at the end of June 2003, we met in Prince George and drove out to Anahim Lake. We were to travel the old Lunaas Pack Trail, the old trail that my dad had used back in the 1930s when packing out of Bella Coola. We were joined by three other guests who were going on the ride as well. The following morning we saddled up in the heat and rode down to Anahim, stopping at the local pub for a beer. We then continued on to Trails End Ranch, west of Anahim Lake about twelve miles. This had been an established ranch years ago but was no longer operating as a cattle ranch. It was now rather run down and had been logged off, and what hadn't been logged showed signs of the mountain pine beetle. We left the horses there overnight, and were picked up and taken back to Wanda and Roger's for the night. Early the next morning we were driven back to Trails End to saddle up and start our second day.

We had a bit of trouble getting over to the old trail, with fences and beaver dams, and the creeks in that area had very boggy bottoms so you had to be careful where you crossed. Roger's horse sunk down into one and there was a lot of mud flying before he scrambled out onto the bank. Leone did a header off her horse when it started to step across a small stream and at the last second jumped it. We took a fence down to get off the ranch and ended up behind water backed up from a beaver dam, but we found a solid dam that we were able to cross the horses on and picked up the old trail and started for the Precipice Valley. Kappan Mountain was in front of us for some time as we travelled down the trail, and there were a fair amount of fresh bear signs, which seemed to bother only me. We also had to cross clearcuts and we would lose the trail on those, but would eventually pick it up and continue. I had been given a little bay mare that was very smooth for riding and an excellent traveller so I was content. When we came to the first steep drop it was suggested that we walk down and lead the horses. Everyone took off their boots and put on the walking shoes that we had all tied to our saddles that morning, and tied our boots to the saddle. Roger, Wanda and I led the horses down the steep trail till we reached the bottom of the hill and the Hotnarko River, which was still no more than a large stream there. On reaching the bottom Roger said to Elaine, "I have some good news and some bad news. The good news is that we have reached the bottom of the hill; the bad news is we have lost one of your boots." It had come untied from her saddle and must have bounced down the steep incline, because nobody saw it. We continued on, crossing the Hotnarko twice and climbing back up a very steep hill to ride along the top for several hours. This was the trail used for all the packing out of the valley in the old days. All I thought was, those poor horses! We slowly dropped down into the Precipice Valley on a much better descent and passed one small homestead nestled in the pine trees close to the creek. We then passed several small, man-made fields and a little farther on came to Lee Taylor's, where we were to spend the night.

The cook had driven down a logging road and was preparing dinner when we arrived. It had been a hot and dusty day, and the mosquitoes and blackflies had kept us busy. We washed our hair under a tap out in the yard, and the water that came out of it could have been ice—it numbed your scalp in an instant. We pitched our tents in the yard and the evening brought cooler temperatures, so we spent a good night.

From the Precipice Valley on, the trail was called the Sugar Camp Trail. Back in the early days it was also called the Zig Zag Trail. We climbed up the side of the mountain for a ways then continued along, looking down onto the old Jim Glenn place, which was now owned by another family. Farther on the trail became very narrow and ran along a steep side hill. It was there that Elaine's mare's hind legs broke away part of the narrow trail, the mare falling partly off the trail. Elaine slid from the horse as it was scrambling to get back on the trail, and its feet appeared to be landing all over Elaine. I leapt from my horse on the high right side, only to slide underneath my horse and come out on the left side. By then Roger was off his too, but by the time both of us reached Elaine the horse was back on the trail. It had not stepped once on Elaine—she was very fortunate to be uninjured. She did say, as she got to her feet, "If you wake up with your hat over your eyes and a horse sitting on you, you are probably on the Sugar Camp Trail!" Later Nancy's horse

*Here's me on the Sugar Camp Trail going down into the Bella Coola Valley.*

broke the trail away also, but it managed to stay on the trail. They were a great bunch of horses: gentle, sure-footed and very trail-wise. I found it a blessing to be able to get off or on either side because I felt safer on foot when things got steep.

Along the last bit of trail before we started down into the Bella Coola Valley, there were a lot of grizzly signs. Every little ways there was a freshly marked tree, with the sap fresh on the bark. A total of thirteen active rub trees on that stretch alone indicated a large and active grizzly population. I felt secure in that both Wanda and Roger packed rifles. We walked down the steep incline to the bottom—for those who were not seasoned riders it was safer, and I hated the steepness so I walked too! In one spot we had to cross over a flat, sloping rock with a drop-off on the low side. As I crossed I could hear the mare's shoes sliding on the rock, and I decided that if I felt a jerk on the halter shank I was just going to let go and keep walking, because it would mean she had slid over the bank. A Native lady once told me that when a pack horse lost its footing in the old days and went over the edge with its pack you just kept going. The Mechams from Firvale, a little farming area farther down the valley, used to drive their cattle up this trail every spring for summer range in the Precipice Valley—what a feat that was. I was told that a lot of the trail had been hand dug by the locals in the valley with pick and shovel in the hungry thirties. It was a way they paid their taxes when times were tough. We stopped for lunch on Sugar Camp Creek at the bottom of the hill, in the shade of the large trees, where it was cooler. Then we rode on to Stuie (the area at the bottom of the hill where we came to Highway 20) on the Tote Road, a very good narrow road that went up the valley towards Hunlen Falls. When we reached Highway 20 at the bottom of the hill, Roger's stock trailer and a five-ton truck were there to take the horses back to Anahim Lake.

I got back to Vanderhoof to find James and Tammie moving into a house they had bought adjoining Jon's property. Jon had bought his own place up the Nechako River from Fort Fraser in 1995 and built a small house, adding to it later. Now James and Tammie were

*James and Tammie at their wedding, on July 26, 2003.*

next door. They got married a short time later, on July 26. It was another big wedding, and was held just outside of Fort Fraser at Tammie's uncle's place. The weather was nice and there was a good turnout of family and friends.

I had parked the 931 track loader down by Joe's cabin earlier in the year, and one day I needed it for something so I went down with the quad to start it, but the thing wouldn't start. I went back home for the battery tester but the battery was good. There had been a loose wire on the starter but it was tight. The fuel gauge said I had lots of fuel but maybe more was needed so I went back home for fuel. After I dumped in the extra fuel I thought I should check the oil, and when I threw open the cover I could not believe it. A pack rat had stuffed dry grass around the motor and apparently was building a nest or something. I cleaned it all out and when I turned the key the loader started without any hesitation. Had it started before, with all the dry grass in it, it would have surely caught fire and I would have had no way to put it out. Someone was certainly looking over my shoulder that day!

Katie and Reagan came out for the cattle drive that year, plus a lot of my lady friends. It was what was referred to as the ladies' cattle drive, although Clifford came out and did the barbecue as usual. A bachelor from Vanderhoof also came out, along with the ten women, so the two guys were sadly outnumbered — but Daniel loved it! Reagan was the youngest to ever go on the drive, at five months old. Katie and the baby had come out with me from town a few days earlier and then Katie drove my truck out to 157 km, following the cattle. Clifford made the usual steak dinner at the loading chute and the evening was an enjoyable one. Wesley arrived later with the truck and cattle liner to haul the cattle the following morning. He and Katie and the baby spent the night in the sleeper, after parking it down by the bridge so those of us at camp would not have to listen to it idle. Apparently Reagan did not appreciate the sleeping arrangement in the truck and fussed all night.

My brother Homer passed away November 27, 2003. He was seventy-three years old. Back in 1983 he had undergone surgery that had left him paralysed from the waist down. He had spent the past twenty years in a wheelchair, not that it seemed to slow him down

*The ladies' cattle drive — (from left) Katie Rempel, Leslie Michaud, Lynda Peebles, Linda Irving, Gail Wilson, Rita Hiatt, Rene Jones, Fran Page, Shelley Funk and Diana holding granddaughter Reagan.*

that much. He had always lived on the rather wild side of life, but he was still too young to have died.

That winter I had a pack of eleven wolves hanging around the ranch hunting moose. I tried my best to get shots but they were always too quick for me. I hated the way wolves killed, tearing animals to pieces and eating them alive. It is nothing like Farley Mowat says in his book about wolves. There is nothing clean about a wolf kill. In winter the snow is red with blood where they kill. If they take down a cow moose with a calf, the calf is generally taken as well because it hangs around looking for its mother. If the cow has twin calves they are both killed along with the mom. In time all the meat is eaten, nothing is wasted, which is the only good thing about it.

If I lost an animal in the winter I would drag it over to the riverbank across from the house. From the upstairs bedroom I would have a clear view of the bait. I even nailed a nail into the window jam, where I could rest my rifle. I was bound and determined to get a wolf. I lost count of how many I hit over the years, but I never did ever drop one right there. I am sure that some of them died of their injuries, but I never hit them well enough. Coyotes are much easier to get than wolves.

One day I took the snow machine up to the Home Ranch to check horses. While I sat on the machine and watched the horses a big grey wolf walked up my snow machine's trail to within fifty yards of me, showing no fear whatsoever. I had not taken the rifle that day so we could only stare at each other. After several minutes he wandered off past the horses and disappeared over the bank of the little creek.

Checking the cows one very dark night towards the end of calving, when I was tired and had very little patience left, one of the cows was having her calf and it was backwards with the hind legs already showing a good ten or twelve inches. I even wondered if the calf was still alive. I tried to get the cow into a smaller corral to put her into the squeeze chute I had finally gotten myself, but she was having none of that. I was alone and roping the cow with a flashlight in one hand was not easy. She would just put her head down and duck behind the other cows, which by now were all up off the bedding ground. I started losing my temper as I followed the cow about, then saw my opportunity to get the rope on the calf's hind legs, while the cow slowed to push between two other cows. Then I quickly wrapped the end of the rope around a handy tree as the cow started to run down a small incline. When she hit the end of the rope that calf came out of her like a cork from a wine bottle. She stopped abruptly and humped up. The calf was very lively, shaking his head and rolling up into a sitting position almost immediately. I grabbed a hind leg and dragged him in front of the dazed cow, which managed a weak moo to her calf. I then went stomping back to the house and bed. The next morning mamma cow was lying down chewing her cud, with baby under her neck, its chin on the ground, eyes following me, and I knew it was ready to jump up and bolt if I got too close. They both looked one hundred percent better than they did in the dark of the night.

One of my big cows had a very small calf in the spring. It was very premature and they don't usually survive when they are that small but this one did. I brought it into the house and put it in a cardboard box on the open oven door of the cookstove, so it could warm up. I think that when it was weighed it was thirty-two pounds. I took it to the barn three times a day to nurse, holding it up the first few times, till it could stand and stretch its neck up to reach the cow's udder. As it got older it would immediately get right under the cow's belly when nursing, where the cow couldn't see it, and then she would get excited: something was nursing, but where was it? I kept the calf in the house for quite awhile, as although it had hair it was very short. When time came to go to the barn for feeding, the calf would run behind me down to the barn and follow me back to the house after. In the evenings just before bedtime I would let it out to run a bit before locking it up. While I was reading in my recliner the little thing came over to me and I picked it up and set it on my lap, where it was content for some time to stay curled up like a cat. Someone who was there took a photo of it. Finally I had to let it go full time with its mother, even though I was afraid it would get stepped on. But it grew up healthy and when market time came in the fall and it was sold it weighed 490 pounds—a bit underweight compared to the other heifers, but it had still done well.

I had an older half-longhorn cow that took to jumping out and hiding when it came time to have her calf. The first time I looked for her for two days with no luck, and on the third day she came back with her calf. The next time she did it I really didn't put much effort into finding her and again, after three days, she came home with her calf. After that I paid her no attention. One year she was late calving and was out in the field when I noticed she was missing at feeding time. A day or two later I was up on the side hill where I could look down on the fields and pastures and I saw her in a little opening among the thick willows in one of the pastures. The river was high with spring runoff, so she had swum the river. Several days later she showed up on the feed ground with her new calf, having swum with it across the river too.

Toby and Doris Cave came out for a few days in May and I am glad they did. My old dog Patch had been failing badly. He was seventeen years old and had not gone far from the house for several years. He had now reached the point where he had not eaten for a couple of weeks and was becoming very weak. Then one day I stood at the window and watched him struggle to get to his feet as he lay on the porch in the sunshine. When he did stand up he fell over, then he looked up and met my eyes. He seemed embarrassed about his unsteadiness. It brought tears to my eyes. There was nothing I could do. I remarked that it was time to put him down. I went to the shop and got a spade and in the soft ground by the hothouse dug a grave. When I returned to the house Toby told me to go for a walk and he would take care of things. I went and knelt down and stroked Patch's head for the last time with tears streaming down my face. I took a long walk and had my good cry. Gone was a companion that had always been there for me, for seventeen years—he had been an exceptional dog.

Patch had always stayed home, except for twice. Once I ran over him with my pickup and he went to Rob's. I had to go over and get him when I found out where he was. He was pleased to see me and held no grudges about the tumble under the truck, and he didn't seem to be injured. Another time, Joe brought home a female dog and nature took its course. Patch would visit her at night; he'd stay home during the day but he was antsy and distracted. The longest he was ever left alone was nearly two weeks, and still he never left. He loved affection and to talk to you by throwing his head back and yodelling while wagging his tail and standing on one front foot then the other. Whenever I headed for town, which seemed to be quite often in his last few years, he would sit in the yard and look away when I looked at him. I think it was called giving me the cold shoulder!

By June the whole country seemed to be on fire. There was a lot of smoke. I had gone into town when Rob phoned me and said the smoke was so bad at home that he couldn't see much and wasn't sure where the fire was. James and Chris Weaver drove home with me. By the time we got to 165 on the Kluskus Forest Road, where we had a fairly good view of the surrounding country, there were no mushroom clouds of smoke near my place so the boys went back to town, as they both had to work the next day. Jon and Dawn came out later, but they returned to town in the morning. For several days the wind came from the west so it took the smoke from the Ilgachuz fire away to the east, as well as the smoke from the big fire at Kluskus. I packed up all my pictures and things that couldn't be replaced and parked the machinery out in the field. The smoke got thick again as the wind shifted, bringing smoke up the valley. I became claustrophobic in it, not being able to see more than a short distance, and the smell frightened me and burnt my nose and throat. I went to town and hoped for the best. A couple days later it rained and I returned home. That was the end of the fires for that season so we had been lucky.

The small creek at Tommy Valley that my driveway passed over had a culvert in it, and that summer beavers kept damming it and flooding the driveway. Joe and I had gone over several times to clean it out. If the day was warm the chore wasn't so bad, but on cool, windy days it was a cold, wet job. While we were there one day a beaver swam about on the pond above the culvert while we pulled branches, mud and rocks from the end of the culvert opening. Once it was cleaned out and the water was pouring through we walked up-stream a short distance and sat on a beaver house, trying to get a shot at the beaver—Joe had his shotgun with him. The beaver seemed to have gone so I became bored and went downstream from the beaver house a bit to where another dam had been constructed above the culvert. I had just begun pulling it apart when the beaver surfaced and Joe opened fire, shooting into the pond around the house and in my direction. I started to run off the dam and caught my foot in some branches and fell on the dam. I covered my head with my arms, expecting to be hit, but I was not—and neither was the beaver. As I've said, Joe does not always see very well. That was enough for that day; we got on our quads and went home.

Because I had had no luck whatsoever relying on the realtors to sell the ranch, Katie said she would list it on a website that advertised ranches and farms and see what she could do. We had made info packages up so she had information to mail out to anyone who in-quired. This sparked some interest. The first to arrive were a couple of guys from Alberta who came out in mid-January to see the place. It was not the greatest time to see the property as we had two and half feet of snow, and although the weather was warm for January we still had to bundle up. In February Katie had another party looking for info—a fellow who had been to the place before. This was more interest than I had seen in three years with the realtors, so my hopes were up that someone would be interested enough to buy the ranch. Through the spring and early summer several more interested par-ties came out. In July I had two different parties come and look at the place. One guy loved it but told me his wife would never live so far from town. The other party returned a couple months later with a serious offer on the place. I signed the papers in October. I then started to pack stuff and haul it to storage in Vanderhoof, as I had to be out by November 1.

I think at the time I was rather numb, wondering if I had done

*Out for a spin in the snow—(from left) Terry, Marianne, Dave, Elaine, Barb and me.*

the right thing. Now I knew how my mom felt when she left the Home Ranch. Sleepy Hollow had been my home for thirty years—I had raised my boys there—and I had lived in the area all my life. There would be so much I would miss. But I had just gotten tired of the worry and stress of running the ranch alone. I was also spending too much time alone, which is not good for a person. I was tired of making decisions then wondering if I had made the right ones. There was a time when I always felt confident they were the right ones, but now I second-guessed myself. And I was not seeing enough of my family. I wanted to spend more time with the grandbabies and watch them grow.

I knew that I would miss the quiet life at times: the unpolluted air, the many birds, my animals, and travelling the backcountry that had always been my home. In summer I could ride my horse whenever I wanted. My quad sat at the back door, ready to tackle unlimited trails, and in the winter the snow machine replaced the quad and took me over all the country a person could want to play in. This I knew I would miss. I would also miss my brother, who had been next door for twenty-one years.

Friends helped me haul my belongings out of Sleepy Hollow. It took many truckloads. James brought the low bed in to 167 on the Kluskus and took out a load on it. Then, on November 6, 2004, I closed the door of my home for the last time. I drove out of the yard on that cool grey day to start a new life.

*A recent family photo — (back row, from left) Reagan, Wesley, me, Jon, Dawn and James, (front row) Katie, Tanner, Rayen, Teagan, Logan and Tammie.*

# Epilogue

It is nearing seven years since I left the ranch, and I think I am finally feeling at home in my more populated surroundings. It has been a long journey, to say the least. I do enjoy the things I never had in the bush, like my automatic washer, Hydro power and my landline phone. In the early hours of the morning, when the highway sounds cease and the village sleeps, the train whistle that can be heard in the silent distance, as the train passes by, is a comforting sound. There is something about that sound, and it seems almost natural to me. It has replaced the night hoots of the owl.

My longing for the isolated backcountry fades as the years pass, but it will never be forgotten! Spring is when my thoughts turn most to the life I had in the bush, when the days warm and the countryside turns green; it is the birth of a whole new year. But I have a lot to be thankful for. I have my new home, my family, friends nearby and my job. I am still able to go on horse rides to the mountains, to snowmobile and do camping trips with my quad. Now, only in my dreams do I walk the trails of my former home.

The Blackwater country, where I spent nearly six decades, will forever be a part of my life. It is where I raised my three boys, and where I saw the passing of my parents. I also witnessed the slow changing of that country, which once teemed with activities. At one time there were a lot of people riding horses through the area, people walking the Mackenzie Trail and canoeing the Blackwater River. Fishing lodges prospered on the many lakes. Float planes flew about constantly from May long weekend into October, taking fishing enthusiasts from one lake to another. And there was an increasing amount of quad and snow machine travel on the trails. The Indian people were a large part of that land.

Then things began to change. Fewer people rode about the country. People stopped hiking the trails and canoeing the river. Business at the lodges slowed, and now some stand deserted, with doors open, windowpanes broken and overgrown yards. The Indians moved away to the towns, abandoning their homes, traplines and horses. The mountain pine beetle invaded the lodgepole pine, turning the country red with dying trees. Now forest fires burn through the dead timber and leave the countryside black and desolate. The trails have become overgrown, or are covered with fallen trees, and the blazed trees that marked those trails are now gone. Having the traplines forgotten allows the beaver population to increase, and they dam creeks and flood trails. There is still some quad and snow machine traffic, but not like there used to be. The moose that were so common in the area are now rarely seen, having fallen prey to the ever-increasing packs of wolves.

One day the new growth of pine will again cover the back-country, restoring it to what it once was. I may not live long enough to see that, but my children will.

# Acknowledgements

I would like to thank all of the people who told me the stories that ended up on these pages, and those who lent me photos. I'd also like to thank Heather Martin, for finding my manuscript when I accidentally deleted it, and my niece Wanda Simpson, for sharing her mother's old letters and photos with me. Elaine Scott, Christine Peters, and Fran and Butch Page all helped by reading my manuscript and offering suggestions. I also appreciate being able to use the following: Earl Payne's journals, *Only In Nazko* by Maurine Goodenough and *Bear Attacks: The Deadly Truth* by James Gary Sheldon. And I'd like to thank the publisher and staff at Harbour Publishing and editors Pam Robertson and Elaine Park. Without them, *Beyond the Home Ranch* would not have been possible.

# Index